ONE HUNDRED
EVENTS
THAT SHAPED WORLD WAR II

First published in the UK in 2016 by
Apple Press
74-77 White Lion Street
London N1 9PF

Conceived, designed, and produced by
Quid Publishing
Level 4 Sheridan House
114 Western Road
Hove BN3 1DD
England

Design by Simon Daly and Lindsey Johns

www.quidpublishing.com

ISBN: 978-1-84543-644-5

Manufactured in China

2 4 6 8 10 9 7 5 3 1

ONE HUNDRED
EVENTS

THAT SHAPED WORLD WAR II

PETER DARMAN

APPLE

CONTENTS

LEFT In the summer of 1940, Winston Churchill's defiance in the face of seemingly insurmountable odds helped maintain British morale.

1943

1944

1945

RIGHT U.S. soldiers at Midway Naval Base in 1942. The Battle of Midway (see pp. 108–109) was a defining moment in the Pacific War.

INTRODUCTION

'Events, dear boy. Events'. This was the reply of British Prime Minister Harold Macmillan (in office 1957–63), when a journalist asked him what could most easily steer a government off course. Had they been posed the same question, the leaders of the Allied and Axis nations in World War II would probably have given the same reply. This book is a compendium of the 100 most decisive events, both on and off the battlefield, that shaped the course of the conflict between 1939 and 1945.

At the heart of the global war, and of the events listed in this book, is Nazi Germany, which between 1939 and 1942 conquered most of mainland Europe and the western half of the Soviet Union. Yet even at the height of its power, the Third Reich had sown the seeds of its own destruction. Hitler's non-aggression pact with the Soviet Union in 1939 was a brilliant piece of realpolitik and paved the way for the speedy conquest of Poland. But it also led to Britain and France declaring war on Germany and turning what Hitler hoped would be a local conflict into a Europe-wide war. From then on, events in large part shaped German strategy, forcing Berlin to react to them rather than act as it desired.

LOOKING EAST

Hitler attacked Britain and France in 1940, resulting in stunning victories but nevertheless leaving Britain undefeated. He then turned his attention to the ultimate aim of Nazi policy: creating 'living space' in the East. But even before he was able to launch Operation Barbarossa, the invasion of the USSR – one of the most pivotal events of the war – Hitler was forced to bail out his Axis ally Italy in the Balkans and North Africa, diverting valuable military resources that should have been dedicated to the Eastern Front. Despite the whirlwind victories won by the Germans in the first weeks of Barbarossa it can be argued that Nazi Germany at the end of 1941

RIGHT The early successes of Hitler's forces were soon overshadowed by remarkable strategic errors, not least the decision to declare war on the USA (see pp. 82–83).

6

was already facing the prospect of ultimate defeat. Not only had it failed to knock the Soviet Union out of the war, Hitler had also declared war on the United States, a truly bizarre decision that pitted the Third Reich against what would become the world's first economic and military superpower.

TAKING ON THE USA

With hindsight, Japan's decision to start a war with the United States in the Pacific was even riskier. In a campaign similar to the one waged by its Tripartite Pact ally in Europe, Japan won a series of staggering victories in the first six months of the Pacific War, but thereafter things went very much against Tokyo's interests. Cracking Japanese naval codes was to prove vital for the U.S. victory at Midway in June 1942, and thereafter Tokyo was fighting a defensive war in the Pacific, as it tried, and failed, to retain the territory and resources it had conquered previously. And as American industrial and military power increased, so did Japan's war-making capacity dwindle, as its aircraft and ships were denied the very thing that had prompted Japan to attack the United States in the first place: oil.

Mostly safe from enemy bombers and armies, World War II was in many ways to become the story of the rise of the United States, which became first the arsenal of democracy, supplying its allies with the material support they required to blunt the Axis alliance, and then a military colossus. For those on the front line this still meant battling a determined and skilful enemy, but from 1943 the Germans and Japanese suffered a series of defeats that made even avoiding ultimate defeat impossible. The bloody clashes at Stalingrad, Kursk, the Solomons, Gilberts, and Marshalls would lead to even more catastrophic defeats for the Axis powers in 1944.

That Germany and Japan were still able to continue fighting after their cities had been reduced to rubble, their economies destroyed, and their armed forces emasculated was testimony to the fanaticism of their regimes. But it did not alter the outcome of the war; it merely added to its butcher's bill.

ABOVE General Dwight D. Eisenhower enjoyed a stellar rise to five-star general and was appointed Supreme Commander of the Allied Expedition, overseeing the invasion of Continental Europe during Operation Overlord (see pp. 178–179).

The Nazi–Soviet Non-Aggression Pact signed on the eve of World War II was a masterstroke by Berlin. It removed the threat of the USSR joining Britain and France in a two-front war against Germany, and paved the way for Hitler to launch the German attack on Poland. The Führer believed that, just as the Western Allies had backed down when he seized the Sudetenland in Czechoslovakia in 1938, so they would not get involved in what he believed was a localised conflict on Germany's eastern border. But his attack on Poland did result in French and British declarations of war and, had those nations acted with determination in the winter of 1939–40, World War II might have ended after less than a year. As it was, Franco-British lethargy would have dire consequences for them both in the summer of 1940.

In the north, the Winter War between Finland and the Soviet Union convinced Hitler and his generals that, in any future conflict with the USSR, the Red Army would be defeated with ease.

1939

NAZI–SOVIET NON-AGGRESSION PACT

DATE

23 August, 1939

SUMMARY

The treaty removed the USSR as a potential enemy of Nazi Germany and gave Hitler a free hand to conquer Poland.

LOCATION

Moscow, USSR

Hitler and the senior members of the Nazi Party looked east to fulfill their dreams of a racially pure 'Thousand-year Reich'. Poland, the Baltic states and the Soviet Union would provide the 'living space' (*Lebensraum*) and resources that Germany needed to become and remain the most powerful nation in Europe.

Buoyed by his successes in absorbing Austria and the Sudeten region of Czechoslovakia into the Third Reich in 1938 – the latter achieved with British and French consent at the Munich Conference – plus the conquest of the rest of Czechoslovakia in March 1939, he was wary of attacking Poland. Though he was confident that Britain and France would not intervene, there was nonetheless still a risk that the two Western powers might revive their old alliance of World War I. If so, Germany would once again be faced with a war on two fronts. Indeed, in April 1939 Stalin had offered Britain and France an alliance that would guarantee the integrity of every state in eastern Europe from the Baltic to the Mediterranean, backed up by the combined military force of all three powers. The Western response was lukewarm, convincing Stalin that Britain and France were uninterested in an alliance with the USSR.

GERMAN OVERTURES

But whereas London and Paris were hesitant about becoming allies with Communist Russia, Hitler took a more pragmatic approach. It was Berlin that made the first moves concerning a non-aggression pact with the USSR. The first feelers, in May 1939 concerning trade discussions, were rejected. At the beginning of August, Nazi foreign minister Joachim von Ribbentrop offered the Soviets a political settlement of the area from the Baltic to the Black Sea. This area contained Poland, Romania and the Baltic states, which had formerly been part of the Tsarist Empire. The Soviets were very interested in recovering these states but did not trust the Nazis. As a result, Moscow was noncommittal.

Hitler, desperate to secure an agreement before the attack on Poland, offered a non-aggression pact and a secret protocol concerning the territorial dismemberment of eastern Europe. Stalin was now very receptive and instructed his foreign minister, Vyacheslav Molotov, to inform the Germans that he was interested in the pact and the secret protocol and to invite Ribbentrop to Moscow. There followed frantic pleadings from the Germans to speed up negotiations to clear the way for the invasion of Poland, which ended when Stalin himself contacted Hitler to propose 23 August. On that day the Nazi–Soviet Non-Aggression Pact was signed in the presence of Stalin himself.

SPHERES OF INTEREST

ABOVE Soviet foreign minister Vyacheslav Molotov (seated) signs the pact, while Ribbentrop (standing third from left) and Stalin (second from right) look on.

The terms of the treaty made public stated that the two countries agreed not to attack each other, not to support any third power that might attack the other party to the treaty, to remain in consultation with each other regarding their common interests, not to join any group of powers that would directly or indirectly threaten one of the two parties, and to solve all differences by arbitration or negotiation. The treaty was to last for ten years, with automatic extension for another five years, unless either party gave notice to terminate it one year before its expiry.

But it was the secret parts of the pact that had driven two ideological enemies into each other's arms. Eastern Europe was divided into German and Soviet spheres of interest. Poland would be divided between the two after being invaded. Lithuania, Latvia, Estonia, and Finland were assigned to the Soviet sphere of interest. The Romanian regions of Bessarabia and Northern Bukovina were also assigned to the Soviets (who occupied them in June 1940).

After hearing that the treaty had been signed, Hitler exclaimed: 'Now Europe is mine!' He was now free to attack Poland with the knowledge that the USSR would not side with Britain and France.

THE RED ORCHESTRA

DATE
....
August 1939

SUMMARY
....
The Soviet spy
network supplied
high-quality
intelligence to
Moscow during
the war.

LOCATION
....
Moscow, USSR

Following the signature of the Nazi–Soviet pact (see pp. 10–11), Stalin ordered the suspension of espionage activity in Nazi Germany. In the mid-1930s, Soviet Military Intelligence, the GRU, had established a network of spies across the world in response to the rise of Fascism in Europe and Japanese expansion in the Far East. This network had been organised by the head of the GRU, Yan Berzin, who was targeted during Stalin's purges and executed in Moscow in 1938.

Before his removal, Berzin had founded a spy network in Germany, headed by Harro Schulze-Boysen, the grandson of Admiral Alfred von Tirpitz, established Richard Sorge in Japan, and set up a network in France and Belgium under GRU agent Leopold Trepper, one of Berzin's protégés. Operating from Belgium, Trepper brought together the various anti-Nazi espionage assets in Europe to form what the Germans would later call the Red Orchestra (*Rote Kapelle*).

RUSSIAN INTELLIGENCE

The Red Orchestra comprised three main sections: the network in France, Belgium and Holland; the Berlin network, which included Schulze-Boysen, an intelligence officer attached to the German Air Ministry; and the Lucy Spy Ring, which operated from Switzerland. With these resources, plus the intelligence collected by Sorge in Japan, the Soviets were privy to high-level intelligence concerning German military plans. For example, Sorge obtained accurate information concerning the launch date of Operation Barbarossa, the German invasion of the USSR, in December 1940 (the operation was launched in June 1941). Other intelligence collected included information on the German attack on Moscow in late 1941 and Operation Blue, the German summer offensive in 1942.

Unfortunately, Stalin's paranoid nature initially worked against the Red Orchestra. The intelligence it supplied in the first half of 1941 regarding a German attack on the USSR was accurate, but when no invasion came the Soviet dictator became increasingly distrustful of its reliability. Thus, by May 1941, reports from Soviet spies regarding a German invasion were being filed in the 'folder of dubious and misleading reports'.

Following the invasion of the USSR, the Red Orchestra continued to send intelligence to Moscow, which was now demanding a constant stream of accurate and timely reports pertaining to German military plans on the Eastern Front. A major problem was establishing radio contact between Moscow and Berlin, which was solved when the Soviets parachuted agents into Germany to set up more efficient communications links. The Red Orchestra continued to send invaluable information, such as the Lucy Spy Ring alerting Moscow to the German offensive at Kursk in 1943.

By this date, however, German intelligence agencies, such as the *Gestapo* (Secret State Police) and *Abwehr* (Military Intelligence), were actively hunting for Red Orchestra agents. They had become aware of the spy network shortly after the launch of Operation Barbarossa but it took a year before the *Abwehr* was able to break the Red Orchestra, in August 1942. Schulze-Boysen was arrested as he tried to send a message concerning *Luftwaffe* deployments around Stalingrad. He and the others that were rounded up faced the full wrath of the Nazis.

Communist sympathisers could expect little sympathy from the Nazis: of the 118 sent to trial, eight (including Schulze-Boysen) were hanged and 41 were guillotined. There were variations on a theme. Arvid Harnack was garroted at Plötzensee Prison in Berlin on Christmas Eve 1942. His wife was guillotined on 16 February, 1943. Those not immediately executed were sent to concentration camps.

Trepper himself was arrested, but, amazingly, managed to escape his captors, who had tried to 'turn' him into becoming a double agent. He convinced the Germans that he would work with them, then contacted Moscow to warn the authorities of his capture before making his escape. He made his way to Paris, where he remained until the war's end.

Eyewitness

ADAM KUCKHOFF WAS A MEMBER OF SCHULZE-BOYSEN'S GROUP, WHO WAS EXECUTED IN AUGUST 1943. BEFORE HE DIED HE WROTE THIS LETTER:

'My dear father,
Be strong! I die just as I have lived: a first-class fighter! It is easy to call yourself a Communist as long as you don't have to pay for it with your life. You don't prove that you are one until the hour of truth. I am a Communist, father!

It is easy for me to die, because I know why I must. Those who are killing me will soon confront a difficult death, I am convinced of it.

Be tough, father! Tough! Don't give in! In each of your hours of weakness, remember this last request of your son, Walter Adam Kuckhoff.'

BRITAIN AND FRANCE DECLARE WAR

DATE

....

3 September,
1939

SUMMARY

....

The German attack
against Poland on
1 September sparked
a general European
conflict two days
later.

LOCATION

....

Berlin, Germany

On the afternoon of 25 August, two days after the signing of his treaty
with the Soviet Union, Hitler gave the order to begin the attack on
Poland. Later that afternoon, however, he received notification from the
British government that it intended to stand by Poland in the event of
a German attack. Hitler backed down, ordering Wilhelm Keitel, Chief
of the High Command of the Armed Forces, to halt military operations,
in order to give him time to negotiate with the British. Subsequent
talks with the British ambassador in Berlin came to nothing and the
Blitzkrieg was launched against Poland on 1 September.

MUTUAL ASSISTANCE

....

Article 1 of the Agreement of Mutual Assistance between the United
Kingdom and Poland, signed in London on 25 August, stated:

'Should one of the Contracting Powers become engaged in hostilities
with a European Power in consequence of aggression by the latter
against the Contracting Party, the other Contracting Party will at once
give the Contracting Party engaged in hostilities all the support and
assistance in its power.'

The rushed British pledge was reinforced by an agreement between
the Poles and the French: the Franco-Polish Military Protocols, signed
in May 1939. Both agreements pledged military action in defence of
Polish sovereignty, thus condemning Germany to a war on two fronts, if
it attacked Poland. Indeed, the French agreement pledged an immediate
French air force offensive in the event of a German invasion of Poland
and a French army invasion of Germany 16 days afterward. In the event
neither promise was fulfilled. Instead, it was to be the Germans who
would move against the French. As for the British pledge of assistance,
its aircraft lacked the range to strike vital German installations and its
army had no way of assisting the Poles. However, Hitler and the German
High Command did not actively seek a two-front war. Why then did the
attack on Poland commence?

First was Hitler's belief that the British and French, just as they had done at Munich in 1938, would cave in to his threats and demands. Even when Britain and France did declare war, on September, he believed it was a sham, a gesture so that both nations would not lose face on the world stage. For his part he stated he had no intention of invading western Europe, declaring in a speech on 19 September: 'I have neither towards England nor France any war claims, neither has the German nation'. He ordered the army in the West to remain on the defensive while the conquest of Poland was completed. As if by mutual agreement the British and French also remained on the defensive. Hitler had always believed that war with Britain and France was inevitable, though he had not envisaged it breaking out until 1943–45.

Flushed with the speed of his victories in Poland, on 25 September (the day Warsaw fell) Hitler summoned his service chiefs to the Reich Chancellery in Berlin. There he informed them of his decision to 'attack in the West as soon as possible, since the Franco-British Army is not yet prepared'. He set the date for the offensive as 12 November, although the invasion of the West had to be postponed due to revisions and opposition from the army's generals.

Despite Hitler's initial view that the declaration of war by Britain and France was a sham, the decision by London and Paris had widened the war to encompass not only most of the European mainland but also Britain's colonies and former colonies. New Zealand and Australia declared war on Germany on 3 September, South Africa on 6 September and Canada on 10 September. What had begun as a conflict localised in eastern Europe was turning into a war of global dimensions.

Eyewitness

ALBERT SPEER, HITLER'S PERSONAL ARCHITECT AND WITNESS TO THE INNER WORKINGS OF THE THIRD REICH, WAS AN OBSERVER OF THE EVENTS OF SEPTEMBER 1939.

'I do not think that in those early days of September Hitler was fully aware that he had irrevocably unleashed a world war. He had merely meant to move one step further. To be sure, he was ready to accept the risk associated with that step, just as he had a year before during the Czech crisis; but he had prepared himself only for the risk, not really the great war.

But all his anxieties seemed to be scattered to the winds in early September, when the campaign in Poland yielded such successes for the German troops. Hitler seemed to recover his assurance swiftly, and later, at the climax of the war, I frequently heard him say that the Polish campaign had been a necessary thing.'

BRITAIN ESTABLISHES THE MOI

DATE

....

4 September,
1939

SUMMARY

....

The British created
their own propaganda
machine to rival that
of Nazi Germany.

LOCATION

....

Senate House
in London,
Great Britain

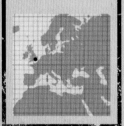

A day after declaring war the British government set up the Ministry of Information (MOI), the department that would be responsible for official publicity and propaganda during the course of the war. For a democracy such as Britain this was a major step and indicated that World War II would be a conflict in which the warring parties would employ propaganda on a vast scale. Total war required the total dedication of all aspects of the state and its population to achieve victory. Propaganda became an important weapon in the war. Thus posters became 'weapons on the wall' and carried simple but effective messages that became famous. 'Dig for Victory', 'We Can Do It' and 'I Want You!' are just a few examples.

PLAYING CATCH-UP

....

Before the war the totalitarian states – Nazi Germany, Fascist Italy, the USSR and Japan – had already subverted the media and the arts to be tools of the state. As such they were well ahead of the Western democracies when it came to propaganda. In Germany the Reich Ministry for Popular Entertainment and Propaganda, headed by Reich Minister Joseph Goebbels, had been established in March 1933. Radios, newspapers, films, posters, mass meetings, lectures and even word-of-mouth propaganda were all means by which the Nazis transmitted their message to the masses.

The Ministry of Information's initial function was threefold and more modest: news and press censorship, home publicity and overseas publicity in Allied and neutral countries. But to fulfill these functions required a large staff and soon the ministry was employing artists, journalists, researchers and film directors. Their output included films, radio programmes, posters, books and exhibitions.

Though the Censorship Bureau of the MOI was responsible for the censorship of newspapers, journals and books, and because of this was much criticised by the British press, in fact the MOI did not peddle wholesale lies and deception. Clearly there was a need to stop information that might be useful to the enemy from being disseminated, resulting in such campaigns as 'Careless talk costs lives' being launched in 1940. But the MOI believed that propaganda should also be truth. The first head of the MOI was the ineffective Lord Hugh Macmillan but his replacement, Sir John Reith, former director of the British Broadcasting Corporation (BBC), was much more effective. He believed that 'news is the shock troops of propaganda' and that propaganda should also relay 'the truth, nothing but the truth and, as near as possible, the whole truth' (ironically an idea shared by Goebbels).

SHAPING PUBLIC OPINION

The MOI went on to achieve some notable successes, which included assisting American coverage of the Blitz and communicating war-related news to the United States before America's entry into the war. In this way it helped to convey a sympathetic view of the 'plucky Brits' bravely enduring in the face of great odds.

On the home front, in addition to its poster and newspaper campaigns, the MOI commissioned films that helped to boost civilian morale. At a time when cinema was the most popular form of entertainment (an estimated 30 million people every week were going to the cinema in 1945, for example), films were a powerful propaganda tool. There were documentaries such as *London Can Take It* (1940) about the Blitz and films made in conjunction with the commercial film industry. These told the human stories of the war, in which all classes united together for the common good in the face of Nazism. They included *In Which We Serve* (1942), *Millions Like Us* (1943) and *The Way Ahead* (1944). They were and remain classics not only of propaganda but also filmmaking.

ABOVE Titled *Unity of Strength Together*, this example of British propaganda by William Little rallied Britain's colonies to the support of the Allied war effort.

THE WINTER WAR

DATE

8 December, 1939

SUMMARY

The Finns stopped the Soviets in their tracks and gave the Red Army some valuable lessons.

LOCATION

Suomussalmi, Finland

Finland was assigned as a Soviet sphere of influence under the terms of the Nazi–Soviet Non-Aggression Pact and Stalin was determined that it should lease to the USSR the port of Hanko in the Gulf of Finland and cede Finnish land near the Soviet border to Moscow. When the Finns refused these demands at the end of October the Red Army invaded Finland with 600,000 troops, supported by 1,500 tanks and 300 aircraft. The Finnish Army totalled 30,000 men but had two advantages: it was led by Field Marshal Carl Mannerheim and it occupied the defences of the Mannerheim Line in the Karelian Isthmus southwest of Lake Ladoga.

STIFF RESISTANCE

Red Army attacks soon foundered against well-sited Finnish machine-gun and rifle positions, barbed-wire defences and minefields. By the beginning of December the Red Army was losing around 10,000 soldiers killed and wounded each day. Finnish losses averaged 250 a day. But the Soviets still retained the initiative and on 8 December launched their offensive against the town of Suomussalmi, which was designed to cut Finland in half by capturing the town and then advancing west to the port of Oulu. To achieve this the Red Army committed 48,000 troops, 335 artillery pieces, 10 tanks and 11 armoured cars against Suomussalmi. Facing them was a single division (the 9th) commanded by Colonel Hjalmar Siilasvuo, a total of 11,500 men.

Instead of remaining on the defensive, Siilasvuo attacked immediately, employing ski troops and snipers to harass and isolate Soviet units. In a month he had inflicted 22,500 casualties on the Red Army and ended the enemy threat in central Finland.

The Battle of Suomussalmi had major repercussions. Stalin 'purged' many of his inept commanders, executing the commander of the 44th Motorised Division and all his staff, for example. During January 1940 the Red Army instigated a new training regime, replacing mass attacks with tactics that co-ordinated infantry, artillery and tanks to take

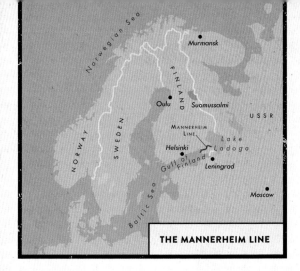

LEFT A map showing Finland's prewar border with the USSR. The Mannerheim Line ran between the Gulf of Finland in the west and Lake Ladoga in the east.

THE MANNERHEIM LINE

Finnish positions, supported by close air support. When the Red Army launched its offensive in Karelia on 1 February, 1940, the combination of artillery barrages and air attacks resulted in the Mannerheim Line being penetrated in 12 days. By the beginning of March the Finns had been forced to sue for peace.

BATTLE-HARDENED

The Winter War cost the Red Army 126,875 dead and 391,783 wounded; the Finns lost 25,000 dead and 45,500 wounded. The Red Army had learned some hard lessons, such as the need for infantry tactics to be flexible, that co-ordination between units was imperative, and that battle training should be realistic. Above all the lesson that winter warfare required warm, camouflage clothing was taken to heart. Notwithstanding the losses suffered during the first weeks of Operation Barbarossa (largely due to an incompetent high command, including Stalin himself), the lessons learned in the Winter War would make the Red Army a more resilient fighting force, as the Germans would discover to their cost during the winter fighting around Moscow in December 1941.

In Berlin entirely different lessons were drawn from the Winter War: that the performance of the detested Bolshevik Slavs had illustrated the racial inferiority of the inhabitants of the Soviet Union. Furthermore, that a small 'Nordic' country had withstood the onslaught of a nation of 180 million Slavs for so long convinced Hitler and his generals that the USSR would quickly collapse when attacked by Germany's armed forces. Such a mind-set would lead to disaster on an unimaginable scale.

THE PHONY WAR

DATE

The winter of 1939–40

SUMMARY

The period of inactivity that rotted the French army from within and made a German victory in the West highly likely.

LOCATION

The Franco-German border

In Britain it was called the Phony War, the French *la Drôle de Guerre* (the Joke War) and the Germans termed it *Sitzkrieg* (Sitting War). But the period of inactivity that marked the situation along Germany's western border in the winter of 1939–40 was a lost chance for the British and French to end the war in 1939. A strong offensive against Germany's western defences, which had been stripped of men and vehicles to support the Polish campaign, might have broken through and ended Hitler's grandiose schemes.

As it was the offensive action undertaken in 1939 was a limited attack by French forces that began on 8 September on a 24km (15-mile) front southeast of Saarbrücken. The French could call on 85 divisions against the Germans' 34, all but 11 of which were reserve units with little training and deficient in weapons and equipment. After advancing 8km (5 miles) and occupying 20 deserted villages French forces halted on 12 September (the Germans had retreated before them). General Gamelin, Chief of the French General Staff, issued an order on that day that they should retreat to the safety of the Maginot Line if the Germans should attack through Belgium. Thus ended the French offensive.

A DEFENSIVE STRATEGY

French and British strategy was based not on hastily mobilised offensives but on a blockade to strangle Germany economically and defensive fortifications that would exhaust the Germans militarily. Crucial to this strategy were the concrete and steel defences of the Maginot Line, which was started in 1930 and completed in 1937. It stretched from the Swiss border north to Montmédy. Unfortunately from that point to the North Sea, along the Belgian border, was an obsolete system of unconnected fortresses.

As the British Expeditionary Force (BEF) was transported across the Channel, to the Arras–Lille sector, the French called up hundreds of thousands of men. By the winter of 1939–40 there were two million

French troops deployed along the border, with little to do. General Charles-Victor-André Laffargue reported: 'Our units vegetated in an existence without purpose, settling down to guard duty and killing time until the next leave or relief'. Boredom quickly became endemic, which led to an alarming rise in alcoholism. The soldiers resented work details, believing them to be futile, a view shared by their junior officers. Another French general, Edmond Ruby, noted: 'Military exercises were considered a joke and work unnecessary drudgery'.

WINTER DISCOMFORTS

To make matters worse, the winter of 1939–40 was one of the coldest in living memory, which further damaged morale. In addition, the Germans were quick to add to the resentment and demoralisation of the French. Using loudspeakers and signs they taunted French troops that they were 'dying for Danzig, for the Poles, for the British'. Across no-man's-land they urged: 'Don't shoot! We won't if you don't'. As the weeks passed even the high command became infected with lethargy. Gamelin himself exclaimed: 'Open fire on the German working parties? The Germans would only respond by firing on ours!'

The lethargy and poor morale had been noted among France's British allies. General Alan Brooke, commander of the BEF's II Corps, observed in November 1939 after watching a parade of French Ninth Army troops: 'Seldom have I seen anything more slovenly … men unshaven, horses ungroomed … complete lack of pride in themselves or their units. What shook me the most, however, was the look in the men's faces, disgruntled and insubordinate looks'.

By the spring of 1940 the French army was far from being a war-winning force.

ABOVE In September 1939, the British government introduced conscription into the armed forces of all men aged 20 and 21.

German military victories in the spring and summer of 1940 left Hitler as the undisputed master of western Europe. The conquest of France destroyed French military power, which had possessed the largest army in the world, and ejected a defeated British Army from mainland Europe. Hitler was now free to concentrate on his main aim: the creation of 'living space' in the East for the Thousand-year Reich. But events conspired to interrupt Berlin's plans for the complete conquest and occupation of Europe from the Atlantic coast to the Ural Mountains. First and foremost was the determination of Great Britain, under the dynamic leadership of Winston Churchill, to carry on fighting. The *Luftwaffe* failed to win the Battle of Britain and the *Kriegsmarine*'s U-boats did not have the numbers to starve the British into surrender. Secondly, Germany's ally Italy was already showing signs of being a liability in North Africa and the Balkans.

1940

RATIONING BEGINS

DATE
....
8 January,
1940

SUMMARY
....
This simple but
effective policy
ensured that the
British people did
not starve during
the war.

LOCATION
....
Great Britain

Rationing in Britain was a war-winning strategy. The government realised that the 55.9 million tonnes (55 million tons) of food imported annually would be a prime target for German U-boats. It therefore introduced rationing to lessen dependence on imports, ensure no one starved and encourage homegrown foodstuffs.

Simple, effective and brilliant, it ensured that everyone, regardless of class or location, had food on a daily basis. The logistics were simple: every person in Britain was given a ration book. They had to register and buy their food from their chosen stores. The storekeeper then crossed the items purchased off the ration book.

SIMPLE AND EFFECTIVE

Ration books were colour-coded. Most adults had buff-coloured books, but green ration books were issued to pregnant women, nursing mothers and children under the age of five. The owner of such a book had first choice when it came to fruit, a daily pint of milk and a double supply of eggs. Blue ration books were issued to children between 5 and 16 years of age and entitled them to fruit, the full meat ration and a pint of milk each day.

Administered by the Ministry of Food, the first foodstuffs to be rationed, on 8 January, were bacon, butter, and sugar. Other items to be rationed included tea and cooking fat in July 1940. A typical weekly allowance for an adult would be 50g (2oz) of butter, 100g (4oz) of bacon and ham, 100g (4oz) of margarine, 225g (8oz) of sugar, 1,800ml (3 pints) of milk, 50g (2oz) of cheese, one fresh egg, 50g (2oz) of tea and meat to the

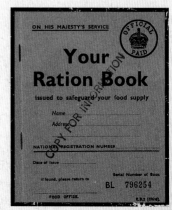

RIGHT Green ration books, such as this for children under the age of five, conferred extra entitlements, including a pint of milk each day.

value of one shilling and sixpence (as it was allocated by price, cheaper offcuts were popular). The jam ration was 450g (1lb) every two months, dried eggs one packet every four weeks and sweets 350g (12oz) every four weeks. In addition, everyone was allowed 16 points a month that could be pooled to purchase canned goods biscuits and dried fruit.

In tandem with rationing the Ministry of Food ran a 'Dig for Victory' campaign that encouraged food self-sufficiency. Vegetables were grown anywhere that could be cultivated, and pigs, chickens and rabbits were reared domestically for meat. And wasting food was made a criminal offence in July 1940.

The Ministry of Food employed 50,000 civil servants and they laboured to ensure that the rationing system was fair and evenly distributed. The so-called black market was smaller than often imagined, though storekeepers did sell small surpluses to favoured customers. But government vigilance restricted the black market: by March 1941, 2,300 people had been prosecuted and severely penalised for fraud and dishonesty. The songwriter Ivor Novello was imprisoned for eight weeks for fraudulently obtaining petrol for his Rolls-Royce.

It is true that people in Britain had much less to eat than they would have wished, and as the war dragged on there was almost nothing that was not rationed or in short supply. Non-food items that were rationed included clothing (June 1941), coal because large numbers of miners were being called up (July 1941) and domestic gas and electricity (by March 1942).

Nevertheless, there was no starvation in Britain during the war and most appreciated the fairness and equality of rationing. Policies such as 'British Restaurants', run by local authorities, were greatly appreciated. Often set up in schools and church halls, they provided cheap meals for workers and fed those bombed out of their homes. By 1944 there were 2,000 British Restaurants in London alone.

ABOVE Storekeepers in Britain kept a record of purchases in each customer's ration book.

THE *ALTMARK* INCIDENT

DATE

16 February, 1940

SUMMARY

The rescue of 299 British POWs led to the German invasion of Norway.

LOCATION

Jøssingfjord, Norway

The Nazi leader regarded the declaration of Norwegian neutrality in September 1940 as a most satisfactory state of affairs, not least because a neutral Norway meant that Swedish iron ore, crucial to the German war effort, could reach Germany in relative safety by remaining within Norwegian territorial waters. However, events during the winter of 1939–40 changed the situation dramatically – and with it the course of the war.

The Soviet invasion of Finland offered a possible pretext for Anglo-French intervention in Scandinavia, specifically the occupation of Norwegian ports so aid could be ferried to the Finns. This came to nothing when Norway refused to co-operate, but the incident that confirmed to Berlin that Norwegian neutrality was in fact not beneficial to Germany was the *Altmark* incident.

In February 1940, British naval vessels intercepted and boarded a German naval auxiliary, the *Altmark*, inside Norwegian territorial waters, in order to free 299 British prisoners on board. The incident convinced the Germans that the Norwegians would offer no resistance to Anglo-French forces should they decide to occupy the country. So Hitler decided that he would act first.

SUCCESSFUL OPERATION

Speed and daring epitomised the German invasion, codenamed *Weserübung*, which commenced on 9 April, 1940. The aim was to overwhelm resistance by bold initial strikes and to seize key airfields and ports to deny any Anglo-French assistance.

The operation was also extremely risky because it violated the principle of concentration of force and invited German forces to be defeated in detail (though only if the Allies could react quickly).

German air-to-ground co-operation was extremely effective and by 10 April the Germans were in possession of all of their objectives. To make matters worse for the Norwegians, Allied forces were not

landed in the country until 14 April, by which time the Germans had
consolidated their hold over central and southern Norway. By 28 April,
the British and French had decided to withdraw from central Norway
and, even though they had pushed German forces out of Narvik, the
Wehrmacht invasion of France and the Low Countries prompted the
evacuation of all Allied forces from Narvik by 8 June. On the same day
the Norwegian government agreed to a cease-fire.

LONG-TERM EFFECTS

The Germans had committed some 100,000 troops to the invasion and
had lost 1,028 killed and 1,604 wounded – remarkably light casualties.
On the other hand, the German navy had lost three cruisers and ten
destroyers, which would reduce the possibility of invading England
later in the year.

Of far greater significance to Nazi Germany was the securing of
an ice-free port through which Swedish iron ore could be shipped.
Throughout the war, Swedish iron ore remained vital to the German
war economy. The steel mills of the Ruhr depended on imported iron
ore for almost three-quarters of their steel-making needs, and Sweden
supplied more than 11 million tons
of that in 1939 alone. And Swedish
ore was high grade, which meant
that it could be used to produce
high-quality steel suitable for
armour plate and gun barrels. For
Sweden, the trade was extremely
lucrative, not only in coal that was
supplied in return, but also 28.3 tons
of gold as payment for iron ore (all of
it looted from Belgium and Holland).

BELOW HMS *Cossack*
docked at Leith in Scotland on
17 February, 1940, after rescuing
299 British prisoners held on the
German supply ship *Altmark*.

27

CHURCHILL BECOMES BRITISH PRIME MINISTER

DATE

10 May, 1940

SUMMARY

The greatest wartime leader assumed the reins of power as Britain entered a period of peril

LOCATION

London,
Great Britain

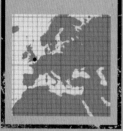

The British and French response to the German invasion of Norway was slow and piecemeal, and against German daring and aggression had predictable results: by 14 April, six days after their attack, the Germans had secured all their initial objectives. On 7 May, during a British House of Commons debate on the Norwegian campaign, Leo Amery, a Conservative member of Parliament, rose to his feet and, pointing at Prime Minister Neville Chamberlain, said: 'Depart I say and let us have done. In the name of God, go'.

Chamberlain, the Conservative prime minister associated with appeasement, had lost the support of his party and the Commons. He resigned on 10 May and Winston Churchill, the First Lord of the Admiralty, replaced him. It was not an automatic choice. Churchill, who had deserted the Conservative Party to join the Liberal Party, only to rejoin the Conservatives years later, was seen as a maverick, unpredictable, even untrustworthy. Furthermore, he was closely associated with the Gallipoli disaster in World War I, which had not been forgotten. However, he had great journalistic and rhetorical skills, and his warnings about German rearmament had proved prophetic. His condemnation of the Munich Agreement had also been correct.

BRITISH GRIT

Though there were many MPs in the Conservative Party and among the opposition who were far from being Churchill supporters, Parliament chose him to be prime minister, preferring dynamism, a strong will and determination (ironically the qualities possessed by Hitler) to negotiation and defeatism.

Leading a coalition government, Churchill epitomised the British bulldog spirit. His pugnacious appearance, cigar and rousing speeches came to represent British grit and determination. In the dark days of the summer of 1940, when Britain and France were defeated in mainland Europe and the British Isles were subsequently besieged by the German navy and air force, his resolute leadership and evocative speeches inspired the British people to fight on against all the odds. Some of his words have entered legend: 'I have nothing to offer but blood, toil, tears and sweat', and, talking of the fighter pilots of the Royal Air Force (RAF) in the Battle of Britain, 'Never in the field of human conflict was so much owed by so many to so few'.

LEFT Winston Churchill in a typically pugnacious pose. His unequivocal defiance of the German threat proved inspirational.

Churchill, like members of the royal family, also toured bombed-out areas during the Blitz to help bolster civilian morale. Above all, it was his indomitable will to go on fighting that rallied the British people. Immediately after the debacle at Dunkirk, for example, he had stated: 'In no circumstances whatsoever would the British Government participate in any negotiations for armistice or peace'.

A RALLYING FIGURE

Of course, Churchill did not single-handedly turn defeat into victory, nor was he without critics (especially among the Conservative Party). But when he came to power he did invigorate the government and inspire the population. In August 1940, for example, a poll showed that 88 percent of the population approved of his leadership (in May 1945 it stood at 83 percent). This made it relatively easy for Churchill to build a social consensus that allowed Britain to weather more easily the severity of wartime austerity and military setbacks. He would also achieve a political consensus by inviting leading Labour Party MPs into his coalition government, such as Clement Attlee (Deputy Prime Minister), Herbert Morrison (Home Secretary) and Ernest Bevin (Minister of Labour and National Service).

THE BATTLE OF SEDAN

DATE

13–15 May, 1940

SUMMARY

The battle that cut Allied armies in France in two by creating the 'panzer corridor' and virtually guaranteed a German victory in the west.

LOCATION

Sedan, France

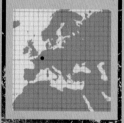

On the eve of the German attack in the west in May 1940, both sides were evenly match in terms of divisions. The Germans committed 136 divisions (though 44 were held back as a strategic reserve) to the offensive. Facing them were 96 French divisions, 10 British divisions, 21 Belgian divisions and eight Dutch divisions – 135 in total. The Allies could muster 4,296 tanks against the Germans' 3,380. But the German army had a plan that would make numbers irrelevant.

The brainchild of Major-General Erich von Manstein, the Chief of Staff of Army Group A, it was termed *Sichelschnitt* (Cut of the Scythe). It comprised a concentrated mechanised strike through the weak French centre in the Ardennes (French and British units would be sucked north by powerful German attacks into Belgium and Holland). The plan was extremely risky because it called for seven panzer divisions – 1,900 tanks, 41,000 motor vehicles and 175,000 men – to travel through the heavily forested Ardennes, often along single, narrow, winding roads. But the plan was bold and innovative and was given the green light.

CROSSING THE MEUSE

The German attack in the West commenced on 10 May. In the Ardennes, three German corps – XV Panzer (5th and 7th Panzer Divisions), XLI Panzer (6th and 8th Panzer Divisions) and XIX Panzer (1st, 2nd and 10th Panzer Divisions) – brushed aside weak French and Belgian defences during 10–12 May and approached the River Meuse. Getting through the Ardennes was only the first part of the operation; if the Germans could not get across the river before the French could recover, the plan would fail.

Heinz Guderian's XIX Panzer Corps reached the river at Sedan during the evening of 12 May. On the opposite side of the waterway was the French 55th Infantry Division, occupying fortified positions on the southern riverbank, with superb observation points obtained from the Marfée Heights south of the German crossing sectors. French infantry also enjoyed fire support from heavy artillery batteries. It was a strong position but would collapse in the face of the German Blitzkrieg.

On 13 May, the assault began, preceded by 750 bombers and Stuka dive-bombers, which pounded the French positions. Guderian's artillery then unleashed a bombardment, supported by direct fire from 700 panzers lined up along the German-held bank of the river. The French, mentally shattered by the intense air and artillery bombardment, were unable to stop riflemen crossing the river in rubber boats. As Guderian himself stated: 'The troops had been ordered to keep up the attack without pause throughout the night'.

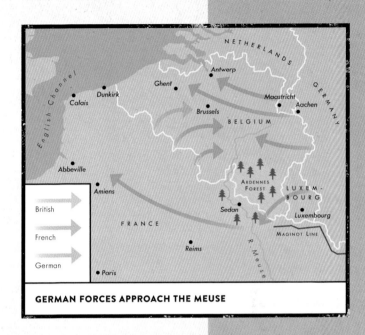

GERMAN FORCES APPROACH THE MEUSE

French resistance began to crumble and by 14 May infantry and engineers had expanded the German bridgehead. Tanks now began to pour across the river and, by the evening of 15 May, six panzer divisions were striking rapidly west in a 'panzer corridor' 76km (47 miles) wide into the rear of the French centre. Worse, the German armoured advance beyond the Meuse between Sedan and Namur threatened the southern flank of French, British and Belgian forces to the north. With air superiority, there was little to stop the advance of the panzers as they left the Meuse and entered the open plains of the French countryside.

To compound the unfolding disaster, the French high command, having first believed that the three German panzer corps would swing east behind the Maginot Line, on 17 May changed their minds and were convinced that they would now turn southwest towards Paris. But the panzers were heading for the English Channel. Bypassing pockets of resistance, the panzers advanced 64km (40 miles) on 18 May, though they only managed 24km (15 miles) on 19 May. This was due to combat support services struggling to keep up with the panzer spearheads rather than enemy action. On 20 May, the panzers reached the Channel coast at Abbeville. It was a stunning demonstration of Blitzkrieg warfare.

ABOVE In only three days, panzer corps swept through the Ardennes forest and closed in on the River Meuse. After capturing Sedan, they moved northwards to complete the encirclement of Allied forces.

HITLER HALTS
THE PANZERS

DATE

24 May, 1940

SUMMARY

With the British
Expeditionary Force
herded into a pocket
around the port of
Dunkirk, Hitler
ordered his panzers
to halt.

LOCATION

Maison Blairon,
France

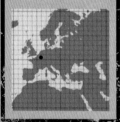

The German breakthrough at Sedan and subsequent armoured thrust to the English Channel had isolated those Allied units to the north, which were forced to retreat to Calais and Dunkirk. These ports represented the sole means of escape for the British, French and Belgian troops trapped against the coast by the enemy advance. The panzers began to push towards the ports but on 24 May were ordered to halt for 48 hours.

The order was issued by Hitler at a meeting of Army Group A's headquarters in the Maison Blairon, a small French château at Charleville-Mézières. It was a decision that incensed General Paul von Kleist, the commander of Panzer Group Kleist (which included Guderian's XIX Panzer Corps). His panzers were only 28.8km (18 miles) from Dunkirk when they were ordered to stop. He wrote: 'There was a channel from Arras to Dunkirk. I had already crossed this channel and my troops occupied the heights which jutted out over Flanders. Therefore, my panzer group had complete control of Dunkirk and the area in which the British were trapped.

'The fact of the matter is that the English would have been unable to get into Dunkirk because I had them covered. Then Hitler personally ordered that I should withdraw my troops from these areas.'

THE PUSH SOUTH

With hindsight, Hitler's decision would appear to be military madness, but closer inspection reveals it to be grounded in reality. First, by 23 May the five armies of Army Group A were extended over 416km (260 miles) and its ten panzer divisions were widely spaced. Second, France had not been defeated. Indeed, there were still large French forces in the field to the south and those panzer divisions would be needed to reduce them. The dash to the Channel had been spectacular but had taken a heavy toll on both men and machines. Kleist himself had reported to Rundstedt, the commander of Army Group A, on 23 May that his group had suffered heavy losses in men and equipment. His tank casualties

(knocked out and broken down) amounted to over 50 percent. In view of this, Rundstedt had said to Hitler at Maison Blairon that it would be wise to conserve the panzers for the push to the south.

The reality was that the ground around Dunkirk was littered with channels and streams and was not ideal tank country. It was terrain where infantry would be much more effective, but Army Group A's infantry had yet to catch up with the panzers. In addition, *Luftwaffe* chief Hermann Göring had assured Hitler that his aircraft could destroy the Dunkirk pocket alone. The army would have nothing to do but conduct mopping-up operations. The army High Command was also reluctant to send the panzers into urban areas, the lessons of heavy tank losses in Warsaw in 1939 being fresh in their minds.

ABOVE Perhaps surprisingly, given the character of some of his later decisions, Hitler's stop order struck a note of caution in an otherwise rapid and hugely successful campaign.

PROTECTING THE FLANKS

There was also another reason why Dunkirk was not the only thing occupying the minds of Hitler and his generals. On 21 May, British and French tanks launched a counterattack at Arras. Spearheaded by the British First Army Tank Brigade, 58 Matilda Mk I and 16 Matilda Mk II tanks rumbled forward, supported by a small French armoured assault. The British tanks caused panic among the soldiers of the 7th Panzer Division and SS Totenkopf Division before being halted. But the attack shocked Hitler and his High Command, who feared for the vulnerable flanks of the panzer corridor. In the subsequent days, it was the French, not the British, who were occupying the Führer's mind.

Hitler was also dismissive of the British. When Kleist spoke to him at Cambrai a few days after his halt order, he informed his general that 'The British won't come back in this war'. But his halt order had given the Allies vital time to strengthen the perimeter and begin the evacuation from the beaches of Dunkirk.

THE MIRACLE OF DUNKIRK

DATE

27 May–4 June, 1940

SUMMARY

The Dunkirk evacuation saved the British Expeditionary Force from annihilation.

LOCATION

Dunkirk, France

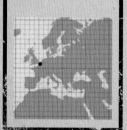

On 25 May, recognising the futility of mounting any more offensives in support of the French army, Lord Gort, the commander of the British Expeditionary Force (BEF), ordered his units to begin the retreat towards the Channel port of Dunkirk. The next day Gort and the French commander of the First Army Group, General Blanchard, made plans to create a defensive perimeter around Dunkirk. The French were intent on fighting on, the British on evacuation, but on 28 May word reached them that the Belgians had surrendered unconditionally. This exposed the northern flank of the Allied pocket to German attack. Evacuation was now the only option.

In Britain, the government had authorised the Royal Navy to commence the evacuation at 18:57 hours on 26 May. Codenamed Operation Dynamo, it was the responsibility of Vice-Admiral Bertram Ramsay. He faced a number of immediate problems, not least that the shallow waters around Dunkirk meant he could not use his largest ships (instead he had a fleet of destroyers, passenger ferry steamers and Dutch coasters). In addition, Dunkirk had been under enemy shelling for days and the inner harbour was out of use. The only option was to use the beaches outside the port.

A VICTORY FOR THE 'LITTLE SHIPS'

On 28 May, the evacuation from the beaches began to pick up speed, aided by the reopening of the harbour – 17,804 men were rescued on that day. But now Dunkirk was under German bombardment, the *Luftwaffe* was operating overhead and U-boats and mines lay out to sea. On 29 May, HMS *Wakeful* was sunk by an E-boat (torpedo boat), HMS *Grafton* was sunk by *U-62* and a civilian ship, *Mona's Queen*, was sunk by a mine. But from 30 May the British effort was greatly aided by the intervention of the 'little ships'. These were hundreds of privately owned boats that sailed across the English Channel to help carry out the audacious rescue. They provided critical help in ferrying men from the shallow inshore waters to the larger vessels waiting offshore. Some 200 of these boats were lost in the course of the four-day operation.

1 June witnessed the second-highest number of men evacuated and the next day it was estimated that only 6,000 British and 65,000 French troops were left in Dunkirk. On 3 June, a further 26,746 men were evacuated from Dunkirk, most from the harbour. During the night of 3 and 4 June, 26,175 French troops were evacuated. Operation Dynamo officially ended at 14:23 hours on 4 June.

The operation had been a great success: 338,226 men had been evacuated from Dunkirk, two-thirds of them French. The BEF left 2,472 artillery pieces, 63,879 vehicles and 508,000 tonnes (500,000 tons) of supplies and ammunition behind. Some 243 ships had been sunk, of which six were Royal Navy destroyers, and the RAF had lost 106 aircraft during the fighting.

For the men on the beaches, the experience had been traumatic. Hunger, exhaustion, the constant bombing and enemy machine-gun fire placed individuals under appalling strain. Maintaining discipline under such circumstances was difficult and in some cases broke down completely. More common was a sort of shell-shock that made men lethargic, except when a boat appeared, which induced a mad rush into the sea. This created its own problems, as small boats were threatened with being swamped by large groups of men.

There were small mercies. *Luftwaffe* bombs sank deep in the sand and their blast was muffled and deadened. This awakened a sense of confidence, reinforced by the unceasing efforts of the Royal Navy and the 'little boats' to get men off the beaches. That the BEF had been evacuated had been a miracle, but as Churchill stated on 4 June: 'Wars are not won by evacuations'.

Eyewitness

CAPTAIN DUGGAN WAS THE MASTER OF *MONA'S QUEEN*, WHICH MADE THE CROSSING TO DUNKIRK ON THE FIRST EVENING OF THE OPERATION.

'Shells were flying all around us. The ship was riddled with shrapnel, mostly all on the boat and promenade decks. Then we were attacked from the air. A Junkers bomber made a power dive towards us and dropped five bombs, but he was off the mark. Then another Junkers attacked us, but before he reached us he was brought down in flames.

Owing to the bombardment, I could see that the nerves of some of my men were badly shaken. I did not feel too well myself, but I mustered the crew and told them that Dunkirk was being bombed and was on fire.'

SEVEN DAYS IN JUNE

DATE

5–9 June, 1940

SUMMARY

The lightning campaign crushed the French army and brought the war in France to an end in 1940.

LOCATION

France

Following the reduction of the Dunkirk Pocket, the German army regrouped for the destruction of the remainder of the French army, which was deployed behind the Somme and Aisne rivers and the Maginot Line. Under the supreme command of General Maxime Weygand, the three French army groups – 2, 3 and 4 – were tasked with conducting a defence in depth behind the two rivers. Unfortunately, they were totally inadequate and were unable to hold off the German army.

Along the 360km (225 miles) of front stretching from the coast to the Maginot Line, the French had 40 infantry divisions (some of which had suffered heavy losses during the fighting in May), three light cavalry divisions with only 36 armoured vehicles between them (out of their original 112), and three armoured divisions (all with less than 40 of their original 200 tanks left). To hold the Maginot Line from the River Moselle to the Jura Mountains, the French had a paltry 17 mountain divisions.

Against the French army, the Germans were able to commit 130 divisions, 10 of which were panzers, dispersed between Fedor von Bock's Army Group B on the line of the Somme east to Bourg, Gerd von Rundstedt's Army Group A from Bourg east to the Moselle and Ritter von Leeb's Army Group C from the Moselle to the French border.

Weygand realised that his forces were inferior in terms of manpower and equipment, so issued instructions for a 'chessboard' pattern of operational bases to be established to face the Germans. Called 'hedgehogs', they were installed in villages and woods and filled with 75mm field guns, which would act as anti-tank weapons. To support

Eyewitness

ON JUNE GENERAL GEORGES WROTE OF HIS FRENCH FOURTH ARMY:

'Exhausted by four days of battle and night marches, the troops no longer have the appearance of organised units. Communications have broken down. The orders, carried by officers bogged down in the columns of refugees, can no longer be carried out when they at last arrive at their destination.'

these defences, the French air force had an operational strength of 599 aircraft, supplemented by some British aircraft: 39 Hurricanes and 82 Fairey Battles. The *Luftwaffe* had over 5,000 aircraft, though this included gliders and transport aircraft. Nevertheless, it was a significant superiority that began to have a telling effect even before hostilities began. During the first three days of June, for example, the *Luftwaffe* attacked 30 French airfields, 60 rail targets and 50 other targets. On 5 June, Operation Red, the codename for the German offensive, began.

ABOVE A still from the U.S. Army propaganda film *Why We Fight*. It shows the reaction of French civilians in Toulon, witnessing the last of the French army fleeing to North Africa.

GERMAN BLITZ

....

For the first two days, the French in their 'hedgehogs' fought well but numbers, firepower and aerial superiority began to tell. In the west, Hoth's XV Panzer Corps annihilated the 'hedgehogs' of the French Tenth Army; in the east, the German Ninth Army pushed French units back to the south bank of the River Aisne. The French air force attempted to strafe enemy armoured columns but German flak defences were formidable. Between 5–9 June, the French lost 130 aircraft. As the Germans established air superiority, the *Luftwaffe* attacked French railways, defences, communications centres and troop columns. The thousands of refugees on the roads were also subjected to air attacks.

By 7 June, the French line was disintegrating. With their defensive positions having been overrun or pulverised by artillery and air attack, German units were able to bypass them. Erwin Rommel's 7th Panzer Division did just that on the morning of 7 June, pushing forward to open ground and advancing 59km (37 miles) south of the River Somme by the day's end. On 10 June, German forces were crossing the lower Seine to the west of Paris and in the east they were pushing from the River Ourcq to the Marne. The city was facing being flanked on two sides, and there were no reserves to save it.

That evening the French government left Paris for Tours on its way to Bordeaux. On 11 June, Paris was declared an 'open city'. To all intents and purposes the campaign in France was over. Fighting would go on until 21 June, when the French capitulated and hostilities officially ceased on 25 June. It was the culmination of a stunningly successful campaign by the German army in the West.

CRACKING THE GERMAN MILITARY CODES

DATE

June 1940

SUMMARY

This vital intelligence work allowed the British to read secret German military communications from 1940 onwards.

LOCATION

Great Britain

Radios had been used for military communications very early in the 20th century. Radio messages can be understood by friend and foe alike and so the practice of encrypting messages, so they became unreadable to all except their intended recipients, was well established before World War I. This cryptography became dependent upon complex electric coding machines. The German Enigma was one such machine, which resembled a typewriter in appearance. It worked by scrambling text typed into it by means of notched wheels or rotors. A similar machine unscrambled the message sent, with its rotors adjusted to the same settings as the sending machine.

The Germans refined Enigma by adding plugs with variable electronic circuits, whose settings operators changed every 24 hours, according to code books listing the daily variations. This resulted in millions of different code variations, leading the Germans to believe that Enigma was unbreakable. Of course no system is unbreakable but notwithstanding this Enigma was already under threat in the 1920s.

BLETCHLEY PARK

Polish intelligence had obtained an Enigma machine in 1929 and the Poles had developed a type of crude computer, called the bomba, which had only limited success in deciphering Enigma. In 1939, in an amazing act of generosity, the Poles gave the intelligence services of Britain and France replica Enigma machines. The French were unable to make much headway in cracking Enigma because France fell in 1940, but Britain's code breakers had the time and resources to study the German machine. The Code and Cypher School was based at Bletchley Park in Buckinghamshire and would eventually employ 6,000 people who were housed in its sprawling grounds. The government made a determined effort to enlist leading mathematicians at Bletchley Park. They included John Jeffreys, Peter Twinn and Alan Turing.

The intelligence gathered was the responsibility of Y Service, which comprised hundreds of interception radio operators drawn from the army, navy and air force. The name given to deciphering Enigma messages was Ultra. The code breakers' first success came on 23 January, 1940, when they cracked the German army's administrative key, which became known as 'The Green'. They also cracked the 'Red' key used by *Luftwaffe* liaison officers co-ordinating air support for army units. German naval codes proved more difficult to crack but the task was aided by the capture of *U-110* in May 1941.

The intelligence summaries generated by Bletchley Park were forwarded to appropriate recipients by Special Liaison Units. These were teams of radio operators who received summaries of the decrypted messages, which were encrypted for safe transmission, and passed them on to officers of the very highest ranks only. These operations were shrouded in the utmost secrecy to safeguard the effectiveness of Ultra.

GERMAN HUBRIS

How successful was Ultra? The short answer was: very successful. Ultra decrypts discovered that the German battleship *Bismarck*, for example, put to sea not to engage the British fleet but to raid the Atlantic trade routes. Bletchley Park was able to read all the Enigma signals of the German *Abwehr* (intelligence), which meant that the British captured every German spy that landed in Britain. Ultra was able to confirm that the German invasion of the USSR would take place in June 1941 (by reading Enigma *Luftwaffe* messages). Finally, in the Atlantic the Allies moved their convoys through the North Atlantic on the basis of Ultra information, when available, to avoid U-boat 'wolfpacks'. Ironically the Germans' faith in the invulnerability of Enigma aided Bletchley Park. Although the Germans realised that the Allies were receiving accurate intelligence, such was their faith in Enigma that they discounted the idea that Allied intelligence could decrypt its signals. When German commanders raised the possibility that Enigma had been cracked they were given short shrift. In 1943, for example, the commander of U-boats suggested that the British had cracked the codes but was told by higher headquarters: 'Decrypting, if possible at all, could only be achieved with such an expenditure of effort and after so long a period of time that the results would be valueless'.

ABOVE The capture of an enigma machine from *U-110* was a huge step towards cracking the German codes and fundamentally altering the course of the war.

BRITAIN INTRODUCES A RADAR NETWORK

DATE

August 1940

SUMMARY

New technology gave the Royal Air Force the ability to concentrate its scarce fighter resources against the *Luftwaffe* during the Battle of Britain.

LOCATION

The south coast of England

As sonar is used to detect enemy submarines, radar is a way of detecting the location and speed of hostile aircraft. Radar makes use of radio waves travelling at 300,000km (187,500 miles) per second to detect distant objects.

In the 1930s, in response to the development of bomber forces by the *Luftwaffe*, the British Air Ministry decided to build a chain of radio detection stations, spaced 32km (20 miles) apart, around the south coast of England. Seven of these stations were in operation by August 1936 and marked the beginning of the Chain Home (CH) radar network.

Eyewitness

OBERFELDWEBEL MANFRED LANGER WAS A PILOT WITH *KAMPFGESCHWADER* 3, A *LUFTWAFFE* BOMBING WING, DURING THE BATTLE OF BRITAIN.

'Day after day we were flying operational duties. The constant run of failures to achieve our goals of destroying our targets due to being constantly intercepted by British fighters was beginning to take its toll. Time and time again we tell our commanding officers that we must destroy the radar systems because we are always being met over the Channel by Spitfires and Hurricanes. The British pilots are very clever, they seem to be able to turn us around and we are forced to return to our bases, not only with bullet holes all over our aircraft, but with dead or injured crewmen that have to be attended to on the return flight.

We became tired and exhausted, each new day brought new missions and then came the night operations. Man can only take so much, he is not a machine, although I think that our commanders thought differently. When the weather is too bad for flying, it is like a dream come true.'

FLOODING THE AIRSPACE

....

The technology used in the CH network was not new but it was entirely suited to providing a radar screen to defend the British Isles from enemy aircraft flying from Europe. Transmitter aerials mounted on tall masts 'floodlit' the airspace in front of them with pulses of radio energy which, when reflected back from an aircraft, were picked up by a receiver aerial. The range of the 'echo' was measured on the screen of a cathode ray tube but the bearing and height of the target could only be determined through triangulation from other stations using a radio direction-finding instrument called a goniometer.

Because the British system used a long wavelength that required large antenna arrays to radiate sufficient power the masts at each station were enormous. Transmission at each station required four masts, each one 110m (360ft) high and 55m (180ft) apart, between which the antenna wires were strung. The returned signal was received by other masts that were 73m (240ft) in height. In addition, the system could not rotate, which meant that once aircraft passed over the CH network it was useless. And yet radar was crucial in winning the Battle of Britain.

When war broke out in September 1939 CH had 18 stations covering the eastern and half the southern coast of Britain, and the network was a vital part of the Dowding System. Named after the Commander-in-Chief of Royal Air Force (RAF) Fighter Command, Air Chief Marshal Sir Hugh Dowding, it integrated technology, ground defences and fighter aircraft into a unified system of defence.

The stations of CH gave a 20-minute warning of the approach of enemy aircraft. The information was reported to a Filter Room, which in turn sent Fighter Command accurate intelligence regarding the location of enemy air fleets. This allowed Fighter Command to deploy its scarce resources to maximum effect, much to the frustration of the *Luftwaffe* (see box).

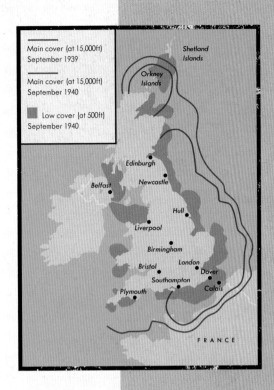

Main cover (at 15,000ft) September 1939

Main cover (at 15,000ft) September 1940

Low cover (at 500ft) September 1940

Shetland Islands

Orkney Islands

Edinburgh

Belfast

Newcastle

Hull

Liverpool

Birmingham

Bristol

London

Dover

Southampton

Calais

Plymouth

FRANCE

ABOVE Britain's Chain Home radar network covered all of Britain's eastern and southeastern coastline, giving Fighter Command 20 minutes to scramble its aircraft.

THE BATTLE OF BRITAIN

DATE

24 August–
6 September, 1940

SUMMARY

This decisive phase
of the battle for
Britain saved the
British Isles from
a German invasion.

LOCATION

Great Britain

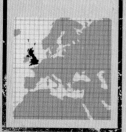

Following the fall of France Hitler turned his attention to dealing with Britain. On 5 June, 1940, he decided to invade the British Isles with an operation codenamed Sea Lion. If an invasion was to succeed, German control of the North Sea and specifically the English Channel was essential. To achieve this the *Luftwaffe* was given the task of first defeating the Royal Air Force (RAF) and then disabling the Royal Navy.

Hermann Göring, head of the *Luftwaffe*, assembled three *luftflotten* (air fleets) for the offensive, a total of 2,800 aircraft (two-thirds of them bombers).

THE FEW

Pitted against the *Luftwaffe* was RAF Fighter Command under Air Chief Marshal Hugh Dowding: 650 fighters and 1,300 pilots. The British also had radar stations that helped to pinpoint enemy aircraft formations, routes and strengths. This information was fed to ground-control systems that allowed fighters to be concentrated against enemy aircraft. Nevertheless, in the first phase of the battle, in which the Germans attempted to lure the British fighters into combat and shoot them out of the sky, the RAF lost 181 fighters in the air and another 30 on the ground (between 8 and 18 August).

On 24 August the Germans changed their strategy to strike targets further inland, the prime targets being fighter airfields and particularly those of No 11 Group, from which the British fighters in the southeast of England were controlled. To guard against losses the *Luftwaffe* sent over a larger proportion of fighters to protect its bombers. The aim was simple: to fatally weaken Fighter Command.

On 24 August the Germans attacked the RAF sector stations of North Weald (Essex) and Hornchurch (east of London). Two days later they attempted to hit the RAF bases at Biggin Hill (Kent), Kenley (Surrey), North Weald and Hornchurch but were beaten off by Hurricane and Spitfire fighters. But on 30 August Biggin Hill was struck twice, resulting in great damage. The next day 39 RAF aircraft were lost defending the air bases at Debden (Essex), Biggin Hill and Hornchurch. Biggin Hill and North Weald were attacked again between 1 and 6 September. Fighter Command was buckling under the strain.

Between 24 August and 6 September the *Luftwaffe* conducted 33 major raids, two-thirds of which were against the sector stations (a sector station controlled three squadrons) and other stations of Fighter Command. Over this period a daily average of 1,000 German aircraft operated over England. The *Luftwaffe* had lost 380 aircraft but Fighter Command had lost 286. Worse, the RAF lost 103 fighter pilots killed and 128 wounded out of a fighting strength at the time of just over 1,000. In addition, the sector station of Biggin Hill had been severely damaged and could control only one squadron instead of three. British fighter aircraft production was not keeping up with losses and the loss of experienced pilots was potentially crippling. If the Germans had kept up the attacks on the airfields and factories, the RAF would have lost the Battle of Britain. On 7 September, however, the Germans changed their strategy. The *Luftwaffe* was directed to strike another target: London.

ABOVE Air-raid wardens were ever-present in British cities during the Battle of Britain. They worked to enforce blackouts and put out incendiary bombs.

A FATEFUL DECISION

The decision to strike London was primarily in retaliation for the RAF raids on Berlin (which caused little damage but which enraged Hitler and had a massive psychological effect on Berliners). An attack on London would also, the Germans believed, result in greater air battles as Fighter Command committed its resources to the defence of the British capital, leading to increased aircraft losses. Hitler also believed that the bombing of London might paralyse the machinery of government.

London was thus bombed and civilian casualties rose but the abandonment of the attacks on the airfields meant that the wastage of Hurricanes and Spitfires was more than offset by factory output. And, crucially, Fighter Command still dominated the skies over Britain. On 12 October Hitler formally postponed Sea Lion until the spring of 1941.

CONVOY HX-72

DATE
....
20–22 September, 1940

SUMMARY
....
One of the most successful U-boat operations of 1940, which showed how devastating Dönitz's tactics could be.

LOCATION
....
Atlantic Ocean

The 'wolfpacks' were the creation of Admiral Karl Dönitz, the head of Germany's U-boat arm. The tactic was quite simple: U-boats would be deployed in lines to scout for enemy convoys. Once a convoy was spotted a U-boat would be designated as 'shadower' and would report the convoy's speed and direction to U-boat Tactical Command. The latter would then contact nearby submarines to converge on the convoy and attack it. Though France had been defeated in June 1940, giving the *Kriegsmarine* access to French Atlantic ports, Dönitz did not have enough U-boats to form comprehensive patrol lines (only 61 submarines by September 1940). The convoy battles of 1940 tended to be conducted by hastily gathered groups. But they were nevertheless deadly.

TARGETING CONVOYS

The British recognised the threat posed by the U-boats and the Admiralty put in place a convoy system on the outbreak of war as a way of protecting Britain's 3,000 oceangoing merchant vessels and 1,000 large merchant coastal ships. A convoy of 45–60 ships, for example, would travel in nine or 12 columns, with 914m (1,000 yards) between columns and 550m (600 yards) between ships. When defended by sea and air assets a convoy was a difficult target to attack – but not impossible, especially in 1940, when many convoys were weakly defended.

Convoy HX-72 left Halifax, Nova Scotia, Canada, on 17 September – 42 merchant ships sailing in nine columns. The armed merchant cruiser HMS *Jervis Bay*, which was then ordered to depart to escort another, westbound, convoy, escorted it. At this point HX-72 was some 800km (500 miles) west of Ireland. The ships of the Royal Navy's Western Approaches Command would escort the convoy when it got to within 640km (400 miles) of the west coast of Ireland. This meant there was a 20-hour gap when the convoy had no escort. It was during this time, late on 20 September, that it was spotted by *U-47*. The submarine reported the position of the convoy to Dönitz, who ordered several U-boats to converge on the convoy in a 'wolfpack'. The conditions – light winds and a full moon – were ideal for a U-boat attack (which was invariably made on the surface at night).

The action began during the early hours of September when *U-99* torpedoed and sank the tanker *Invershannon*, after which it sank the *Baron Blythswood* and the *Elmbank*. Having used up its torpedoes *U-99* sailed for home. Other U-boats now joined the 'pack' during daylight hours: *U-47*, *U-48*, *U-65*, *U-46*, *U-43* and *U-32*. The *Blairangus* was torpedoed and sunk by *U-48* but the arrival of a Royal Navy escort group forced the submarines to withdraw, though they continued to shadow the convoy.

The arrival of *U-100*, commanded by Joachim Schepke, on the evening of 21 September, caused havoc among the merchant ships. Sailing on the surface *U-100* penetrated the convoy and began firing its torpedoes, hitting and sinking three merchant ships: the *Dalcairn*, *Canonesa* and *Torinia*. The convoy scattered but this only increased its vulnerability. The *Broompark* was hit and damaged by *U-48* and in the early hours of 22 September *U-100* torpedoed and sank the merchant vessels *Empire Airman*, *Scholar*, *Frederick S. Fales* and *Simla*. Later *U-32* torpedoed and damaged the *Collegian*.

WREAKING HAVOC

In total Dönitz's first 'wolfpack' had sunk 11 merchant ships, totalling 73,890 tonnes (72,727 tons). These ships had been carrying over 101,600 tonnes (100,000 tons) of U.S. supplies and 45,720 tonnes (45,000 tons) of fuel. Britain was soon facing a crisis as Dönitz's submarines sank 343 ships in the Atlantic between June and December 1940.

Fortunately for the British the ability to read German naval Enigma signals after the capture of *U-110* in May 1941 enabled the Royal Navy to provide evasive routing around U-boat concentrations. In addition, increasing the number of escorts for convoys and the introduction of greater air cover also helped to reduce the U-boats' effectiveness. But in 1940 these developments were still in the future.

ABOVE After the losses inflicted by U-boats in 1940, the U.S. Navy ramped up the production of destroyer escorts (DEs), which provided protection to convoys.

BRITAIN INTRODUCES SONAR

DATE

September 1940

SUMMARY

The technology that
allowed British
warships to detect
submerged U-boats
played a crucial role
in the Battle of
the Atlantic.

LOCATION

Atlantic Ocean

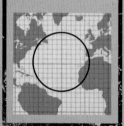

In World War I the British recognised that a way of defeating German U-boats was to give Royal Navy vessels the ability to detect a submerged submarine and equip them with a weapon that had a good chance of destroying it once it had been detected. The weapon was the depth charge, which was first used in 1915. The technology to detect undersea vessels would take longer to develop. The work, which was carried out by a department called the Anti-Submarine Division, was called ASDIC.

LIMITED PROTECTION

The British echo-ranging detector was housed in a dome on the underside of a vessel's hull and sent out impulses that, when they struck an object such as a U-boat, returned a pulse echo that gave the target's range and bearing. However, early ASDIC devices were unable to determine its depth. The U.S. Navy had a similar system called Sound Navigation and Ranging (SONAR). Sonar would eventually be the name by which undersea detection systems would be commonly called.

The early Type 123 and Type 129 ASDIC systems had other limitations, such as a short-range effectiveness – 1.2km (1,300 yards) – in good sea conditions. In addition they 'lost' a target during the final 182m (200 yards) of an attack approach, which allowed a U-boat to use the 'blind zone' for evasive manoeuvres. ASDIC was also effective only at low speeds. Above 28km/h (15 knots) the noise of the ship going through the water drowned out the system's echoes.

During searches it was Royal Navy procedure to sweep the ASDIC in an arc from one side of an escort's course to another. Ships working together as escorts for a convoy would deploy in a line some 1.6–2.4km (1–1.5 miles) apart to create a wide ASDIC arc. Once a U-boat was detected a warship would move towards the target and, working on the German vessel's speed and bearing, would plot a course to pass over the submarine. As it did so it would release depth charges in a pattern that resembled a stretched diamond in shape. To disable a U-boat a depth charge had to detonate within 6.1m (20ft) of its hull. Since early ASDIC systems were incapable of determining a submarine's depth the depth charges launched had variable depth settings.

Notwithstanding ASDIC's deficiencies (such as being unable to detect U-boats on the surface) it made a valuable contribution to the British effort in the Battle of the Atlantic at a time when other systems were unavailable. Between September 1939 and September 1940, for example, ASDIC made 25 detections of U-boats, which resulted in the sinking or scuttling of 15 submarines. As detection systems improved sonar became much more effective and by the war's end it had been involved in more than half of the 246 U-boat sinkings.

Eyewitness

LIEUTENANT ANTHONY D'EVELYN TREVOR SANGSTER WAS SERVING ON BOARD THE DESTROYER AND CONVOY ESCORT HMS *VENOMOUS* IN THE ATLANTIC IN 1942.

'The old *Venomous* was coming back into the picture. We had just started a square-mile search of 2-mile sides when our Asdic operator yelled: "Torpedo, torpedo, Green 40 to 70" (40–70 degrees on starboard bow). "Hard a starboard, steady on 110", ordered the Captain quite quietly.

And on the Asdic loudspeaker dwarfing the "ping" of our own transmission everyone could hear the tube-train kind of roar picked up from torpedoes. There was a horrible thud in our own ears, and the loudspeaker roar decreased, there was another horrible thud and the roar ceased altogether. *Marne's* stern had been blown off and the other torpedo had hit *Hecla* again. Immediately, a shaded blue lamp started flashing us from *Marne*, "U-boat my starboard quarter!" "Hard a starboard—full ahead both engines", and off we went cutting past *Marne's* stern. After a minute with no report from radar, the Captain cried, "Fire a Snowflake". With a swish the rocket ascended and far above the magnesium burst into light and floated down on its parachute and there at Red 10 was a submarine powering away on the surface — 400 yards away. At full ahead

Venomous had sunk her stern as her screws bit into the water. There were lots more orders. B gun (4.7 inches) got off two rounds, whose charges were supposed to be non-flash for night-fighting, but we on the bridge were all blinded. The port Oerlikon opened up and tracer crowded round the conning tower of the enemy. I was adding to the din being the Gunnery Officer controlling B Gun. By the next time a Snowflake went up, there was no submarine, just our bow wave spoiling the calm dark sea.

And then we saw it, just near our bow, the still-bubbling swirl of a submarine's dive. The anti-submarine Bo'sun broadcast:

"Stand by emergency pattern — shallow setting — Fire One! Two! Three!"

Venomous careered on and once the mine explosions were over the Captain reduced to 15 knots so as to use his Asdic. We never got contact with the Asdic. We went on searching for an hour and a half. *Hecla* had meanwhile sunk and we kept on hearing shouts from the water and the occasional torch was seen. We stayed at action stations all night, and reduced to two watch defence stations at dawn.'

ITALIAN FIASCO IN GREECE

DATE

....

28 October, 1940–
19 March, 1941

SUMMARY

....

The Italian campaign
in Greece destabi-
lised the Balkans
and delayed
the launch of
Operation Barbarossa.

LOCATION

....

Albania and Greece

Following the stunning *Wehrmacht* victories in the West in 1940,
Nazi Germany was desirous of a stable Balkans, which was either neutral
or, preferably, pro-German. It was essential that events in the Balkans
did not interrupt preparations for Operation Barbarossa, the invasion of
the USSR. On 28 October, 1940, however, the Italians, without alerting
Berlin, invaded northwestern Greece from their colony of Albania
(Hitler and Mussolini had met at the Brenner Pass on 4 October, 1940).

A PIECE OF THE ACTION

The German victories in the West had made Mussolini thirst for his own
military glory, especially along the Adriatic seaboard which he viewed
as an Italian domain. Albania had already become part of the 'New
Roman Empire'. Greece and Yugoslavia would soon follow. To achieve
his aim of conquering Greece in 10 days Mussolini assembled 162,000
troops under the command of Visconti Prasca, against which the Greeks
could muster around 260,000 men in total. The Italians had more
aircraft, more tanks and more artillery and yet the Italian advances
were sluggish from the start.

Attacking at three points the Italians immediately ran into well-
organised Greek mountain defences, In addition, the 150,000 soldiers
under the command of General Alexander Papagos were well led and
highly motivated, in sharp contrast to their Italian opponents. The
Greeks launched a series of counterattacks, the most successful of which
trapped the elite Italian Third Alpine Division near the village of
Vovousa on 3 November.

Things got worse for the Italians on 22 November when the Greeks
launched their own counteroffensive that defeated Mussolini's prized
unit: the mechanised Tenth Army. The Greeks captured Italian-held
Koritsa in Albania on 22 November and the vital Albanian port of
Sarandë on 4 December. The Italian army, badly led, poorly supplied
and demoralised, was collapsing against an enemy that lacked modern

armaments. Greek artillery was of German or French origin and so neither spares nor ammunition were readily available, anti-tank and anti-aircraft artillery was lacking and there was a shortage of modern transport vehicles. In the air the Italians could muster up to 200 fighters in Albania, which were greatly superior to their Greek opponents in terms of armament and performance.

However, the Greeks did receive supplies shipped by the British from North Africa, among which was captured Italian equipment from Libya. The British also sent a detachment of RAF aircraft – Blenheims of 30 Squadron – to assist the Greeks in November. Eventually four RAF squadrons were sent to aid the Greeks.

THE JUNIOR PARTNER

The Italian fiasco brought about a change in the relationship between Mussolini and Hitler. The latter made no attempt to disguise his displeasure at the Italian campaign, which had destabilised the strategic position in the Balkans. It was at this time that Nazi Germany became the dominant partner in the alliance. For the first time Hitler began advising the Italians how to run their war. He informed Mussolini, for example, that Italian aircraft in Albania should be recalled to Italy where they could perform a more useful service by attacking British bases in the Mediterranean than they could in Albania. There was also the realisation in Berlin that the Italians would be unable to defeat the Greeks without assistance.

This view was confirmed at the beginning of January 1941 when the Italians launched a new offensive in Albania to retake territory that had been lost to the Greeks. But once again Greek resistance was fierce and the Italians gained almost no territory but incurred heavy losses. The Italians launched a spring offensive on the Albanian Front on March 9, launching seven of their 28 divisions in Albania into the attack along a 32km (20-mile) front, supported by 159 fighters and 160 bombers. The 14 Greek divisions holding the entire Albanian front were near to exhaustion but they managed to hold their positions. The offensive ended in failure 10 days later.

It was a humiliating defeat for Mussolini and a setback for Hitler's plans. The Germans would be forced to invade Yugoslavia and Greece in April 1941, which would delay the start date of Barbarossa.

OPERATION JUDGEMENT

DATE

11 November, 1940

SUMMARY

The daring Royal Fleet Air Arm attack on the Italian navy confirmed to the Japanese that an attack on Pearl Harbour was viable.

LOCATION

Taranto, Italy

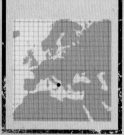

The Italian navy (*Regia Marina*) posed a major threat to the Royal Navy in the Mediterranean in 1940. Possessing 84 surface ships, 67 torpedo boats, and 116 submarines, it had the potential to wreak havoc on British shipping transporting men and supplies to North Africa and Malta. The main strength of the Italian navy was based at Taranto, southern Italy, and so the British decided to attack the base using torpedo-bombers.

The plan, codenamed Judgement, would be the first aerial raid launched from an aircraft carrier against a fleet in a defended harbour. Taranto was a rich target. On 11 November, the day of the raid, the outer harbour contained six battleships, three heavy cruisers and seven destroyers, while in the inner harbour were four heavy cruisers, two light cruisers, 21 cruisers and a number of submarines and smaller ships. To defend shipping the harbour defences comprised 22 searchlights, 21 batteries of 102mm anti-aircraft guns, 84 37mm and 20mm cannon, 109 machine guns and 27 anti-aircraft balloons. The Italians did not have radar but they did have listening devices (airphonic stations) along the Gulf of Taranto coastline. In addition, they had laid 4,200m (4,593 yards) of anti-torpedo nets, though there was a space of 4.2m (14ft) between the bottom of the nets and the bottom of the lagoon. The Italians knew this but believed that the harbour was too shallow for torpedoes dropped by aircraft.

REPURPOSING THE FAIREYS

The aircraft detailed to attack the ships at Taranto were aged Fairey Swordfish, fabric-covered biplanes that were obsolete by 1940. However, they were also agile, rugged, reliable and highly manoeuvrable. What's more, the fact that they were covered with fabric meant anti-aircraft shells passed straight through them instead of exploding. A torpedo was slung under the fuselage of each aircraft and had been adapted with 'air tails' to ensure it did not dive too deep before reaching its running depth.

Eyewitness

THE DISPATCH OF ADMIRAL SIR ANDREW CUNNINGHAM, COMMANDER-IN-CHIEF, MEDITERRANEAN, TO THE BRITISH ADMIRALTY, 16 JANUARY, 1941.

'There can be little doubt that the crippling of half the Italian Battlefleet is having, and will continue to have, a marked effect on the course of the war. Without indulging in speculation as to the political repercussions, it is already evident that this successful attack has greatly increased our freedom of movement in the Mediterranean and has thus strengthened our control over the central area of this sea. It has enabled two battleships to be released for operations elsewhere, while the effect on the morale of the Italians must be considerable. As an example of "economy of force" it is probably unsurpassed.'

The first wave of Swordfish (12 aircraft) flew off HMS *Illustrious* at 20:30 hours on 10 November, 288km (180 miles) southeast of Taranto, followed by a second wave of nine aircraft. The first wave attacked before midnight, the second wave just after, all aircraft meeting intense anti-aircraft fire as they attacked the ships below. Indeed, the Italians continued to shoot at the Swordfish even when they were at sea level, inflicting damage on their own ships and on the town of Taranto itself.

After the raid the battleships *Littorio*, *Caio Duilio*, and *Cavour* were either sunk or beached to prevent them sinking. The heavy cruiser *Trento* was damaged, as were the destroyers *Libeccio* and *Pessagno*. Two fleet auxiliaries were also damaged and two Swordfish were lost during the raid. It had been a daring operation that delivered a huge psychological blow to the Italian navy. Alarmed, the Italians sent the battleships *Vittorio Veneto*, *Cesare* and *Doria* with the 10th and 13th Destroyer Divisions to Naples.

Taranto convinced Japan's naval air arm that it was possible to conduct a torpedo attack against warships in a shallow harbour. In January 1940, therefore, the Combined Fleet formally requested the Imperial Navy Ministry to supply the fleet's carrier torpedo aircraft with weapons that could be launched in the 12–13m (40–45ft) depths of Pearl Harbour. Just as modified British torpedoes had been successful at Taranto so would specially adapted Japanese weapons triumph at Pearl Harbour.

Once again, the German war machine proved all-conquering, as Hitler unleashed his army against Greece and Yugoslavia in the spring, before launching the greatest land invasion in history — Operation Barbarossa — in June. German panzer spearheads cut through Red Army units to penetrate hundreds of miles into Soviet territory in the summer. Hundreds of thousands of Red Army troops were killed or captured as the Germans laid siege to Leningrad and then launched an assault on Moscow — Operation Typhoon. But Typhoon failed and the Red Army then launched a winter campaign that forced the Germans onto the defensive.

In the Pacific, a belligerent Japan launched a surprise attack on the U.S. Fleet in Pearl Harbour to make World War II a truly global conflict. But whereas Japan had not declared war on the USSR when its German and Italian allies had launched Barbarossa, Hitler and Mussolini both declared war on the USA, thus guaranteeing American involvement in the European war.

1941

U.S. CONGRESS PASSES THE LEND–LEASE ACT

DATE

....

11 March, 1941

SUMMARY

....

The Act allowed Britain to purchase vital military goods, food and raw materials from the United States.

LOCATION

....

Washington, D.C., USA

The government and people of the United States were largely determined to stay out of the European war that had broken out in September 1939. The Neutrality Act of that year allowed belligerents to purchase materials from the United States but only on a 'cash and carry' basis. A major problem for Britain was that the Johnson Act of 1934 forbade the extension of credit to countries that had not repaid American loans made to them in World War I, which included Britain.

President Roosevelt was sympathetic to the plight of Britain and, like the vast majority of Americans, viewed Nazi Germany with extreme distaste. However, among the U.S. military there was a view, especially after June 1940, that the Germans would win the war and that any military supplies sent to the British would fall into German hands. Far better to equip U.S. forces with these supplies. This was the opinion of General George C. Marshall, the U.S. Army's Chief of Staff.

AMERICAN LARGESSE

....

Things came to a head in December 1940 when Prime Minister Churchill informed President Roosevelt that Britain would no longer be able to purchase American supplies. As a result Roosevelt proposed a Lend–Lease Act to Congress whereby the United States would provide Britain with the supplies it needed to fight Nazi Germany, but would not insist on being paid immediately. Payment would be deferred, with the Americans initially 'lending' the goods. Congress passed the Lend–Lease Act on 11 March, 1941.

Britain was the initial beneficiary of the act, receiving $7 billion at the outset, but when the war had ended in 1945 expenditure under the act had reached $50 billion, with 30 countries receiving Lend–Lease aid, including the Soviet Union.

It is important to realise that Lend–Lease aid regarding military vehicles, ships, and aircraft was not immediate; indeed, up to the Japanese attack on Pearl Harbour Britain was still paying dollars for

Eyewitness

LEND–LEASE WAS NOT ENTIRELY ALTRUISTIC ON THE PART OF THE UNITED STATES. THERE WERE MANY U.S. POLITICIANS WHO RECOGNISED THAT, IF BRITAIN WAS DEFEATED, THE NAZIS WOULD PROBABLY TURN THEIR ATTENTION TO THE UNITED STATES ITSELF. REPUBLICAN FRANK KNOX WAS AN ADVOCATE OF LEND–LEASE, AS HE STATED:

'We can be very sure that the devious diplomatic, economic and political methods which Germany has employed towards all the countries near her would also in the future be employed in the regions to the south of us. First would come economic penetration, near economic dependence, then political immigration and political interference. After that we would see the establishment of puppet regimes under Nazi or native control, and finally the arming of those countries and their military domination by Nazis.

I believe that our people now are determined to put forth their full efforts for saving Britain and thus saving themselves from the burdens of future militarism and war and from an overturn of American life.'

the majority of supplies it was receiving from the United States. Of the 2,400 aircraft exported to Britain between March and December 1941, for example, less than 100 were supplied under Lend–Lease. The rest were purchased for cash. Nevertheless, access to U.S. supplies was immediately beneficial to British industry, for example. Prior to Lend–Lease the British had imported iron ore from Narvik. The fall of Norway closed this supply source. But after March 1941 America was able to supply not ore but finished steel. This in turn allowed British industry to plan ahead, knowing there would be no raw material shortages.

The immediate help of Lend–Lease was not so much actual deliveries of goods as the promise of substantial aid to follow, which in turn allowed the British government and people to organise their war economy, safe in the knowledge that they would not starve in the interim.

ENTER THE DESERT FOX

DATE

March–April 1941

SUMMARY

The arrival of Rommel and his *Afrikakorps* saved the Axis war effort in North Africa from total collapse.

LOCATION

North Africa

Mussolini dreamed of making the whole of North Africa part of his new Roman Empire. In the Italian colony of Libya he had up to 300,000 troops under the command of Marshal Rodolfo Graziani, facing only 36,000 British troops in adjacent Egypt. On paper it seemed a mere formality that once an offensive was launched Egypt would fall with ease.

The Army of Libya began its war of conquest in September 1940 but the offensive was a halfhearted affair. Soon the Italians were being pushed back into Libya by the British Western Desert Force, commanded by General Richard O'Connor. Using aggressive armoured tactics the British captured Sidi Omar on 16 December, Bardia on 16 January, 1941, and the port of Tobruk on 22 January. By this time Graziani had a field army of just 40,000 soldiers. The Italians were defeated at the Battle of Beda Fomm on 3–5 February, by which time the British had captured 130,000 soldiers. With their army near to total collapse, on 1 February the Italians officially asked for German assistance. The next day Hitler informed Erwin Rommel that he had been appointed commander of the *Deutsches Afrikakorps* (DAK).

LEADING FROM THE FRONT

Rommel, a favourite of the Führer, had led the 7th Panzer Division, the 'Ghost Division', during the spectacular campaign in France in 1940. A brilliant tactician and leader, he was the epitome of a panzer division commander, always leading from the front, where he could exploit rapidly developing situations. He arrived in Tripoli on 12 February, 1941, to be informed by a German liaison officer that the Italian army was near total collapse. Though nominally under the command of the Italians, Hitler had told Rommel that he would always have direct access to him. This gave him the latitude to make his own decisions, especially given the fact that the Italians in North Africa were thoroughly demoralised and defeated.

Ten days after his arrival at Tripoli the first elements of the DAK arrived. Eventually Rommel would have the 5th Light Division (renamed 21st Panzer Division) and 15th Panzer Division to support the Italians. By an amazing stroke of luck the British had halted their advance at Sirte. If they had pressed on to Tripoli, most likely they would have captured the city and ended the Axis war effort in North Africa there and then. As it was, their failure to do so and the arrival of Rommel prolonged the North African war for another two years.

Displaying the boldness that would be his hallmark in the desert war, Rommel attacked the British on 20 March with just his 5th Light Division and available Italian troops (he had disregarded German High Command orders that he should wait for a second panzer division). During the remainder of March and the first half of April, Rommel's offensive drove the British relentlessly back east, forcing them to relinquish Benghazi and leave behind an encircled Tobruk. By 12 April the DAK had taken Bardia and reached the Egyptian frontier.

THE TACTICIAN'S PLAYGROUND

ABOVE Erwin Rommel earned the respect of Allied commanders for his bold tactics on the battlefield and the respect he showed to those he had defeated.

Why had the 'Desert Fox' been so successful? Undoubtedly Rommel himself made success possible. He combined mobility and deception to defeat his enemies. During his first campaign, for example, the Germans used lines of trucks to create dust clouds to provide the illusion of greater armoured strength.

It is a myth that the DAK had greater numbers of tanks in the desert war, or that they were technically superior. However, in North Africa the DAK used them in combination with other weapon systems to defeat the British. Anti-tank screens, which contained the famous 88mm anti-aircraft gun used in the anti-tank role, were used to defeat enemy armour, which allowed the panzers both to outflank enemy tanks and destroy enemy infantry. British tactics tended to be unimaginative and predictable whereas Rommel's were just the opposite. As he himself said: 'The desert is a tactician's paradise and a quartermaster's nightmare'. The 'Fox' was at large and the war in North Africa was set to continue.

BALKAN INTERLUDE

DATE

....

6 April–1 June, 1941

SUMMARY

....

The conquest of
Yugoslavia and
Greece was a
spectacular success,
but delayed the
start of Operation
Barbarossa.

LOCATION

....

The Balkans

The overthrow of a pro-German government in Belgrade, Yugoslavia, on 27 March was interpreted by Hitler as a personal affront. He ordered an immediate attack on Yugoslavia, which was to be conducted 'with pitiless harshness'. Greece, which had repulsed an Italian invasion and was being reinforced with British troops, was also a target.

The German Balkans campaign began on 6 April, the Yugoslav Army quickly disintegrating under relentless air and ground assaults. An armistice between the Germans and Yugoslavs was signed in Belgrade on 17 April. The conquest of Greece took longer but again German air and ground operations overcame Greek and British resistance, conquering the Greek mainland by 3 May. To secure his southern flank Hitler authorised the airborne assault on the island of Crete, which was launched on 20 May and brought to a successful conclusion by 1 June.

A PYRRHIC VICTORY

....

On paper the conquest of the Balkans had been a textbook demonstration of the power of Blitzkrieg warfare. But a closer examination reveals that it not only adversely affected preparations for Operation Barbarossa, the German invasion of the Soviet Union, but also had repercussions during the actual operation itself.

The Balkan campaign postponed the start date of Barbarossa from mid-May. On 7 April the High Command of the German army again delayed the start of Barbarossa to mid-June. And on 17 June Hitler himself set the start date for the invasion of the USSR as 22 June. The delays were caused by practical reasons. Divisions that had fought in Yugoslavia and Greece had to be redeployed to their start lines facing the Soviet border. Some units could not be redeployed in time. Thus the 2nd and 5th Panzer Divisions were in southern Greece at the end of May 1941 and were not available for the start of Barbarossa. The situation was such that when the attack was launched on 22 June Army Group South was lacking a third of its armoured strength.

Moving units from the Balkans to the Eastern Front, and having to travel to railheads, inflicted great wear and tear on engines, especially those of the panzers. This resulted in a high rate of mechanical failure during Operation Barbarossa.

THE END OF AIRBORNE

There were other repercussions of the Balkan campaign that impinged on the conduct of Barbarossa. The conquest of Crete had been daring and brilliant but it had not come cheap. The Germans suffered over 5,000 casualties on Crete out of a committed force of 13,000. Losses had been particularly high among the paratroopers: one in four dropped on the island had been killed. These casualties shocked Hitler and resulted in no more large-scale airborne operations being launched by him in the war. Henceforth the paratroopers would be employed as infantry, a waste of a valuable resource. The high casualties on Crete resulted in a lack of qualified personnel among the 7th Flieger Division, making the launching of large-scale airborne operations impossible anyway.

Mention must also be made of *Luftwaffe* losses on Crete. The assault on the island had involved 700 Ju 52 three-engined transport aircraft. By the end of Operation Mercury, the codename of the attack on Crete, the *Luftwaffe* had lost 119 Ju 52s, the destruction of which left the *Luftwaffe's* transport squadrons sorely depleted on the eve of Barbarossa (and there were too few to carry large numbers of paratroopers, even if the High Command had been inclined to sanction airborne drops).

ABOVE The German losses sustained during the airborne invasion of Crete were substantial and led directly to a change in the tactics used for future campaigns.

SOVIET–JAPANESE NEUTRALITY PACT IS SIGNED

DATE

13 April, 1941

SUMMARY

The pact that saved the Soviet Union from a two-front war in 1941 and went a long way to denying Nazi Germany total victory in that year.

LOCATION

Moscow, USSR

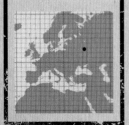

In 1931 Japan had occupied Manchuria, renaming it Manchukuo, which brought the Japanese into contact with the Soviet puppet state of Mongolia. The border between Manchuria and Mongolia had always been ill defined and the issue of a disputed border led to a series of clashes between Japanese and Red Army troops. These clashes culminated in the Battle of Khalkhin-Gol in August 1939, in which Soviet forces commanded by Georgi Zhukov inflicted a heavy defeat on the Imperial Japanese Army in the so-called Nomonhan Incident. For the Japanese it had been a salutary lesson in the superiority of Red Army tactics, armour and leadership.

Japanese military humiliation was compounded by what many in Tokyo regarded as political betrayal when Germany and the Soviet Union signed their non-aggression pact in August 1939. That its ally Germany had concluded a treaty with their mutual enemy, Soviet Russia, was a bitter pill to swallow. Following Germany's lead, Japan embarked on a policy of normalising relations with Moscow.

A BROADER ALLIANCE

In September 1940 Japan signed the Tripartite Pact with Germany and Italy. Article 3 of the pact stated that 'Germany, Italy and Japan agree … to assist one another with all political, economic and military means when one of the three contracting powers is attacked by a power at present not involved in the European war or in the Chinese–Japanese conflict'. Japan hoped to build on this by bringing the Soviet Union into a coalition of itself, Germany and Italy that would deter the Western powers from hostilities in the Far East while Tokyo was establishing its Greater East Asia Co-Prosperity Sphere. The first step towards this aim was taken in April 1941 when the Soviet–Japanese Neutrality Pact was signed in Moscow. Both parties agreed to friendly relations and to 'mutually respect the territorial integrity and inviolability of the other Contracting Party'.

The German invasion of the Soviet Union in June 1941 put an end to notions of a coalition involving the USSR. As Germany had not been attacked Japan was under no obligation to join the war against the Soviet Union. However, Berlin encouraged it to do so, to attack in the Far East, avenge Nomonhan and to seize Soviet territory.

WAIT AND SEE

Ostensibly it appeared a golden opportunity for Japan but closer inspection revealed several problems. First, despite many in the Imperial Japanese Army thirsting for revenge, there was no guarantee that a war with the Red Army in 1941 would fare any better than the one in 1939. Japan was still involved in a drawn-out war in China and, if the decision were taken to attack Soviet forces in Mongolia, it would take time to assemble the necessary forces. Even if a large force was assembled there was no guarantee that it would be victorious as there was no guarantee that Germany would triumph against the Soviets. The senior leadership of the army preferred to wait and see how events turned out on the Eastern Front before committing Japanese troops against the formidable Red Army in the Far East.

The Imperial Japanese navy was set against a war with the Soviets and the July oil embargo imposed on Japan by the British, Americans and Dutch-in-exile forced Tokyo's hand. The oil of the Dutch East Indies had to be secured before, as Prime Minister Tojo Hideki had stated in November 1941: 'Ships will stop moving'. To do so would mean war with Britain and America. To embark upon a war with the Soviet Union as well would be the height of folly.

In the autumn of 1941 the Soviet Far Eastern reserves were transferred west when Moscow learned from the Red Orchestra that the Japanese would not attack in Mongolia. Had they done so it is unlikely that the Soviet Union would have been able to withstand a two-front conflict in 1941 and World War II might have ended very differently.

ABOVE The Soviet–Japanese Neutrality Pact allowed Stalin to focus his forces on the fight against Axis forces in the west.

THE CAPTURE OF *U-110*

DATE

9 May, 1941

SUMMARY

Top-secret material captured from a U-boat helped the Allies to break the Enigma code.

LOCATION

East of Cape Farewell, Greenland

In May 1941, the Type IXB U-boat *U-110* was operating in the North Atlantic east of Cape Farewell. Commanded by Captain Fritz-Julius Lemp, on 9 May it sank two merchant ships, but Lemp left his periscope up too long (to confirm a kill) and was spotted by the British corvette HMS *Aubretia*. The ship rushed to the scene and began depth-charging. The destroyers HMS *Bulldog* and HMS *Broadway* joined in; the three vessels forced the U-boat to surface and its captain to order abandon ship. Lemp assumed the submarine would sink, together with the top-secret material it was carrying. He was wrong.

A boarding party commanded by Lieutenant David Balme made several trips between the U-boat and HMS *Bulldog*, during which Balme retrieved an Enigma machine and a set of current codebooks. Great care was given to the transfer of the latter as they were printed in ink that disappeared if they were dropped in seawater. Once notified, the British Admiralty realised that if the Germans discovered the submarine had been captured they would order their codes and signals to be changed. Therefore the boat was scuttled while being towed to Britain.

CRACKING THE CODE

The Enigma used by the German army had been decrypted as early as 1932 by Polish cryptographers, but until the capture of *U-110*, German naval codes had remained unbroken. The documents captured from *U-110* were delivered to Bletchley Park on 13 June. They included the so-called 'Offizier' messages, which were important messages, enciphered on the Enigma machine using the U-boat officer's settings, before being enciphered again using the settings circulated to all Enigma operators. Thanks to these documents, the Bletchley Park code breakers were eventually able to work out a method for reading 'Offizier' messages.

Once Bletchley Park had cracked the naval codes the information was put to use in the Battle of the Atlantic and thus saved Britain from

near-certain defeat. The Royal Navy did not have any spare destroyers to form an anti-U-boat force at that time, but the intelligence supplied by Bletchley Park allowed the Submarine Tracking Room in the Admiralty to route convoys away from the 'wolfpacks'.

ABOVE The capture of the *U-110* was the first time the Allies had seized an Enigma cipher machine together with its codes, radiographs and other related documents.

INTO ACTION

....

The Enigma intelligence became operational in June 1941 and was an immediate success. In April, for example, the tonnage of British shipping lost to the U-boats had been 688,000; in May it was 511,000.

By June, however, this fell to 432,000 tons, by July to 121,000 tons, and by August to 80,000 tons.

In January 1942 the Germans changed the Enigma machine by adding another wheel and their ciphers were only broken again in December. However, the Enigma settings gained from *U-110* had carried the Allies through a critical time, when the Third Reich was on the verge of victory against Britain and before the United States had entered the war.

As an addendum, it is interesting to note that in addition to the capture of the Enigma machine, other codebooks and cipher books were also found on *U-110*. There were also some vital charts, the most important of which were the special grid charts used for positioning U-boats throughout the Atlantic, and other charts showing all the German minefields and swept channels that Britain was subsequently able to use for raids against German targets.

GERMANY INVADES RUSSIA

DATE

22 June–5 August, 1941

SUMMARY

The first seven weeks of the invasion of the Soviet Union conquered great swathes of territory but failed to destroy the Red Army.

LOCATION

The Soviet Union

Hitler had boasted before the launch of Operation Barbarossa, the invasion of the Soviet Union: 'We have only to kick in the door, and the whole rotten structure will come crashing down'. The invasion of the USSR was a vast and complex military operation and only a brief summary can be given here. But the war on the Eastern Front would determine the ultimate outcome of World War II, would shape the postwar world, and Barbarossa is thus one of the most important events of the conflict.

Three army groups – North, Centre and South – supported by Finnish units and German units in Norway, would destroy the Red Army in western Russia in a Blitzkrieg campaign, after which the *Wehrmacht* would capture the Ukraine, the western USSR, Leningrad and Moscow. The final objective of Barbarossa would be a line stretching from Archangel in the north to the River Volga in the south to create a vast area of 'living space' that would be colonised by the Aryan 'master race'.

BATTLE-HARDENED AND READY

In mid-1941, after two years of unbroken success, the *Wehrmacht* was a finely honed military machine, well led at all levels, equipped to fight rapid mechanised campaigns and its ranks filled with veterans. To subdue the 'Bolshevik Slavs', Hitler amassed three million German and Axis troops, 3,300 tanks and 2,232 aircraft.

Facing them were 5.5 million Red Army soldiers (though not all were deployed along the USSR's western border), 29,484 tanks, and 19,533 aircraft organised in so-called fronts: Northern, Northwestern, Western and Southwestern. However, Stalin's purges of the 1930s had robbed the Red Army of many experienced commanders, there was a lack of radios, and a shortage of 76.2mm ammunition, which adversely affected the performance of the Red Army's KV-1 and T-34 tanks. Tank training was generally poor and many vehicles required major overhauls. As a result only 7,000 tanks were combat-ready.

When Barbarossa was launched on 22 June, defending Red Army units were quickly rendered helpless by *Luftwaffe* attacks that destroyed large numbers of Soviet aircraft on the ground and then began to provide close air support for ground units. On 22 June, 2,500 Soviet aircraft were destroyed for the loss of 39 *Luftwaffe* aircraft. German army units began to pour through the many breaches in Red Army lines, the panzers driving deep into enemy territory to encircle Soviet armies in huge pockets.

Like rabbits caught in headlights Red Army units were gripped with inertia and indecision (this spread all the way up to the Kremlin; Stalin made his first broadcast to the people on 3 July, 12 days after the start of the invasion). The command system broke down and the few counterattacks were uncoordinated and possessed inadequate resources. With total German air superiority (by 1 July Soviet aircraft losses totalled 4,900 machines), whole armies were herded into pockets. On 3 July the Germans liquidated the Białystok Pocket, for example, taking 290,000 prisoners.

The losses suffered by the Red Army during the opening phase of Barbarossa were staggering. By 9 July, for example, the Western Front alone had lost 418,000 killed, wounded, and missing, 4,800 tanks and 9,427 artillery pieces. By the middle of July the panzer pincers were closing around Smolensk and in the north the Germans were nearing Leningrad. Eleven days later the Germans sealed the Smolensk Pocket, trapping 700,000 Red Army soldiers. When the pocket was liquidated on 5 August, 30,900 were taken prisoner. The Soviets had lost 3,200 tanks, 3,100 artillery pieces and 1,000 aircraft in the battle for the pocket.

But the Russians kept on fighting, much to the surprise of the Germans, and traded space for time, conducting a scorched-earth policy as they withdrew. The vast expanses of the Soviet Union began to take a toll on German vehicles and infantry marching on foot. The pace of the advance slackened as supply lines became stretched. Most worrying for the Germans was that by the end of October 1941, despite its losses, the Red Army still had 2.2 million troops fighting on the Eastern Front.

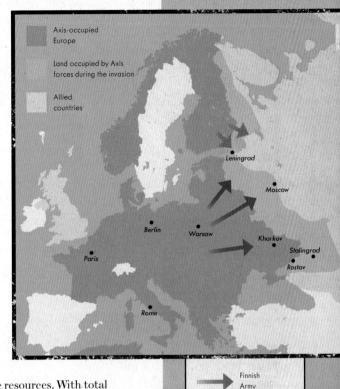

Axis-occupied Europe

Land occupied by Axis forces during the invasion

Allied countries

Finnish Army

Army Group North

Army Group Centre

Army Group South

ABOVE Supported by the *Luftwaffe*, German and Axis forces made rapid progress into the USSR in the summer of 1941. Soviet losses in this period were staggering, but they nevertheless continued to fight.

MOVING SOVIET INDUSTRY EAST

DATE

4 July, 1941

SUMMARY

Factories were moved east, allowing the Red Army to fight on.

LOCATION

Urals, Western Siberia, and Central Asia

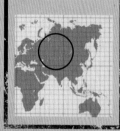

By the end of 1941, the USSR had lost the grain lands of Belorussia and the Ukraine, one-third of its rail network, three-quarters of its iron ore, coal and steel supplies, and 40 percent of its electricity-generating capacity. And yet not only was the Red Army able to continue fighting, the huge material losses it had suffered were largely replaced by the relocated Soviet heavy industry.

Two days after the launch of Barbarossa, on 24 June, the Council of Evacuation was established with the aim of evacuating plant and materials from the German advance. On 4 July, the council ordered Nikolai Voznesensky, director of five-year planning, to organise the movement of industry and workers east.

A MASSIVE UNDERTAKING

Some 3,000 agents controlled the movement, which was well underway by August 1941, the three main receiving areas further east being the Urals, Western Siberia and Central Asia. The railway network was crucial to this operation, and though the process was often haphazard and far from orderly on account of the rapid German advance, the results were impressive. On 7 August, for example, 3,000 rail carriages evacuated iron and steel manufacturing equipment from the Dnieper area. In the week from 8 August, 26,000 rail carriages evacuated industries in the Ukraine, while in Moscow 80,000 carriages transported 498 factories, including 75,000 lathes.

The reality behind the numbers was often harsh. Boxcars were converted for long journeys, each one equipped with bunk beds, an iron stove and a paraffin lamp. A workshop superintendent whose task was to oversee the loading and unloading of the plant and equipment at its destination supervised each train. When they arrived in the east, the workers and their families were housed in wooden barracks and then the plant had to be reassembled, often in subzero temperatures. Living conditions were hard, but the authorities tried to ensure that

Eyewitness

ELENA FOMINA, EVACUATED FROM LENINGRAD TO THE DZHUVALINSKY
DISTRICT OF SOUTH KAZAKHSTAN IN 1941, WAS ONE OF AN ESTIMATED
25 MILLION CIVILIANS EVACUATED EAST DURING THAT YEAR.

'Finally, the chairman of the collective farm came and
explained that he will wait for the chairman of the village
council. When, in the evening, he came, by his instructions I
was given three kilos of potatoes and two kilos of flour.
I had to stay in the barn one more night. Finally, the
chairman of the village came. He inspected my property and
decided that the barn is too large or too posh for me. He
took me and showed me where he permitted me to live and
fear gripped me. It was something like a slum. I flatly
refused and asked to be sent back to the district, but the
chairman refused and he decided to give me another
apartment. He has sent me to one evacuee [post] where there
were 10 people in 3.5 metres of living space, where there was
no oven. However, there I met people who were ours, the
Soviet people. I had no bedding. I put down the straw and
the kids could relax on it. It was better than nothing.
One child, five years old, was seriously wounded, and was
almost dying.'

those engaged in industrial production received larger food rations,
higher-quality housing, and better medical care.

The relocation was a massive undertaking. In the last three months of
1941, 455 factories had been moved to the Urals, 210 to western Siberia
and 250 to Central Asia and Kazakhstan. Such dislocation necessarily
had an adverse effect on the war economy. By September 1941, for
example, although small arms and artillery production had increased,
there was a shell 'famine'. Despite a goal of six million artillery shells in
the third quarter, only two million were produced. And tank production
was a fraction of the number required to replace losses. Nevertheless, the
decision to relocate Soviet industry allowed the USSR to continue the
war after the catastrophic losses it had suffered in 1941.

THE BATTLE OF MOSCOW

DATE

....

2 October–
4 December, 1941

SUMMARY

....

The German offensive
failed to win
the war on the
Eastern Front
in 1941, saving
Stalin's regime.

LOCATION

....

Western USSR

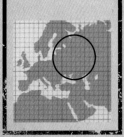

By the autumn of 1941 the Germans were ready to initiate what they believed would be the final offensive on the Eastern Front: Operation Typhoon, the capture of Moscow. Though Leningrad still held out, which meant that Army Group North could not contribute to the offensive, and Army Group South had been committed to the conquest of the Donets Basin, Rostov and the Crimea, Hitler and the Army High Command believed that a reinforced Army Group Centre would be capable of destroying the Red Army in front of Moscow and capturing the city before the end of the year.

The city would be encircled in giant pincers. The Ninth Army and Third Panzer would drive to the north of Moscow and the Second Panzer Group and Second Army would attack from the south. In the centre the Fourth Army and Fourth Panzer Group would prevent the Red Army from striking the flanks. To achieve these aims the *Wehrmacht* assembled 1.929 million troops, 14,000 artillery pieces, 1,000 tanks and 1,390 aircraft. They faced Soviet forces under the command of Georgi Zhukov: Ivan Konev's Western Front (six armies), Semyon Budyonny's Reserve Front (five armies) and Andrei Yeryomenko's Bryansk Front (three armies). In total the Red Army defending Moscow totalled 1.25 million troops, 7,600 artillery pieces, 990 tanks and 670 aircraft.

SLOWING PROGRESS

....

Typhoon opened on 2 October and initially the Blitzkrieg carried all before it. Huge numbers of Red Army soldiers were encircled around Bryansk and Vyazma. The Vyazma Pocket was crushed by 15 October, with 650,000 Red Army soldiers captured and large numbers of tanks and artillery pieces being destroyed. But by this date German units were experiencing severe difficulties. It was no longer summer, when the ground was dry; the fall rains reduced roads to rivers of mud into which wheeled vehicles sank. They had to be towed by tracked vehicles, which in turn wore out the latter.

Eyewitness

ERNST JAUERNICK WAS A GERMAN INFANTRYMAN DURING OPERATION
TYPHOON. HERE HE DESCRIBES THE FINAL STAGES OF THE OFFENSIVE.

'We have now begun the last great raid on Moscow — but we lack almost everything. We have not yet been assigned winter clothing and our Motorised units have no lubricating oil. We receive little in the way of food. In the autumn it was the mud that was our enemy, but this cold may finish us off completely. Our poor horses are being pushed to the very limits and are suffering horribly. We can no longer offer them straw to lie on or hay to eat. They get ice-cold water to drink and have to nibble on small branches we gather from the forest. At night they have little shelter from the freezing cold, often having to lie with their bellies in the icy snow.'

By mid-October some German spearheads were only 100km (62 miles) from Moscow but the mud had restricted their movement to 5–10km (3–6 miles) a day. Soviet resistance in the Bryansk Pocket ended on 25 October, the Red Army losing 50,000 dead. But Zhukov was feeding units into the battle in front of Moscow, having received reinforcements from the Far East to bolster his forces. And Red Army troops had a massive advantage over their enemies: they had winter clothing; the Germans did not.

The arrival of subzero temperatures in mid-November hardened the ground and allowed the Germans to commence the second phase of Typhoon. Once more the panzers advanced but now many armoured divisions were down to 17 operational tanks each. German units, lacking air support, winter clothing and supplies, were now facing increasing numbers of Soviet T-34 tanks, against which the Germans' 37mm anti-tank rounds were useless. By 22 November the lead units of the Third Panzer Group were only 48km (30 miles) north of Moscow. But by this date the combat strength of most German infantry units was less than 50 percent and many mechanised units were stranded due to lack of fuel. Typhoon ground to a halt on 4 December. The next day Zhukov unleashed his counteroffensive and within days the German army was fighting for its life on the Eastern Front.

The failure to capture Moscow not only saved Stalin and his regime, it delivered a huge psychological blow to the hitherto invincible *Wehrmacht*. Zhukov's offensive would eventually falter but the Germans were faced with continuing the struggle on the Eastern Front into 1942.

THE DEFENCE OF LENINGRAD

DATE

12 November–
30 December, 1941

SUMMARY

The Red Army
offensive ended
Hitler's dream of
encircling Leningrad
in 1941.

LOCATION

Western USSR

The city of Leningrad had been a prime objective of Operation Barbarossa, Hitler believing that the capture of the city was a necessary part of the destruction of the Soviet state. Leningrad had a population of 2.5 million and was the target of Field Marshal Ritter von Leeb's Army Group North, which in June 1941 comprised the Eighteenth and Sixteenth Armies and the Fourth Panzer Group.

As elsewhere on the Eastern Front those Red Army formations defending Leningrad suffered massive casualties as they were pounded by German air and ground attacks at the start of Barbarossa. Between 23 August and 30 September, the Leningrad Front alone suffered 116,316 casualties. By the end of September the city was in danger of not only being encircled but also destroyed. As the weather deteriorated Army Group North made one last effort to encircle the city before the onset of winter. But Stalin and the Headquarters of the Main Command (*Stavka*) were determined to use every means to prevent this happening.

WINTER TAKES ITS TOLL

Leeb's now diminished forces were tasked with attacking towards Tikhvin, east of Leningrad, to reach Lake Ladoga to sever the city's last rail links with Moscow and encircle Leningrad (and link up with the Finns in the north). The offensive began on 16 October, 39th Panzer and 38th Corps hitting the junction of the Soviet Fourth and Fifty-Second Armies. It was snowing heavily but the Germans made good initial gains, driving east towards Tikhvin. On 8 November they captured the town and cut the last rail line between Moscow and Lake Ladoga. However, by this date many German divisions were ghost units, many of their soldiers having died in the extreme cold and their vehicles having broken down. Indeed the cold was inflicting more casualties than Red Army bullets. The offensive ground to a halt, leaving the Germans in possession of a great bulge with Tikhvin as its eastern tip. The conditions were ideal for a Soviet counteroffensive.

For the Tikhvin Offensive the Stavka assembled the Fourth, Fifty-Second and Fifty-Fourth Armies, a total of 17 rifle and two tank divisions, one cavalry division, three rifle and two tank brigades, and three tank and two ski battalions. In all, 192,950 troops, facing 120,000 German troops, 100 tanks and assault guns, and 1,000 artillery pieces and mortars.

The offensive began on November in thick snow. German weapons jammed in the cold and many of their horses collapsed and died in the snow as Red Army units attacked. Soviet tactics were often poor, especially in the Fifty-Second Army where many frontal assaults resulted in high casualties. Tikhvin itself was attacked on three sides and came under intense pressure. German units put up a desperate defence but were being literally ground down. In early December, for example, the 18th Motorised Division lost 9,000 men in fierce fighting. Leeb recognised that his divisions were slowly being destroyed and asked Hitler permission to withdraw from Tikhvin. On 8 December the Führer gave permission for his units to withdraw to the Volkhov River.

Buoyed by the successes in the north Stalin believed, wrongly, that Army Group North was on the verge of collapse. He therefore ordered the newly created Volkhov Front, made up of the Fourth, Fifty-Ninth, Second Shock and Fifty-Second Armies, to expand the offensive to achieve the complete lifting of the Leningrad blockade. At the same time the Leningrad Front would assist the Volkhov Front by destroying German units dug in around the city.

ABOVE A Soviet poster from 1941 with a call to all Russians: 'Let's shield Leningrad!' Stalin's Tikhvin Offensive against German forces around Leningrad was the USSR's first significant victory in the war.

The success of the offensive would hinge on the armies of the Volkhov Front reaching and establishing bridgeheads on the Volkhov River. In the event the Fifty-Fourth Army suffered heavy casualties and failed to establish any bridgeheads across the river. The Fourth and Fifty-Second Armies finally reached the river near Kirishi, Gruzino and north of Novgorod on 27 December, seizing bridgeheads and expanding them. By 30 December the three armies had driven the two German corps back to the positions from which they had begun their own Tikhvin offensive on 16 October. But the Soviet armies were exhausted and at the end of their supply lines and so advanced no further.

Though it did not achieve what Stalin had desired, the Tikhvin Offensive, the Red Army's first large-scale military success in World War II, had saved Leningrad from encirclement.

WOMEN ON THE HOME FRONT

DATE

December 1941

SUMMARY

In an effort to maximise production output, Britain, the USA and the USSR were quick to mobilise their female population to undertake vital war work.

LOCATION

Great Britain, USA, and USSR

From early 1941 it became compulsory for British women aged between 18 and 60 to register for war work. The realisation that the war would be a long one, together with the U-boat threat to Britain's merchant marine, occasioning the increased exploitation of land for producing food, plus millions of men called up for the armed forces, gave the government no option but to call on Britain's female population to aid the war effort.

Large numbers of women had already volunteered for war work, of course. Many had joined the Women's Voluntary Service (WVS), which helped with organising evacuations, shelters, clothing exchanges and mobile canteens. It had over one million members during the war. The Women's Land Army (WLA) trained women for agricultural work and contained many young women from the towns and cities. The Auxiliary Territorial Service (ATS) was formed in 1938 and was in France with the British Expeditionary Force (BEF) in 1939. Most women in the ATS served in anti-aircraft duties. The 93rd Searchlight Regiment, for example, was all female.

The National Service Act (No. 2) of December 1941 made the conscription of women legal. At first only single women aged between 20 and 30 were called up, but by mid-1943 almost 90 percent of single women and 80 percent of married women were employed in essential war work. By 1944, seven million women were engaged in war work in Britain.

AN ARMY OF MILLIONS

American women were also recruited to aid the war effort, a staggering six million entering the workforce for the first time during the war. The poster 'We Can Do It!' came to symbolise not only U.S. industrial might but also the essential role women were playing in the economy. The poster showed 'Rosie the Riveter', a fictitious factory worker modelled on Michigan factory worker Geraldine Doyle.

American women also served in uniform. The Women's Army Corps (WAC) was a part of the U.S. Army and although its members were not trained for combat, they served overseas as stenographers, telegraph and teletype operators and radiographers. Over 150,000 women served in the WAV during the war.

WOMEN AT THE FRONT

Hundreds of thousands of Russian women served in uniform during the war, the difference between them and their U.S. counterparts being that many saw action. More than 70 percent of the 800,000 women who served in the Red Army during the war fought at the front, 100,000 of them being decorated for their bravery. Faced with fighting an enemy intent on wiping out the USSR, the Soviets had to mobilise all sections of society, which included women, to resist the Nazi aggressor. By 1943 eight percent of Red Army personnel were female, being trained in all-women units and then being posted to the front to fight alongside men.

Many Soviet women achieved excellent combat records. The sniper Lyudmilya Pavlichenko, for example, was credited with killing 309 Germans. Female Red Army personnel often suffered the same fate as their male counterparts: being shot out of hand if captured. This was because in Nazi eyes women in uniform were not proper soldiers but partisans. Those women soldiers who were not executed on the spot were often sent to concentration camps, where the 'women murderers from Russia', as the SS termed them, were invariably murdered.

The Germans were initially reluctant to mobilise women for the war effort, mostly because Nazi ideology regarded the main role of women as the mothers of future generations of racially pure Germans. The notion of female emancipation was a sign of decadent social democracy. To ensure women remained at home the Nazis offered incentives to have large families. These included marriage loans (given only to women who were 'genetically healthy'), child allowances and family subsidies. Those who were not 'genetically healthy' could be sterilised.

It was only when the tide of war had turned against Germany that the Nazis grudgingly accepted that women could be useful outside the home. By 1944 there were 500,000 German women in uniform serving as support troops, 100,000 being in *Luftwaffe* anti-aircraft batteries. But by then it was too late to make a difference to the outcome of the war.

ABOVE The skills of women with prewar engineering and manufacturing experience were increasingly utilised, such as in the production of armaments shown here.

JAPAN BRUTALLY REPRESSES THE CHINESE

DATE

3 December, 1941

SUMMARY

The Japanese policy
in China led to a
rapid expansion
of the Communist
Red Army.

LOCATION

Northern China

The Sino-Japanese War had begun in 1937 but tensions between China and Japan predated the conflict. The Chinese Nationalist Government under Chiang Kai-shek was already engaged in conflict against the Chinese Communist Party (CCP) and dissident warlords, in addition to attempting to unify and modernise a backwards country, when the Japanese declared war. Between 1934 and 1937 the Japanese expanded their control in North China, which flared into open war in July 1937.

The Nationalist Chinese were no match for a Japanese army equipped with modern weapons and a Japanese air force flying modern aircraft. Chiang's armies suffered a number of defeats but the sheer scale of the theatre of war and the problem of controlling a hostile population in occupied China led to the war dragging on, much to the frustration of the Japanese.

To add to their woes the CCP was active in the areas under their control. Under the direction of Mao Tse-tung the CCP mounted a series of small-scale offensives between August and November 1940 in Shansi, Chahar, Hopeh and Henan, which inflicted substantial damage in Japanese rear areas. The so-called Hundred Regiments Campaign, when 400,000 Eighth Route Army soldiers fought the Japanese in North China, destroyed 1,600km (1,000 miles) of road, 480km (300 miles) of railway track, 260 railway stations and scores of bridges and tunnels, albeit at great cost in CCP lives.

INDISCRIMINATE KILLING

In response, the commander of Japan's North China Area Army, General Yasuji Okamura, received permission from Imperial General Headquarters in Tokyo to implement a new 'pacification' policy in those areas where the CCP was active. Army Order No. 575, approved on 3 December, 1941, became known as the Three Alls Policy ('Kill all, burn all, destroy all').

Japanese control in occupied areas was mostly confined to major cities and railways ('points and lines'). They did not have the manpower to maintain a presence in the vast Chinese countryside. Three Alls divided North China into three areas: pacified, semipacified and unpacified. To bring about total pacification Okamura was authorised to destroy villages, confiscate food stocks and order the Chinese peasantry to build protected villages. It also permitted the execution of 'enemies pretending to be local people'.

At first Three Alls was brutally successful and resulted in the reduction of territory under CCP control and a depletion of the Communists' military strength. In response Mao assumed personal control over the party and military strategy. Conventional warfare was abandoned in favour of a guerrilla campaign.

The reality of Three Alls was Japanese brutality on a massive scale. In May 1942, for example, the Japanese Army broke 128 river and lake dykes in central and western Hebei, flooding 6,752 villages and hamlets. Around two million Chinese were affected by this devastation. At the end of the year the Eighth Route Army estimated that the Japanese had constructed throughout North China 15,360km (9,600 miles) of walls and ditches, 29,846 blockhouses, and 9,243 forts or strongholds. But the cost had been high. Japanese intelligence estimated that in North China the population had shrunk in base areas from 44 million to 25 million.

In total Three Alls was the subject of over 100 campaigns launched by Okamura, resulting in an estimated 2.7 million Chinese deaths. Designed to undermine peasant support for the Communists, it often had the reverse effect, stiffening the resolve of the peasantry and driving them into the arms of the CCP. The policy contributed to an increase in size of the Chinese Red Army to one million men by the end of 1942. Three Alls had spectacularly backfired.

UNREPENTANT WAR CRIMINAL

Yasuji Okamura never faced trial for the hundreds of thousands of Chinese deaths at his hands during the war in China. In August 1945, on hearing that Japan had surrendered, he signalled to the General Staff: 'Such a disgrace as the surrender of several million troops without fighting is not paralleled in the world's military history, and it is absolutely impossible to submit to unconditional surrender of a million picked troops, in perfectly healthy shape, to the Chungking forces of defeated China'.

He actually did surrender, to Chiang Kai-shek. Because he was a rabid anti-Communist he became Chiang's adviser (who absolved him of responsibility for any war crimes). He returned to Japan in 1949 and died in his house in 1966.

THE ATTACK ON PEARL HARBOUR

DATE

....

7 December, 1941

SUMMARY

....

The surprise
Japanese attack
brought the USA into
the war on the side
of the Allies.

LOCATION

....

Hawaii

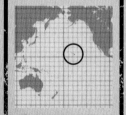

By late 1941 the Japanese had established a large empire in the
Far East, occupying Taiwan, Korea and parts of China (where they
were fighting a protracted war). With the defeat of France and
Holland in 1940 and what appeared to be the impending defeat
of Britain, Tokyo saw an opportunity to seize the Far Eastern
colonies of the European powers. The main impediment to these
plans was the United States, which was already assisting the
Chinese and would not stand by and watch the Japanese conquer
Southeast Asia. This was confirmed when the Americans placed a
U.S. oil embargo on Japan following Tokyo's occupation of French
Indochina in July 1941 (with Vichy agreement). The British and
Dutch governments (the latter in exile) also impounded Japanese
funds, which meant Japan could not purchase oil from U.S.
suppliers or the Dutch East Indies. These economic sanctions
forced the Japanese towards war.

SURPRISE ATTACK

....

The Japanese war plan was to cripple the U.S. Pacific Fleet (based
at Pearl Harbour) with a surprise attack, then seize the Philippines,
Malaya, Burma and the Dutch East Indies while the Americans were
disabled. The Japanese would then bargain from a position of
strength to negotiate a settlement with the United States.

The six aircraft carriers of the Japanese navy's First Air Fleet left
Tankan Bay in the Kuril Islands on 26 November, 1941. Commanded
by Vice-Admiral Chuichi Nagumo, the fleet sailed well to the north of
the Hawaiian Islands before turning southeast. The Japanese force
was grouped into carrier divisions, each with its own air group.
Division 1 comprised the carriers *Akagi* and *Kaga*, Division 2 *Hiryu*
and *Soryu* and Division 5 *Zuikaku* and *Shokaku*. Each carrier had a
complement of 21 A6M Zero fighters, 18 D3A Val dive-bombers
and 27 B5N Kate torpedo-bombers.

On the evening of 6 December the Japanese fleet was 800km (500 miles) north of Pearl Harbour, unspotted by the Americans. The ships then headed southward to enable their aircraft to be launched the following morning. The 213 aircraft of the first wave took off at 06:00 hours on 7 December. Among them were 89 Kates, 40 of which were armed with specially adapted torpedoes with 'air tails' to allow them to be dropped in the shallow waters of Pearl Harbour.

THE SECOND WAVE

An hour after the first wave had been launched the second wave took off from the carriers: 50 Kates, 40 Zeroes and 80 Vals. By this time the first wave was approaching the target. If total surprise was achieved, the torpedo-bombers would attack the warships in the harbour, closely followed by the bomb-armed Kates. The Val dive-bombers would attack the naval air base on Ford Island. The fleet received the radio message 'Tora, Tora, Tora', signalling that total surprise had been achieved.

The battleships *West Virginia*, *Arizona*, *Nevada*, *Oklahoma* and *California* and a target ship, the *Utah*, were all hit. All began to sink except the *Nevada*, which began to steam out of the harbour. The battleship *Pennsylvania* in dry dock was also hit.

At 08:50 hours the aircraft of the second wave appeared over Pearl Harbour to continue the attack. Less than a third of the 143 United States Army Air Force (USAAF) on Oahu survived the air attacks. By 10:00 hours the aircraft were returning to their carriers, leaving five battleships and three destroyers sunk or sinking, three battleships and two cruisers damaged and 3,478 military personnel killed or wounded.

Pearl Harbour had been a brilliant tactical success but a major strategic blunder. The surprise attack launched before a declaration of war enraged U.S. public opinion (reinforcing a widespread image of the Japanese as being unscrupulous). On 8 December President Roosevelt addressed an emergency session of Congress, asking for a declaration of war against Japan. The United States would thereafter mobilise massive resources to wage war against the Japanese Empire.

ABOVE Three battleships of the U.S. Navy burn after the attack on Pearl Harbour. In the foreground, the USS *Arizona* was crippled and would eventually sink.

BELOW In the aftermath of Pearl Harbour, war against Japan was declared in an emergency session of Congress.

JAPAN CONQUERS MALAYA AND SINGAPORE

DATE

8 December, 1941

SUMMARY

The conquest of Malaya and Singapore gave the Japanese passage from the Pacific to the Indian Ocean and was a disaster for the British in the Far East.

LOCATION

Malaya

On 8 December, 1941, the day after the attack on Pearl Harbour, the Japanese invaded British-controlled Malaya. For the Japanese, Malaya was a great prize, producing 38 percent of the world's rubber and 58 percent of its tin. At its southern tip lay the island of Singapore, Britain's naval base and the key to her power in the Far East.

The Japanese Twenty-Fifth Army, commanded by the brilliant General Tomoyuki Yamashita, which had been given jungle training, was given the task of taking Malaya and Singapore. Mustering 60,000 men at the start of the campaign, it was supported by the 459 aircraft of the 3rd Air Group, to which the Japanese navy added a further 159 aircraft. Vice-Admiral Ozawa's Southern Squadron of one battle-cruiser, ten destroyers and five submarines also supported the invasion. Crucially, the Japanese brought 200 light tanks with them to invade a country that the British regarded as totally unsuited to tanks.

General Arthur Ernest Percival was the overall commander in Malaya and initially had around 80,000 British and Commonwealth troops to defend against a Japanese attack. However, many, especially the Indian units, were only partially trained.

IMMEDIATE RETREAT

When Japanese troops struck Malaya from the landward side via Thailand's Kra Isthmus they caught the British totally off-guard (Japanese troops had landed in Thailand on 8 December and in northern Malaya, at Kota Bharu, on the same day). The British plan was to rush into Thailand to forestall any invasion, but their troops now found that the Japanese were behind them. They therefore withdrew, triggering a never-ending cycle of retreat that repeated itself all the way down the western side of Malaya.

Japanese aircraft flying from Indochina and Thailand destroyed the few British aircraft remaining in northern Malaya (the total RAF strength at Percival's disposal was 158 aircraft) and then bombed the airfields, making aerial reinforcement impossible. The British battleships *Repulse* and *Prince of Wales* were sunk on 10 December, which allowed the Japanese to launch seaborne assaults behind British positions as they advanced south.

On land Japanese tactics were bold and aggressive, outflanking British positions by infiltrating through the 'impassable' jungle.

Percival began to receive reinforcements from India and Australia in January but many were untrained and of poor quality and did nothing to improve deteriorating British morale. On the other side Japanese spirits were soaring as units advanced without meeting any effective British checks.

On 31 January British forces completed their withdrawal to Singapore Island, having retreated 560km (350 miles) in 58 days. Percival estimated that he had 85,000 men, including 15,000 admin staff and noncombatants, to defend the island. The reality was that he had more but morale was now crumbling. Japanese aircraft now began to bomb Singapore City itself, damaging the water supply system. Food for the soldiers and one million civilians began to run short.

By 13 February the British were penned into a 45km (28-mile) perimeter and morale was shot. Deserters flooded into the city and hid in cellars, emerging at night to loot stores and houses. Ironically, by this date Yamashita's divisional commanders were reporting that their ammunition and food were almost exhausted. The general gave orders that attacks were to continue, to convince the enemy that his ammunition supplies were unlimited. It worked: on 15 February the British sent forward a delegation under a flag of truce to discuss terms of surrender.

For the loss of 9,824, of which 3,000 were fatalities, the Japanese had conquered Malaya and Singapore. British and Commonwealth losses were 9,000 killed and wounded and 130,000 taken prisoner.

Japan now had complete control of the lines of communication across the central Pacific, they had captured Hong Kong, and the Philippines were now isolated.

Eyewitness

A BRITISH OFFICER IN MALAYA GIVES ONE REASON WHY THE CAMPAIGN FAILED.

'It's like this. Before the war we would be working from a map to conduct our manoeuvres. Our colonel or the brigadier would say: "Now this is thick jungle here and this is mangrove swamp. We can rule this out. In this sector all we have to concern ourselves with is the road."

Thus we based our strategy on that type of operation. We kept to the roads everywhere. Why, I went through a mangrove swamp the other day and nowhere did I sink down in the mud over my ankles. Anyhow, you can walk on the roots in almost any swamp and in that way avoid sinking. And the Japanese did.'

THE PHILIPPINES IS LOST

DATE

8–31 December, 1941

SUMMARY

The fall of the Philippines was a stunning Japanese tactical success but did not signify a strategic victory.

LOCATION

The Philippines

The Philippines group contains over 7,000 islands, the most important of which, Luzon, contains Manila and in 1941 was the location of the fortified defensive position of Bataan (with the fortified island of Corregidor nearby). General Douglas MacArthur, the commander of all forces in the Philippines – 22,400 U.S. troops, 3,000 Philippine Constabulary and 107,000 men of the partly trained and armed Philippine Army – had long warned of a Japanese attack. If it happened his plan was to launch a counterattack against an invasion together with a B-17 bomber strike against the Japanese air bases on Formosa, Taiwain. If this failed he would order a retreat to the Bataan Peninsula, there to hold out until the U.S. Pacific Fleet sent reinforcements.

Japanese plans had written off the Philippine Army, which meant that Tokyo expected an easy victory. The task of conquering the Philippines was given to General Masaharu Homma and his Fourteenth Army (50,000 veteran troops). Homma was given 50 days to complete the task, which was made much easier when the Japanese achieved surprise, despite Manila having been notified of the attack on Pearl Harbour.

A SINGLE DEADLY STRIKE

On 8 December Japanese aircraft attacked Clark Field near Manila, where the majority of U.S. aircraft in the Philippines was located. Most of the aircraft were on the ground when the Japanese struck, 18 B-17s, 56 fighters and a number of other aircraft being destroyed for the loss of seven Japanese fighters shot down. MacArthur had lost over half his aircraft in one strike. The Japanese had achieved surprise and gave the Americans no time to recover.

The first landings took place on 10 December, at Aparri and Vigan in northern Luzon, and at Legaspi in the south two days later. The Japanese established air bases and transferred aircraft from Formosa. Surviving U.S. aircraft were transferred to the island of Mindanao. But Homma followed, his troops landing on Mindanao on 20 December and on the island of Jolo on Christmas Day. Thus did the Japanese gain air and naval bases for operations against the Dutch East Indies. As anticipated the poorly equipped and trained Filipino Army was no match for its veteran opponents. The campaign was turning into a victory parade. There were only two significant American forces to deal with: General Jonathan Wainwright's North Luzon Force and General George Parker's smaller South Luzon Force.

WITHDRAWAL

....

With air and naval superiority (Japanese bombers had wrecked the naval base at Cavite), Wainwright's troops were unable to halt the invasion of Luzon when it commenced on 22 December.

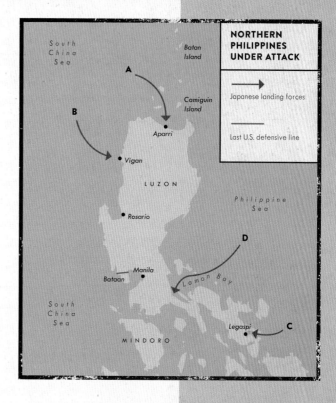

Two days later a smaller Japanese force landed in the south, at Lamon Bay, to threaten the South Luzon Force. U.S. forces were now risking being trapped between two Japanese pincers. MacArthur had no choice but to withdraw into Bataan, declaring Manila an open city on the 26th.

The decision to abandon Manila took the Japanese by surprise but was an inspired decision; to have remained would have led to the destruction of MacArthur's entire army. As it was the year ended with his troops in Bataan. Had Homma annihilated MacArthur's forces he could have moved his troops south to assist the seizure of the entire Southern Resources Area. It was not the strategic victory that Homma had hoped for. For the moment his soldiers were tied down in the Philippines.

Though the Japanese campaign in the Philippines was a foregone conclusion, it would delay Tokyo's timetable by five months (Corregidor would not fall until early May 1942). This crucial period allowed the United States to organise its resources to prevent a Japanese takeover of the entire western Pacific. Mention must also be made of the population of the Philippines, which, to the great consternation of the Japanese, helped to support a guerrilla war against the invaders that lasted until the end of the war.

ABOVE The first of the Japanese forces landed at Aparria (A), Vigan (B) and Legaspi (C) and pushed towards Manila. Two days later, additional forces landed at Lamon Bay (D). Air bases were quickly set up, establishing air supremacy and hastening the defeat of the Allied forces.

GERMANY DECLARES TOTAL WAR

DATE

11 December, 1941

SUMMARY

The decision of
Hitler, and therefore
Mussolini, to declare
war on the United
States condemned
them to battling
what would become
a military and
economic superpower.

LOCATION

Berlin, Germany

On 11 December, 1941, during a long speech in the Reichstag, Hitler announced that according to the Tripartite Pact Germany and Italy, alongside Japan, felt themselves compelled 'together to carry out the struggle for defence, and thereby for the upholding of freedom and independence of their peoples and empires against the United States of America and England'. A formal declaration of war had been delivered to the Americans earlier that afternoon in what appeared to be one of the strangest decisions of World War II.

The reference to the Tripartite Pact was nonsense because Japan had instigated war with the United States. Thus neither Germany nor Italy was compelled under the terms of the pact to join the war against the United States. In addition, the parlous military situation on the Eastern Front in December 1941 made the decision to declare war even more bizarre. And yet according to the Nazi worldview (*Weltanschauung*) it was both predictable and sensible.

AN INEVITABLE CONFLICT

At the heart of Nazi ideology were the notions of space and race. Germany needed 'living space' (*Lebensraum*) to survive and thrive. This space was to be found in the East, which was to be ruthlessly exploited at the expense of the indigenous Slav population, whom the Nazis considered racially inferior. Eventually a German-dominated and racially pure Europe would face a contest with the other emerging great power: the United States. As Hitler himself had stated: 'It is thoughtless to believe that the conflict between Europe and America would always be of a peaceful economic nature'. What is more, according to Nazism, the Jews, the great racial enemy of Nordic Germans, controlled U.S. politics and culture and the white population of the United States was dominated by Jewish capital. A clash with America was therefore not only inevitable but also desirable in order to crush a Jewish-dominated power, leaving the Thousand-year Reich as the only world power.

Once war in Europe had broken out in September 1939, in Hitler's eyes President Roosevelt had done nothing to convince the Führer that the United States desired to remain neutral. On 10 June, 1940, for example, Roosevelt publicly promised to 'extend to the opponents of force' the material resources of the United States. The actions of the Americans over the coming months convinced Hitler that the United States was becoming the 'arsenal of democracy'. First came the destroyer deal of September 1940 whereby the U.S. supplied Britain with 50 old destroyers in exchange for leases on British territories. Far more worrying was the Lend–Lease Act of March 1941. To Berlin this confirmed that the United States was committed to aiding Germany's enemies.

There were a number of incidents in the Atlantic between U.S. ships and U-boats in 1941 that threatened to lead to conflict. However, Roosevelt did not have the backing of the American people to declare war on Germany, and Hitler and the Nazis were preoccupied with events on the Eastern Front from June. But when the Japanese attacked Pearl Harbour in December, Hitler was determined to seize the chance that fate had offered him.

He gave his U-boats licence to attack U.S. vessels in the Atlantic on 8–9 December, before he had declared war. He believed that the United States would be preoccupied in the Pacific, which would work to Germany's advantage in the Atlantic. Notwithstanding the difficulties encountered on the Eastern Front, Hitler was confident that the war in Russia would be won in 1942, allowing Germany to focus its resources against the Americans. The reality, of course, would be very different.

ITALY DECLARES WAR

Mussolini's declaration of war on the United States, on 11 December, 1941, was an exercise in self-delusion.

'This is another day of solemn decision in Italy's history and of memorable events destined to give a new course to the history of continents. The powers of the steel pact, Fascist Italy and Nationalist Socialist Germany, ever closely linked, participate from today on the side of heroic Japan against the United States of America.

The Tripartite Pact becomes a military alliance which draws around its colours 250,000,000 men determined to do all in order to win. Neither the Axis nor Japan wanted an extension of the conflict.

One man, one man only, a real tyrannical democrat, through a series of infinite provocations, betraying with a supreme fraud the population of his country, wanted the war and had prepared for it day by day with diabolical obstinacy.

The formidable blows that on the immense Pacific expanse have been already inflicted on American forces show how prepared are the soldiers of the Empire of the Rising Sun. I say to you, and you will understand, that it is a privilege to fight with them. Today, the Tripartite Pact, with the plenitude of its forces and its moral and material resources, is a formidable instrument for the war and a certainty for victory. Tomorrow, the Tripartite Pact will become an instrument of just peace between the peoples.

Italians! Once more arise and be worthy of this historical hour!

We shall win.'

SAVING THE SUEZ CANAL

DATE

18 November–
20 December, 1941

SUMMARY

The Eighth Army's
Operation Crusader
saved Egypt from
German invasion
and safeguarded
the Suez Canal.

LOCATION

North Africa

In July 1941, following the unsuccessful British operations Brevity (May 1941) and Battleaxe (June 1941), Archibald Wavell was replaced as head of Middle East Command by General Sir Claude Auchinleck. British losses in tanks had been heavy and London feared that a fresh assault by the *Deutsches Afrikakorps* (DAK) would threaten Egypt and the Suez Canal.

The Western Desert Force, now renamed the Eighth Army, was therefore rebuilt to allow it to launch a fresh offensive against the DAK. Rommel had six Italian divisions and three German ones to defend against the British attack, which would be spearheaded by three armoured divisions that had a combined strength of 700 tanks, plus another 500 being repaired or en route. Some of these tanks were U.S. Stuart light tanks armed with a high-velocity 37mm gun that was at least equal to the German Panzer III.

AUCHINLECK'S OFFENSIVE

Auchinleck did not launch his offensive, codenamed Crusader, until his preparations were complete, which included appointing Lieutenant-General Sir Alan Cunningham as commander of the Eighth Army. Auchinleck's plan was simple: he would use one of his two divisions to outflank the DAK to the south and push Rommel out of eastern Cyrenaica. The fact that Rommel was obsessed by the British-held port of Tobruk, being concerned that he might be trapped between the garrison and the Eighth Army, initially aided Auchinleck's plan.

The offensive commenced on 18 November, spearheaded by Major-General Gott's 7th Armoured Division, which broke though Axis defences. Rommel rallied his forces and, on 20 November, launched a counterattack with the 15th and 21st Panzer Divisions against Bir el Gubi, which knocked out many of the 7th Armoured Division's tanks.

The climax of Crusader came on 23 November when the British New Zealand Division stormed the DAK headquarters. Once more Rommel launched a counterattack that captured 3,000 Eighth Army soldiers, but lost 70 tanks out of his 160 remaining. However, his forces had reached the Egyptian border.

But Rommel's tanks were desperately short of fuel, which was threatening his chances of victory. Once more German tactics were superior to those of the enemy, the DAK integrating tanks, anti-tank guns, artillery and aircraft that destroyed British armoured formations that were invariably dispersed and small.

Despite his supply problems Rommel continued with the offensive between 29 November and 1 December. But by this time the DAK was too weak and his assault against Sidi Omar failed, his panzers suffering badly at the hands of dug-in infantry supported by artillery. Another attack, against El Duda on 5 December, also failed and two days later Rommel was forced to face reality and order a retreat back to Gazala. Now British material superiority began to tell as the Eighth Army, despite its losses, continued to attack. By 15 December it had only 200 tanks left but the DAK was down to 30. On 20 December, therefore, Rommel gave the order to retreat.

Despite British attempts to trap the DAK, Rommel escaped, but Auchinleck could feel very satisfied with the results of Crusader. The whole of Cyrenaica had fallen to the Eighth Army and the DAK had lost 33,000 troops compared to British losses of 18,000. In addition, the DAK had lost 300 tanks against 278 for the British. The problem for Rommel was that the British could make good their equipment losses far quicker. The Desert Fox was back to square one in the seesaw war that the conflict in North Africa had become.

For the time being Auchinleck had saved Egypt and the Suez Canal.

Eyewitness

GENERAL F. W. VON MELLENTHIN WAS A MEMBER OF THE DAK STAFF DURING OPERATION CRUSADER AND RECALLED HOW LOSSES DEPRIVED ROMMEL OF VICTORY IN NOVEMBER AND DECEMBER 1941.

'On paper we seemed to have won the Crusader battle. But the price paid was too heavy; the *Panzergruppe* had been worn down, and it soon became clear that only one course remained — a general retreat from Cyrenaica.

[11 December] Although the British attacks were repulsed, it became clear that the fighting power of the Italians had decreased to an alarming degree; we were in danger of exhausting our last stocks of ammunition and were in no condition to meet a strong armoured thrust around the southern flank.'

In the Pacific, the Japanese won a series of stunning victories in Malaya, Borneo and the Philippines, fatally wounding the power and prestige of the European colonial powers in the region: Britain, France and Holland. But in May and June, Japanese expansion was checked at the naval engagements at Coral Sea and Midway. Tokyo believed that it could hold the perimeter of its Greater East Asia Co-Prosperity Sphere, but the reality was that it had no way of striking at an American economy that was rapidly gearing up for war.

On the Eastern Front, the Germans launched a summer offensive that initially won a large amount of territory. But the offensive came to a halt in the rubble of Stalingrad, where the Red Army engaged the Germans, while preparing a counterattack that would trap the enemy invaders in the city. In North Africa, meanwhile, Axis forces were defeated at El Alamein, and U.S. and British forces landed on the coast of North Africa. For the Axis powers, the writing was on the wall.

1942

THE WANNSEE CONFERENCE

DATE

....

20 January, 1942

SUMMARY

....

The systematic
murder of the
entire Jewish race
was agreed at a
conference held
in a pleasant
Berlin suburb.

LOCATION

....

Wannsee, Berlin,
Germnay

The outbreak of World War II had seen a rapid acceleration in the imprisonment and murder of those groups deemed to be enemies of the Nazi New Order. At the top of the list were the Jews. As German armies conquered Poland, France, the Low Countries, Yugoslavia, Greece and then vast tracts of the western USSR, they found themselves in control of millions of Jews. On 31 July, 1941, Hermann Göring, *Luftwaffe* chief and Plenipotentiary of the Four-Year Plan, ordered Reinhard Heydrich, head of the SD (*Sicherheitsdienst*, the Nazi Party's intelligence and security agency), to 'present to me, as soon as possible, a draft setting out details of the preliminary measures in the organisational, technical and material fields for the achievement of the "Final Solution of the Jewish question"'.

THE 'FINAL SOLUTION'

....

On 20 January, 1942, Heydrich assembled the major representatives of the agencies involved in the 'Final Solution' at a villa in the exclusive Berlin suburb of Wannsee. Chief among the 15 delegates were: Gestapo chief Heinrich Müller; Dr. Otto Hoffmann of the Race and Settlement

RIGHT Presented in dry bureaucratic language, the agreement reached at the Wannsee Conference plotted a course to the mass murder of the Jews and other minority groups.

Office; Karl Eberhard Schöngarth, SD chief for the Government General (occupied Poland); and Dr. Rudolf Lange, commander of the SD for Latvia. The Gestapo's Adolf Eichmann, who at the conference took the minutes, had sent out invitations.

The wording of the subsequent minutes was bland and couched in bureaucratic tones but was clear enough. Those areas under German control were to be swept for Jews, who would be rounded up and sent to ghettos in the east, prior to being sent further east. But of course these were just steps towards the complete elimination of European Jewry.

The murder of Jews was already in full swing: the four SS *Einsatzgruppen* (Special Action Squads) were following closely behind German armies in Russia, rounding up thousands of Jews, gypsies and communists and shooting them. What Wannsee did was to direct the entire apparatus of the Nazi state towards the murder of European Jewry.

Jews were rounded up, herded into freight trains and sent to camps that were to become extermination centres. The first death camp, at Belzec near Lublin, in Poland, was set up towards the end of 1941 and became operational in the spring of 1942. It was capable of murdering up to 15,000 Jews a day in death chambers, into which exhaust fumes from diesel engines were pumped. Other death camps were established at Auschwitz, Sobibor, Treblinka, and Majdanek. At Auschwitz a new and more effective chemical agent, Zyklon-B, was introduced to kill Jews in gas chambers. Its use would soon spread to other camps.

By the end of the war the Germans had murdered up to six million Jews, plus gypsies, political prisoners and 'Asiatic inferiors'. After 1945 many Germans denied any knowledge of the Holocaust but the involvement of tens of thousands of train drivers, German firms building crematoria to burn the bodies from the gas chambers, to say nothing of the tens of thousands of administrative staff involved in the smooth running of the concentration camp system, is testimony to the fact that the Holocaust was an open secret in which a great percentage of Germany's population was complicit.

WANNSEE PROTOCOL

This is an extract from the protocol as agreed at the Wannsee Conference.

'The Jews should in the course of the Final Solution be taken in a suitable manner to the east for use as labour. In big labour gangs, separated by sex, the Jews capable of work will be brought to these areas for road building, in which task undoubtedly a large number will fall through natural diminution. The remnant that is finally able to survive all this … must be treated accordingly, since these people, representing a natural selection, are to be regarded as the germ cell of a new Jewish development, in case they should succeed and go free (as history has proved).'

AREA BOMBING DIRECTIVE

DATE

14 February, 1942

SUMMARY

The Royal Air Force (RAF) was authorised to conduct a nighttime area bombing campaign against Germany's towns and cities.

LOCATION

London, Britain

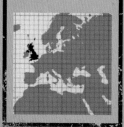

The British Butt Report of August 1941 revealed that fewer than a third of the RAF's bombers dropped their bombs within 8km (5 miles) of the target and 90 percent of bombs dropped fell outside the target area. Clearly, nighttime precision bombing was not working. As a result of the Butt Report the Air Staff issued the Area Bombing Directive on 14 February, 1942.

TARGETING CIVILIANS

Henceforth bombing would be directed towards undermining the morale of the German workforce by destroying residential housing, amenities and services. This would increase levels of absenteeism from German companies engaged in war production and thus undermine production of war materials. That such bombing would result in large numbers of civilian fatalities was omitted from discussions but was understood to be a truism. It was pointed out that the Germans had tried the same strategy during the Blitz, which had failed to break British morale. There were two reasons why this was dismissed. First, what would be done to Germany by the RAF would be ten times worse than the damage inflicted on Britain by the *Luftwaffe*. Second, the destruction of German cities had the overwhelming support of the British public.

The man charged with implementing the RAF's new bombing strategy was Air Chief Marshal Arthur Harris (who took up his post eight days after the Area Bombing Directive), the commander of Bomber Command, who would be nicknamed 'Bomber Harris'. When he assumed command Harris stated that he had only 300 bombers to call on, of which only 50 were four-engine 'heavies'. This amounted to a third of Britain's bomber force, the rest being diverted to attacking U-boat pens or sent to the Mediterranean or Far East. Harris immediately called for more bombers, particularly four-engine types, and navigational aids to get them to the target. He received a bonus with the new Gee target-finding device, which allowed aircraft to identify

LEFT Crew prepare to board an RAF Avro Manchester in 1940. The Manchester was a precursor to the Avro Lancaster, one of the RAF's most effective weapons in the campaign against German cities.

locations up to 400km (250 miles) away by receiving radio pulses transmitted by three Gee stations in Britain.

The basic theory of area bombing was to drop ordnance in the centre of a city, which would not only destroy housing but also infrastructure. Bomb loads were a carefully selected mixture of high-explosive bombs to smash roofs and blow out windows and doors, and incendiaries to set fire to exposed interiors.

The first area bombing raid was carried out before Harris arrived in post, on the night of 14–15 February, against the city of Essen, the home of the giant Krupp armaments concern. The raid caused little damage. Harris took up his position on 22 February and on 28 March launched a much more effective raid, against Lübeck. This was the first raid to use the 'double-blow' tactic whereby a second wave of aircraft arrived over the target several hours after the initial strike, to increase chaos and confusion below. Lübeck's wooden medieval city centre burned, killing 300 people, injuring 800 and making 16,000 homeless.

Great success followed at the end of April when Harris managed to assemble 1,000 bombers for a 'double-blow' against the city of Cologne. The RAF destroyed 3,300 buildings, seriously damaged 2,000, and moderately damaged 7,400. Civilian casualties were relatively light – 500 killed and 500 injured – but 45,000 citizens were made homeless overnight. Area bombing was judged a success and would increase in intensity until the end of the war.

Eyewitness

THE FOLLOWING IS FROM A PAMPHLET DROPPED BY ALLIED PLANES ON GERMANY IN THE SUMMER OF 1942.

'We are bombing Germany, city by city, and ever more terribly, in order to make it impossible for you to go on with the war. That is our object. We shall pursue it remorselessly. City by city; Lübeck, Rostock, Cologne, Emden, Bremen, Wilhelmshaven, Duisburg, Hamburg — and the list will grow longer and longer. Let the Nazis drag you down to disaster with them if you will That is for you to decide. We are coming by day and by night. No part of the Reich is safe. People who work in [factories] live close to them. Therefore we hit your houses, and you.'

HEAVY BOMBERS ENTER THE FRAY

DATE

3 and 4 March, 1942

SUMMARY

The Avro Lancaster, one of the most effective heavy bombers of World War II, was introduced.

LOCATION

Heligoland, German coast

On the night of 3 and 4 March, 1942, the RAF's 44 Squadron conducted a so-called 'gardening mission' to lay mines in the sea off the German coast, close to Heligoland. All four aircraft dropped their mines and returned safely to base. This type of mission had been carried out many times by RAF aircraft, but this particular sortie was different: it was the operational debut of the four-engined Avro Lancaster heavy bomber.

A STALWART OF THE RAF

The Lancaster was not the first four-engined RAF bomber. The Short Stirling (2,368 produced) had entered service in February 1941 and the Handley Page Halifax (6,176 produced) a month later. But the Stirling gave poor performance and the Halifax was underpowered. They both paled beside the Lancaster, which was reliable, well armed and had excellent range. Carrying standard fuel and a 4,540kg (10,000lb) bomb load, the Lancaster had a range of 1,670km (1,040 miles). With one 1,818-litre (400-gallon) fuel tank and a bomb load of 3,180kg (7,000lb) this increased to 4,310km (2,680 miles), meaning it could reach every target in Germany. In total 7,379 Lancasters were produced during the war, of which 3,345 were lost during a total of 156,000 sorties.

In August 1942 the Lancaster was joined in the skies over occupied Europe by the Boeing B-17 Flying Fortress (12,731 produced) and Consolidated B-24 Liberator (16,188 produced) four-engined bombers of the U.S. Eighth Air Force, which was based in Britain. The British conducted area bombing by night and the Americans carried out precision daylight raids. Against *Luftwaffe* fighters and flak defences the bombers suffered high losses. To the Lancaster losses must be added 4,754 B-17s and 2,112 B-24s lost on missions in the European theatre of operations. The tonnage of bombs dropped on enemy targets by Allied bombers totalled 2.7 million by the end of the war in Europe.

Eyewitness

THIS IS AN EXTRACT FROM AN OFFICIAL NAZI REPORT
FROM THE RHINELAND CITY OF AACHEN IN 1945.

'The necessity, because of the suspension of public transport, of having to go to work over piles of rubble and through clouds of dust; the impossibility of washing oneself properly or of cooking at home because there was no water, gas, or electricity; the difficulty of shopping for food because most of the stores had been destroyed or closed of their own accord; the continual explosions of delayed-action bombs or duds, or the blowing-up of parts of buildings which were in danger of collapse.'

In all there were 1.44 million bomber sorties and 2.68 million fighter sorties flown. At its peak the Eighth Air Force could dispatch more than 2,000 four-engined bombers and 1,000 fighters on a single mission.

Against such air power Nazi Germany's economy buckled. By 1945 bombing had destroyed or heavily damaged 3.6 million homes, killing 300,000 civilians, wounding 780,000, and rendering 7.5 million homeless. The German economy was powered by coal and the *Wehrmacht's* aircraft and panzers by oil. Sources of both fuels were targets of the bomber offensive. The only crude oil that Germany could call on was that supplied by Romania's Ploesti oil fields and Hungarian oil fields. Both were attacked by four-engined bombers, the Ploesti fields being continually bombed by the Americans in 1943–44 until the Red Army overran them in August 1944. Germany's 13 synthetic oil plants were also targeted, every one being bombed by July 1944. By the end of 1944 a lack of oil was badly affecting *Luftwaffe* training and missions, as well as panzer operations on the ground. Tanks and vehicles were literally running out of fuel. It is no coincidence that in 1945 the German army was using over a million horses to transport artillery and supplies.

The bombing offensive against Germany's rail and waterway network was designed to interrupt the supply of coal to power stations, to reduce war production and make it difficult to move what was produced to the front. The four-engined bombers struck a decisive blow. Attacks against marshalling yards, bridges and railway lines damaged the supply network and reduced carrying capacity. In August 1944 the Third Reich possessed 900,000 freight carriages. Following an intensive bombing campaign this number had dropped to 214,000 carriages by the beginning of March 1945.

THE FALL OF BURMA

DATE

April 1942

SUMMARY

The defeat of British and Chinese forces in Burma constituted a grave threat to India and was another blow to Britain's military prestige.

LOCATION

Central Burma

The Japanese Fifteenth Army, commanded by Lieutenant-General Shojiro Iida, invaded Burma on 12 January with a westwards advance on Moulmein and Tavoy from Thailand. The British commander in Burma, Lieutenant-General Thomas Hutton, was defeated at Moulmein in January and at Sittang in February, his British, Burmese, and Indian troops retreating north after having lost all their heavy equipment. Hutton was replaced in March by Lieutenant-General Sir Harold Alexander, the latter's forces strengthened so that British capability was once again two divisions. But converging Japanese columns were closing in on the capital Rangoon so Alexander had to abandon the city on 7 March.

NATIONALIST SUPPORT

With their forces disintegrating the British accepted an offer of help from Chinese Nationalist leader Chiang Kai-shek, who sent his Fifth and Sixth armies (the equivalent of two Western corps) down the Burma Road. Accompanying them was Chiang's chief of staff, U.S. General Stillwell, who would command both armies.

In mid-March Alexander established a defensive line running south of Prome and Taungoo, then east to Loikaw. The British Burma Corps, commanded by Major-General William Slim, held the right. The Chinese Fifth Army held the centre (the Rangoon–Mandalay road and railway) and the Chinese Sixth Army held the mountainous jungle region, on the left.

In early April both sides received reinforcements. Iida received two veteran divisions from the Malaya campaign and Alexander the Chinese Sixty-Sixth Army. On 10 April the Japanese struck against the Burma Corps. For nine days the Battle of Yenangyaung raged, with the British forced to evacuate the Yenangyaung oil fields and Magwe.

On 18 April the Japanese 56th Division opened a new phase of the campaign when it struck the Chinese Sixth Army in the Loikaw–Taunggyi region. Stilwell launched a counterattack but the Japanese avoided him and struck north towards Lashio, the starting point of the Burma Road (the overland route to China). While this was happening the remainder of the Fifteenth Army was wearing down the British and Chinese south of Mandalay.

The Japanese 56th Division captured Lashio on 29 April then struck west, towards Maymyo and Mandalay. Alexander had no option but to order a retreat across the Irrawaddy River. The British fought a desperate rearguard action to allow Allied units to retreat during the evening of 30 April. Japanese troops entered the town the next day.

Iida did not allow the British any respite, pushing on towards the Indian frontier in an attempt to trap the enemy. The Japanese advance halted at the Chindwin River where they regrouped. What was left of the Chinese armies had scattered, across the mountain border to Yunnan, to the Himalayan foothills of northern Burma, or across the mountains to India.

The longest retreat in British military history had cost Alexander 30,000 casualties among the 42,000 involved in the Burma campaign. Half were reported as 'missing' and were Burmese who had abandoned their weapons to return to their homes. Chinese losses were huge among the 95,000 men sent to Burma; only the 38th Division withdrew as a fighting unit. Japanese losses totalled 7,000.

As in Malaya well-trained Japanese troops had outflanked and outfought their enemies to win a stunning victory. By conquering Burma the Japanese severed land communications between China and its allies and had a country that could act as a bulwark to protect the western approaches to the Southern Resource Area. Burma could also be used as a springboard for an invasion of India.

ABOVE Indian troops arrive in Singapore in November 1941. The better equipped, highly motivated Japanese forces inflicted a hugely significant defeat on the British-led forces.

JAPAN'S SOUTHERN RESOURCE AREA

The primary strategic purpose of the leaders of the Japanese Empire at the beginning of the war was the occupation and development of what was called the Southern Resources Area: the Dutch East Indies and adjacent regions. It was this part of the Pacific that contained most of the raw materials, specifically oil, considered essential to Japan's economic welfare and military potential. Lines of communication between the Japanese homeland and the Southern Resource Area, once seized, also had to be maintained. To guarantee the permanency of its empire, Japan had to cripple Allied naval strength in the Pacific and establish a strong defensive perimeter to protect the homeland and its new economic adjunct to the south.

BATAAN DEATH MARCH

DATE

9 April, 1942

SUMMARY

The brutality the Japanese displayed towards U.S. and Filipino prisoners of war was a foretaste of things to come in the Pacific War.

LOCATION

Bataan Peninsula, Philippines

The Japanese attack on the Philippines began on 8 December, 1941, the main drive of Lieutenant-General Homma's Fourteenth Army being a landing at Lingayen Gulf prior to a drive towards Manila. General Douglas MacArthur, the overall commander in the Philippines, abandoned Manila and ordered his forces to withdraw to the Bataan Peninsula. On paper Bataan and the island fortress of Corregidor were excellent defensive positions. Unfortunately the American and Filipino troops were short of ammunition, food and medical supplies. The Japanese commenced a siege and soon the defenders were suffering from disease and having to subsist on starvation rations. Japanese attacks began on 14 January, 1942, and continued until 9 April when the garrison was forced to surrender.

CONTEMPT FOR THE POWS

The Japanese were faced with the unexpected problem of what to do with around 12,000 American and 66,000 Filipino captives. Their plan was to move them out of Bataan quickly so they could launch attacks on Corregidor, the island across from Bataan. Moving a large number of men who were suffering from malnutrition, malaria, and intestinal infections in hot conditions would have been cruel enough, but their misery was made worse by the attitude of their Japanese guards.

The reasons that Japanese soldiers abused Allied soldiers were many. White Westerners in particular were viewed as arrogant colonists who oppressed the indigenous peoples of Asia, and like the countries they served were also weak and immoral. The surrender of large numbers of British and American soldiers during the early phase of the war in the Pacific appeared to confirm this. This made them contemptible in the eyes of Japanese soldiers who were highly trained, disciplined and indoctrinated in a military culture that demanded absolute obedience to the emperor and those appointed by him to lead them. To retreat or to be taken prisoner, both of which the defenders of Bataan had done, were acts of profound dishonour. Guarding prisoners of war was also regarded as a dishonourable act, which resulted in the Japanese inflicting great cruelty on the defenders of Bataan.

ENDLESS MARCHING

....

The 'death march' began on 10 April, a long line of prisoners trudging up the east coast of Bataan towards the town of San Fernando. Abie Abraham was one of the American captives: 'The men started to march in a long column on the dusty road. For many of the bloody, frail men this was the last march. The sun beat down unmercifully on the marchers with a continuous drum by the Japanese guards to hurry. Furthermore, the Japanese treated the POWs with savage brutality'. Ferron Edward Cummins: 'A typical day on the "March" was endless marching, a few hours towards San Fernando and then turning around and marching back a few hours. Monotonous, one foot in front of the other. Always hungry and thirsty, dejected and depressed. Trying to stay alert for the irate behaviour of the guards and trying to help ailing and weary comrades'. Albert Brown remembered the fate of those who could not maintain the pace: 'Those who fell out of line or failed to follow orders were met with beheadings, stabbings or shootings'.

The prisoners were forced to march 104km (65 miles) over the course of six days. When they reached San Fernando around 11,000 had died on the march, the vast majority of them Filipinos. But their ordeal was not over. They were loaded into boxcars for a four-hour ride in sweltering conditions. Up to 115 men were forced into boxcars designed to hold 30–40 men for the 4-hour journey. The survivors then had to walk another few miles to reach their prison camp, Camp O'Donnell.

Those prisoners who survived the 'death march' and Camp O'Donnell faced a fresh hell when they were sent to Japan to become forced labourers. During the journey, many died due to the inhumane conditions or, tragically, when the boat they were sailing on was sunk by a U.S. submarine.

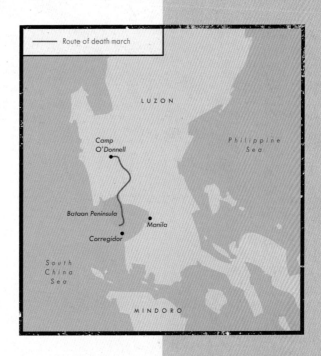

ABOVE U.S. and Filipino prisoners of war endured a terrible forced march along the 104km (65-mile) route to Camp O'Donnell.

WAR BONDS ARE INTRODUCED

DATE
....
15 April, 1942

SUMMARY
....
This simple but
brilliant plan
enlisted the American
public in financing
the war effort.

LOCATION
....
United States

It is a truism that wars are expensive, and World War II was prohibitively expensive in monetary terms. In April 1942, for example, the United States was spending $100 million a day on war purposes (this would rise to $200 million a day by the end of the year). The anticipated billions of dollars of war expenditure had to be paid for by the American people and there were many in the Roosevelt administration that argued the answer lay in higher taxes. However, many politicians in Congress argued the opposite: that raising taxes would damage civilian morale and actually work against the war effort. Henry Morgenthau, secretary of the Treasury, argued successfully that it would be more productive to get the majority of the American people to participate on as large a scale as possible in the financing of the war. This would be achieved by appealing to their patriotism rather than relying on coercion.

On 15 April, 1942, Morgenthau issued Treasury Department Order No 45 as follows: 'The name of the Defence Savings Staff, established

SERIES E SAVINGS BOND

Introduced on 1 May, 1941, the Series E Savings Bond was the same as the War Bond. It was initially called the 'Defence Bond' in 1941 and the 'War Bond' from 1942 to 1945.

As with War Bonds, its purchase was promoted by U.S. financial institutions, community leaders, voluntary committees, and the media. Available in denominations of $25, $50, $75, $100, $200, $500, $1,000, $5,000 and $10,000, bonds were purchased for 75 percent of their face value.

In 1956, the fifteenth anniversary of the first sale of the Series E Savings Bond, more that 40 million Americans held these bonds.

by Treasury Department Order No. 39, dated 19 March, 1941, is hereby changed to War Savings Staff, effective immediately'. War Bonds were born. In the same month he vowed to increase War Bond sales to $1 billion a month by July 1942. At its simplest a War Bond was an investment in the country and an investment in a citizen's personal future. A single $25 bond was purchased for $18.75. The government used the latter sum to finance the war effort and 10 years from the time the bond was purchased it could be redeemed for $25. Under the War Bond Program, Morgenthau arranged that the Federal Reserve would support Treasury borrowing and would purchase bonds not bought by the public at an agreed rate. This was unnecessary because War Bonds were a huge success.

There was a massive drive to encourage people to purchase War Bonds, supported by a nationwide poster campaign that depicted among others Uncle Sam imploring people to purchase bonds. Celebrities such as Bob Hope, Frank Sinatra, Bette Davis and Marlene Dietrich toured the country, putting on live shows and radio programmes to promote War Bond sales. The 'Stars Over America' bond campaign involved no fewer than 337 stars and sold $838,540,000 worth of bonds.

Even children were involved, being able to purchase 25-cent War Stamps to paste into War Bond booklets, and schools had their own War Bonds drives.

By the end of the conflict War Bonds totalling $185.7 billion had been purchased. The U.S. government had spent $300 billion fighting the Axis powers and supplying its allies and the War Bonds had played a crucial part in bringing about the Allied victory.

ABOVE War bonds made a large contribution to the U.S. war effort. They encouraged active participation from the American people and bolstered war coffers.

THE DOOLITTLE RAID

DATE
....
18 April, 1942

SUMMARY
....
The first American
air raid to strike
the Japanese home
islands had major
consequences for
the conduct of the
Pacific War in 1942.

LOCATION
....
Tokyo, Japan

In the weeks after Pearl Harbour the Americans sought ways to strike back against a rampaging Japan. One involved flying B-25 Mitchell twin-engine bombers off the deck of an aircraft carrier to bomb Tokyo.

Two U.S. Navy captains, Francis S. Low and Donald B. Duncan, convinced Admiral Ernest J. King, Chief of Naval Operations, and General Henry H. Arnold, Commanding General, Army Air Forces, that it would be possible to fly bombers from the deck of an aircraft carrier. With Arnold's permission, the USS *Hornet* set sail in April 1942, loaded with 16 B-25s and escorted by the carrier USS *Enterprise*, heading west from San Francisco. On the morning of 18 April, the *Enterprise* detected a Japanese warship and, given the possibility that the carriers had been spotted, it was decided to launch the bombers 240km (150 miles) further from Japan than originally planned.

JAMES H. DOOLITTLE
....

The man leading the air strike was Lieutenant-Colonel James H. Doolittle, who had trained the aircrews and modified the aircraft. All 16 aircraft took off from the *Hornet* successfully (the first time they had done so from the deck of a carrier) and dropped their bombs in the Tokyo area. The plan had been for the bombers to fly on to 'friendly areas' of China. Because they had taken off further out than anticipated all but one of the aircraft went down in Japanese-occupied China (the other landed in the USSR).

Of the 80 crewmen, 71 made it back, one died, and eight were captured. Of the latter, four were executed as war criminals and the others were freed when the war ended, albeit after suffering harsh treatment. The Japanese retaliated instantly against the Chinese for assisting the airmen, killing many peasants.

The raid had been nothing more than a minor irritant to the Japanese but had a major psychological effect on the nation as a whole. The army and navy had failed to protect the home islands but, more importantly, the raid cleared the way for an advance east to capture Midway Island, an important forward fuelling station for U.S. submarines in the central Pacific. This would push Japan's defensive perimeter further east. Midway was 3,600km (2,250 miles) from Japan but only 1,760km (1,100 miles) from Oahu in Hawaii.

Not only would seizing Midway reduce the possibility of another Doolittle raid, according to Admiral Isoroku Yamamoto, the Commander-in-Chief, Combined Fleet, it would also enable him to draw out and destroy the U.S. Navy's aircraft carriers in a pivotal battle. Yamamoto approved an assault plan in April and submitted it to Admiral Osami Nagano, Chief of the Naval General Staff. Nagano, who had always given Yamamoto free rein, ordered the Combined Fleet to seize and occupy Midway Island and key locations in the western Aleutian Islands, in co-operation with the Japanese Army. The scene was set for the Battle of Midway, the turning point of the naval war in the Pacific.

ABOVE Pilot James H. Doolittle (front left) and crew. Although small, the Doolittle raid had a significant psychological impact.

Eyewitness

LIEUTENANT TED LAWSON PILOTED ONE OF THE B-25s THAT FLEW FROM THE USS *HORNET* TO ATTACK TOKYO ON 18 APRIL.

'With full flaps, engines at full throttle, and his left wing far out over the port side of the *Hornet*, Doolittle's plane waddled and then lunged slowly into the teeth of the gale that swept down the deck. His left wheel stuck on the white line as if it were a track. His right wing, which had barely cleared the wall of the island as he taxied and was guided up to the starting line, extended nearly to the edge of the starboard side.

We watched him like hawks, wondering what the wind would do to him, and whether we could get off in that little run towards the bow. If he couldn't, we couldn't.

Doolittle picked up more speed and held to his line, and, just as the *Hornet* lifted itself up on the top of a wave and cut through it at full speed, Doolittle's plane took off. He had yards to spare. He hung his ship almost straight up on its props, until we could see the whole top of his B-25. Then he levelled off and I watched him come around in a tight circle and shoot low over our heads, straight down the line painted on the deck.'

U.S. GETS WARNING OF THE MIDWAY ATTACK

DATE

....

May 1942

SUMMARY

....

The cracking of Japanese naval codes by the Americans allowed them to anticipate and prepare for a Japanese strike against Midway Island.

LOCATION

....

Pearl Harbour, Hawaii

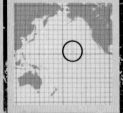

The Americans had always taken a keen interest in Japan's expanding navy and the threat that it posed to U.S. interests in the Pacific. As a logical extension of this, U.S. Navy intelligence had embarked on a campaign to intercept and decrypt Japanese naval communications. This predated World War II by nearly 20 years. In 1921, for example, U.S. Navy intelligence agents had broken into the Japanese Consulate in New York and copied Japanese diplomatic codes. In the 1920s and 1930s the U.S. Navy achieved some success in cracking Japanese naval codes used for communications between surface forces, though the Japanese did not always entrust important secret topics to radio communications.

JAPANESE CODE

....

JN-25 was the Japanese navy's most widely used fleet cryptographic system. The original version, JN-25A, was effective from June 1939 to December 1940, when it was superseded by JN-25B. From December 1941 increased radio traffic from Japanese warships engaged in operations against British and American targets and bases allowed U.S. Navy intelligence cryptanalysts to crack the current version of JN-25 just in time for the battles of Coral Sea and Midway. The code was cracked by Commander Joseph J. Rochefort, commander of Station Hypo (Pearl Harbour, Hawaii), assisted by teams at Station Cast (Cavite, Philippines), and at the British Far East Combined Bureau (before the Philippines surrendered on 9 April the codebreakers at Cavite were evacuated to Australia, to the main British station at Brisbane).

By April 1942 intercepts had identified that location AF was to be the target of a major Japanese attack. But it was unclear where AF was. Some believed it to be the Aleutians, others Midway Island. Rochefort was able to solve the mystery by requesting a message in plain English be sent from the base commander at Midway to Pearl Harbour stating that drinking water was running low due to a breakdown of the water plant. Soon afterward a JN-25 message noted that AF had freshwater problems.

JN-25 EXPLAINED

The following is the U.S. National Security Agency's explanation of
Japan's JN-25 naval code:

'JN-25 consisted of a codebook with approximately 27,500 entries and
an additive book for super enciphering the codebook values. The additive
book consisted of 300 pages, each page containing 100 random five-digit
groups. It should be noted that this additive book for JN-25 was not a one-
time pad: the five-digit groups were re-used, as needed.

In studying JN-25, U.S. cryptanalysts had to collate large numbers of
Japanese messages over time. Their first goal was to recover the indicator in
each message which showed where in the additive book numbers were
taken; then recover and strip away the additives themselves to get down to
the codebook values; and, finally, recover the meanings in plaintext
Japanese of the underlying codebook values, which would allow messages
to be read, at least in part.

Navy cryptanalysts used IBM machines to correlate and compare values
in JN-25-based communications. This allowed them to identify depths,
which were the key to recovering the numerals used in messages. This
method also enabled them to identify a "garble check" the Japanese used to
ensure each message had been copied and decoded correctly. This was of
prime value in helping to strip away the additive numbers and get to the
underlying codebook values.

Once the additive had been stripped away, U.S. cryptanalysts took
advantage of stereotyped messages to recover some basic text.'

Rochefort's team was therefore able to convince Admiral Chester
W. Nimitz, Commander-in-Chief, Pacific Fleet (CinCPac), that the
next major Japanese attack in the Pacific would be in the Midway Island
chain. It was a remarkable intelligence coup that allowed Nimitz to
adapt his plans to meet and defeat the Japanese navy at Midway.

Interestingly, many of Rochefort's men were bandsmen from the
battleship USS *California*, which had been damaged during the Pearl
Harbour attack. He believed that their musical skills might make them
good codebreakers, perhaps equating the ability to quickly read and
play music with excellent mathematical problem-solving.

THE BATTLE OF
THE CORAL SEA

DATE

7–8 May, 1942

SUMMARY

A tactical Japanese
victory was in fact
a strategic setback
for Tokyo.

LOCATION

Coral Sea,
South Pacific

As a result of the Doolittle raid the Japanese High Command decided to expand its defensive perimeter in the central and southern Pacific, with far from beneficial results. On 1 May, 1942, the commander of the Japanese Combined Fleet, Admiral Isoroku Yamamoto, ordered Admiral Shigeyoshi Inoue, commanding at the base at Rabaul, to seize bases in the southern Solomon Islands and capture Port Moresby, New Guinea.

To achieve these aims the Japanese dispatched the small carrier *Shoho*, four cruisers, and an assault force of transports south through the Solomons towards Tulagi. A larger force was assembled to assault Port Moresby by sea. In addition, a strike force of the fleet carriers *Shokaku* and *Zuikaku*, supported by two heavy cruisers and six destroyers, moved south from the central Pacific to enter the Coral Sea from the east to provide support.

A RAID FORETOLD

Unfortunately for the Japanese, U.S. Naval intelligence knew of these plans and reported them to Admiral Nimitz, Commander-in-Chief, Central Pacific, who sent two task forces to counter the enemy's moves. Task Force 17, built around the carrier USS *Yorktown*, was commanded by Rear-Admiral Frank Fletcher and included three heavy cruisers and six destroyers. Task Force 11, commanded by Rear-Admiral Aubrey Fitch, comprised the carrier USS *Lexington*, two heavy cruisers and seven destroyers. Task Force 44 sailed from Sydney to join the American forces. Commanded by Rear-Admiral J.G. Crace RN, it was made up of two Australian cruisers, one U.S. cruiser and one U.S. destroyer.

On 3 May, the Japanese occupied the island of Tulagi unopposed and the *Shoho* task force sailed north to join the Port Moresby assault force that was then leaving Rabaul. The next day aircraft from the *Yorktown* bombed Tulagi but inflicted only minor damage. Between May the *Yorktown* rejoined Fletcher's fleet (the three combined task forces were now designated Task Force 17) in the central Coral Sea. At the same time the Japanese fleet carriers were sailing into the sea from the northeast, and the *Shoho* force and the Port Moresby assault force were approaching the Coral Sea from the Solomon Sea to the north. Both sides launched scout aircraft to search for each other, without success. That changed the next day.

A MAJOR VICTORY

During the morning of 7 May, U.S. scout aircraft spotted the two Japanese fleet carriers and reported their position. Just over an hour later the Lexington launched 28 dive-bombers, 12 torpedo-bombers and 10 fighters. Twenty minutes afterward the *Yorktown* launched 23 dive-bombers, 10 torpedo-bombers and eight fighters. En route the aircraft sighted the *Shoho* and attacked it. The carrier sank at 11:35 hours. By that time the Port Moresby assault force, aware of Crace's blocking force and having been bombed by land-based aircraft, had turned back permanently. It was a major strategic victory for the Allies.

Back in the Coral Sea, Admiral Takeo Takagi, commander of the carrier strike force, received intelligence regarding the position of the U.S. carriers and launched his aircraft. They failed to detect Task Force 17 and were intercepted by enemy aircraft during their return flight. Many were shot down while others ran out of fuel and had to ditch in the sea. Only four out of the 27 Japanese aircraft dispatched returned.

On 8 May both sides detected each other at around the same time, launching their carrier aircraft simultaneously. U.S. aircraft attacked the *Shokaku*, damaging its flight deck. Meanwhile, Japanese aircraft struck when the U.S. carriers' combat air patrols had too little fuel to intercept them. *Yorktown* suffered minor bomb damage but *Lexington* was hit. It caught fire and was abandoned.

Both sides were now too battered to continue the battle and so withdrew. The Japanese had won a minor tactical victory but the Allies had scored a strategic success by halting the assault on Port Moresby.

BELOW USS *Yorktown* photographed from a Douglas TBD-1 torpedo plane that had just taken off from the carrier. The *Yorktown* suffered minor damage in the battle.

ASSASSINATION OF REINHARD HEYDRICH

DATE

27 May, 1942

SUMMARY

Action by Czech paratroopers removed one of the most talented and brutal individuals among the Nazi hierarchy.

LOCATION

Prague, Czechoslovakia

Reinhard Heydrich, the blonde, blue-eyed head of the SD (*Sicherheitsdienst* – the Nazi Party's intelligence and security body) and head of the SS security police who had organised the Wannsee Conference, was one of the most able individuals of the Nazi elite. A womaniser and workaholic, Heydrich had a callous, untrusting nature and kept files on all the leading Nazis, even Hitler reportedly. As a reward for his efforts and in recognition of his talents, in September 1941 Heydrich was appointed Protector of Bohemia and Moravia (the part of Czechoslovakia that did not include the Sudetenland and what became the separate state of Slovakia), where the Czech resistance had been active.

HEYDRICH'S REGIME OF TERROR

As soon as he took up his post Heydrich unleashed a wave of terror, hundreds of suspected terrorists being shot and hundreds more members of the Czech intelligentsia being arrested and sent to concentration camps. As he stated himself in October 1941: 'I must unambiguously and with unflinching hardness bring the citizens of this country, Czech

or otherwise, to the understanding that there is no avoiding the fact they are members of the Reich and as such they owe allegiance to the Reich'. Two weeks after his appointment Heydrich had all but destroyed the Czech resistance movement.

Following the terror came an attempt to enlist the support of ordinary Czech industrial workers and farmers. The black market was suppressed and its food given out in worker cafés. Food rations and free shoes were also issued and pensions were increased. To Czech

RIGHT Even by the standards of the time, Reinhard Heydrich's ideological commitment was extreme. He was a leading proponent of many of the most brutal Nazi policies.

workers he offered wages and benefit packages equivalent to those of their German counterparts. Heydrich even requisitioned luxury spa hotels in Bohemia as holiday homes for Czech workers. The result was a 73-percent reduction in acts of sabotage in Bohemia and Moravia within six months.

It is important to state that the protectorate did not become a workers' paradise. It was a Nazi client state ruled over by an SS overlord. SS occupation policy was designed to produce a grudging consensus between rulers and ruled by a continuous swing between severity and leniency. However, it was apparent to the Czech government-in-exile in London that Heydrich the 'benefactor' was winning over the Czech people. Something had to be done to reverse this and the decision was taken to mount an assassination attempt on the Reich Protector himself.

The operation, codenamed Anthropoid, involved dropping British-trained Czech soldiers into the country by parachute. The paratroopers struck in Prague on 27 May, 1942. Amazingly, Heydrich had taken to riding through the city in an open-top car, which made him an easy target. The assassination attempt resulted in Heydrich being fatally wounded by splinters of his car when a grenade exploded near it. He died of septicemia in a Prague hospital on 4 June.

RUTHLESS MEASURES

As anticipated the Nazi response was brutal. Goebbels wrote a few days after the event: 'The Führer foresees the possibility of a rise in assassination attempts if we do not proceed with energetic and ruthless measures'. Those ruthless measures included the deportation of 3,000 Jews from the Terezin ghetto in Bohemia to death camps in Poland. Lidice, a mining village near Prague, was selected for annihilation because the Nazis believed its inhabitants had aided Heydrich's killers. All men over the age of 15 were shot and the women were sent to Ravensbrück concentration camp, where 53 died. A few of Lidice's 104 children were given to SS families for 'proper upbringing'; 82 were gassed in concentration camps. Retaliations continued for months afterward, with hundreds of resistance activists and their families rounded up and shot.

The Czech government-in-exile and its British sponsors had achieved their ambition of inducing the Czech people to resist their occupiers by provoking German reprisals for the death of Heydrich. But the Czech people paid a high price.

THE BATTLE OF MIDWAY

DATE

....

4–5 June, 1942

SUMMARY

....

One of the most
decisive battles
in history halted
Japanese expansion
in the Pacific.

LOCATION

....

Central Pacific

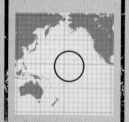

To Admiral Isoroku Yamamoto, Commander-in-Chief, Combined Fleet, the capture of Midway Island and the western Aleutians would extend Japan's defensive perimeter and draw America's aircraft carriers into a decisive engagement where they could be sunk. To achieve his objective Yamamoto assembled over 160 ships that were divided into three main groups: an Aleutian strike force, a mobile strike force, and a reserve.

Forewarned by cryptanalysts of the Midway attack, Admiral Chester Nimitz, Commander-in-Chief, Pacific Ocean Areas, organised Task Force 16, comprising the carriers *Enterprise* and *Hornet*, supported by six cruisers and nine destroyers. In addition, the carrier *Yorktown*, damaged at Coral Sea, was hastily repaired and sailed from Pearl Harbour at the end of May. *Hornet* and *Enterprise* were under the command of Rear-Admiral Raymond A. Spruance.

THE ATTACK BEGINS

On 2 and 3 June, fog helped screen the approach of the Japanese Midway strike force, under Admiral Chuichi Nagumo, from U.S. scout aircraft. Nagumo launched his attack on Midway Island at 04:30 hours on 4 June. American aircraft spotted the formation of Japanese aircraft and Spruance was ordered south to attack the Japanese carriers. Meanwhile the Japanese aircraft bombed Midway and caused some damage, though crucially they did not put its runway out of action. It was a small return for the 38 aircraft that Nagumo lost and another 30 too badly damaged to fly again.

American aircraft from Midway then attacked Nagumo's carriers but were shot out of the sky before they reached them. The admiral was considering a second strike against Midway when he received news that a second wave of U.S. aircraft from Midway was approaching. These aircraft reached his carriers but, amazingly, inflicted no damage. But Spruance, learning of the Japanese attack, decided to launch his own aircraft, at 09:00 hours, to strike while Nagumo's first wave was on deck refuelling.

JAPAN'S CARRIER FLEET IS DECIMATED

The first 15 aircraft from *Hornet* did not get close enough to the enemy ships before being shot down. *Enterprise*'s torpedo-bombers suffered a similar fate, losing 10 out of 14 for no damage to the enemy. But the dive-bombers from *Hornet* and *Enterprise* had more luck, hitting the Japanese carriers as their aircraft were being refuelled and rearmed. The bombs and torpedoes in *Akagi*'s hangar deck exploded, the ship being reduced to a blazing wreck. *Kaga* was also hit and soon ablaze. It sank that evening with the loss of 800 men. *Soryu* was hit by two bombs and within 20 minutes was aflame and had to be abandoned.

The fourth Japanese carrier, *Hiryu*, became separated from the others. It launched its aircraft against *Yorktown*, resulting in the American carrier being crippled and abandoned. However, aircraft from *Enterprise* and *Yorktown* in turn attacked *Hiryu* and reduced it to a burning wreck. Japan had lost four of its main carriers in a single day. Yamamoto called off the Midway operation in the early hours of 5 June and on the same day aircraft from *Enterprise* and *Hornet* sank the cruiser *Mikuma* and badly damaged the cruiser *Mogami*.

The Japanese lost four carriers at Midway, half their carrier force, with one cruiser sunk, 322 aircraft lost and 2,500 men killed. U.S. losses amounted to one carrier, one destroyer, 147 aircraft, and 307 men killed. It was a turning point in the Pacific War because Japan never recovered from Midway, being unable to replace the four carriers lost or the experienced naval pilots who died there. After Midway Japan was on the defensive, holding the Southern Resources Area, but ominously for Tokyo it could not match the 13 aircraft carriers the Americans were constructing. If the Americans could defeat a Japanese fleet with an inferior number of ships and aircraft, what would they be able to achieve with superior numbers of ships and aircraft? For Japan the writing was on the wall.

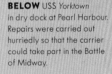

BELOW USS *Yorktown* in dry dock at Pearl Harbour. Repairs were carried out hurriedly so that the carrier could take part in the Battle of Midway.

THE OSS IS ESTABLISHED

DATE

....

13 June, 1942

SUMMARY

....

The forerunner
of the Central
Intelligence Agency
was instrumental
in waging a secret
war against the
Germans and
Japanese.

LOCATION

....

Washington, D.C.

On 13 June, 1942, President Roosevelt established by a presidential military order the Office of Strategic Services (OSS) to provide intelligence needed for wartime activities. The new organisation was placed under the direct control of the Joint Chiefs of Staff and was headed by General William J. Donovan. It comprised three branches: Secret Intelligence Branch, Special Operations Branch and Morale Operations Branch. The theory was that U.S. military personnel (both men and women), organised in small groups and trained in commando skills, could be parachuted into enemy-occupied territory to harass the opposition and support and raise local resistance groups.

EFFECTIVE INTELLIGENCE

Members of OSS Operational Groups had to have a working knowledge of a foreign language. They also had to be fully indoctrinated in the OSS's philosophy: bright people could get things done. A typical Operational Group was made up of two officers and 13 other ranks (all non-commissioned officers). All members of the team were fully trained in weapons skills and operational techniques, with two being specialists: one a medical technician and the other a radio operator. OSS Operational Groups would go on to mount operations in enemy-occupied Asia, North Africa, Norway, Italy and France.

The OSS also ran a small army of spies, saboteurs, cryptanalysts, analysts, and scientists. It worked closely with the Federal Bureau of Investigation (FBI) to arrest Nazi spies operating in the United States.

The OSS conducted hundreds of operations during the war but two examples will give a flavour of the type of work it carried out. Before the Allied invasion of Sicily in July 1943, the OSS made a deal with the father of American organised crime, Charlie 'Lucky' Luciano, who at the time was languishing in an American jail. Senator Estes Kefauver provides the details: 'The proffered deal was that Luciano would use his Mafia position to arrange contacts for undercover American agents and that therefore Sicily would be a much softer target than it might otherwise be'. Luciano also organised Mafia 'hits' on Sicilian fascist leaders. In return the gangster was allowed to run his mob activities unimpeded from his prison cell until 1946, when he was granted deportation to Italy for his wartime 'assistance'.

The second example was very different. OSS Detachment 101, operating on the Indian frontier, was ordered to plan and conduct operations against the roads and railways leading to Japanese-occupied Myitkyina in northern Burma. The detachment originally numbered 21 partially trained agents but grew steadily to support the campaign to retake Myitkyina in the summer of 1944. By the latter date Detachment 101 controlled up to 10,000 guerrillas who played a key role in Stilwell's capture of the city in August.

THE SOE

Britain's equivalent to the OSS, the Special Operations Executive (SOE), was set up in 1940 to strike back against German-occupied Europe. Potential recruits, who included civilians and women, were often selected because they were fluent in a foreign language or were well acquainted with an area of enemy territory. Agents were trained in a wide variety of skills, including forgery, survival, reconnaissance, burglary, codes, and ciphers. Because agents worked behind enemy lines radio communications was a vital skill. Most messages sent from agents were transmitted in Morse code using a variety of radio sets.

The work was vital but dangerous and many SOE agents paid the ultimate price. Violette Szabo parachuted into France in 1944 to assist partisans trying to halt the advance of German panzers to the Normandy beaches. She was captured, interrogated, revealed nothing, and was sent to Ravensbrück concentration camp where she was shot as a spy. Noor Inayat Khan, codenamed 'Madeleine', was flown into France to assist the resistance as a wireless operator. She kept on working until she was betrayed and captured. She too revealed nothing under interrogation and was also shot as a spy. Of the 39 female SOE agents sent to occupied France, the Germans executed 15. Of the 470 SOE agents sent into France, 118 failed to return.

THE FALL OF TOBRUK

DATE
....
21 June, 1942

SUMMARY
....
The fall of the port of Tobruk to Rommel's Panzer Army Africa was a great material and psychological blow to the Allied war effort in North Africa.

LOCATION
....
Tobruk, Libya

The Italians had fortified Tobruk, a small town on the Libyan coast, during the 1930s with coastal batteries, a 50km (31-mile) long perimeter of concrete posts, minefields and gun positions. Inside the town were headquarters bunkers, underground supply dumps and a water desalination plant. It also had a sheltered, deep-water harbour. Its position meant that Tobruk was also of strategic importance because it was the only major port between Tripoli and Alexandria, which meant that in Italian hands it was a threat to Egypt and the Suez Canal.

THE IMPORTANCE OF TOBRUK

Fortunately for the British, Tobruk had been captured by the Australian 6th Division in January 1941. In the seesaw war in North Africa the port retained its great strategic value. Churchill himself stated: 'Tobruk was crucial to the protection of Egypt and the Suez Canal – and therefore to the entire Middle East. Were the Middle East to be lost; Spain, Vichy France, and Turkey would embrace the Axis powers and a "robot new order" would be created in a world in which Hitler dominated all Europe, Asia and Africa'.

The Battle of Gazala (26 May– 11 June, 1942), fought to the immediate west and southwest of Tobruk, had resulted in a major defeat for the Eighth Army, the remnants of which fell back east to the Egyptian frontier. Tobruk was isolated and on 13 June Rommel's grandly titled Panzer Army Africa once more encircled the port. If Rommel managed to capture the port, it would greatly shorten his supply lines and allow him to build up his strength for an invasion of Egypt and the capture of the Suez Canal.

On 15 June General Hendrik Klopper, commander of the 2nd South African Division, was promoted to Garrison Commander of Tobruk and ordered to hold the port at all costs. On paper his defences were formidable: fortified positions, minefields, 35,000 troops and enough supplies and ammunition to withstand a three-month siege. However, the defences had suffered damage during previous Axis attacks and the minefields around the port were in a state of disrepair. In addition, Tobruk had no air cover, meaning the *Luftwaffe* was free to pound the defences with impunity.

On 20 June the attack began, 150 *Luftwaffe* aircraft bombing the town and its defences at dawn. Then the panzers and infantry advanced, piercing the British lines. The battle was fought over a large area and Klopper's command network soon broke down, sowing confusion among his troops. By 16:00 hours Rommel's forces had captured all the airfields around the port and three hours later his panzers were rumbling into the bomb-wrecked town.

At 08:00 hours on 21 June Klopper surrendered. It was a disaster for the British in North Africa. Some 19,000 British, 9,000 white South African, and 9,000 Indian and 'native' South African troops were captured. In addition, 2,032 tonnes (2,000 tons) of gasoline, 5,080 tonnes (5,000 tons) of provisions, and 2,000 vehicles fell into Axis hands.

A delighted Hitler made Rommel a field marshal, the youngest in the German army, and began to think of Panzer Army Africa conquering Egypt and linking up with his forces in the Caucasus. Churchill called the loss of Tobruk 'a disgrace'. The race was on to see who could rebuild their forces for the crucial battle for Egypt.

> ## Eyewitness
>
> FRED VAN ALPHEN STAHL, 2ND ANTI-AIRCRAFT REGIMENT, WAS A SOUTH AFRICAN CAPTURED WHEN TOBRUK FELL TO ROMMEL.
>
> ---
>
> 'Of course your first feelings as a prisoner of war are, this is the end. You imagined going to the army you could lose an arm, you could lose your life, you could lose your legs, your sight, but you never gave prisoner of war a thought, and so this, this is the end … I wasn't busy fighting at the time. We had been fighting in the Gazala handicap and on the rearguard coming back, and they said right now you are all moving … we didn't even realise it was Tobruk … and the next morning … a signal just came in and they said destroy your guns, destroy your vehicles, Tobruk has fallen, you are now prisoners of war.'

LEFT Erwin Rommel speaking with officers at the port of Tobruk. Despite the success of the June offensive, the Allies' material advantage soon told.

THE BATTLE OF GUADALCANAL

DATE

7 August, 1942

SUMMARY

The beginning of the campaign in the Solomon Islands foreshadowed the defeat of Japan.

LOCATION

Guadalcanal, Solomon Islands

The Allied campaign in the Solomon Islands, the gateway to northern Australia, of which Guadalcanal was a part, lasted longer than any other Allied campaign of the Pacific War, from August 1942 until March 1944. Its successful conclusion foreshadowed the defeat of Imperial Japan itself.

AN AMBITIOUS PLAN

Following the victory at Midway the U.S. Joint Chiefs put in motion a campaign to capture the Japanese South Pacific base of Rabaul on New Britain. The campaign was an ambitious one and would involve mutually supporting advances along the western and eastern edges of the Solomon Sea. The western flank would be the responsibility of General Douglas MacArthur whose forces would advance over Papua New Guinea's Owen Stanley Mountains and march northwest along the coast of New Guinea. The eastern flank would advance through the Solomon Islands to New Britain.

The initial phase of the eastern campaign would take place in the U.S.-designated Pacific Ocean Areas, the responsibility of Admiral Chester Nimitz, commander of the U.S. Pacific Fleet. Thus a naval officer, Admiral William F. Halsey, was put in command of a combined force of U.S. Navy ships, U.S. Marines, U.S. Army troops and U.S. Army Air Forces aircraft. The first phase, codenamed Watchtower, called for the capture of the island of Tulagi. However, the Japanese airfield on nearby Guadalcanal meant that island was added to the list of objectives.

On 7 August, elements of the U.S. 1st Marine Division (19,000 men), under Major-General Alexander A. Vandegrift, waded ashore on Guadalcanal and Tulagi. The Marines' transport ships were supported by eight cruisers (three of them Australian), 15 destroyers and five minesweepers located immediately offshore. Further out to sea was another U.S. armada of three aircraft carriers, a battleship, six cruisers, 16 destroyers and five oilers. The few Japanese defenders fled into the jungle, allowing the Marines to capture the airfield on Guadalcanal.

As the Marines formed a defensive perimeter Admiral Halsey, commander of the escorting carrier task force, withdrew his ships from the waters around Guadalcanal, fearing they would fall victim to Japanese land-based aircraft at Rabaul and Kavieng. At this time Henderson Field could not receive aircraft, which meant the Marines on the island were isolated (it was not until 20 August that Marine aircraft were able to land on the airfield).

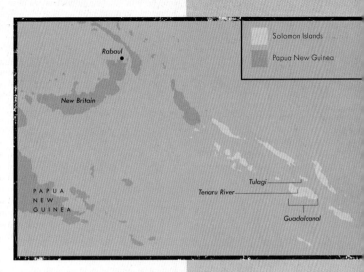

The U.S. landings prompted a determined naval and aerial response from the Japanese, their aircraft raiding Marines positions on Guadalcanal, either Henderson Field or U.S. supply ships at Lunga Point. Japanese ships offshore also bombarded the Marine perimeter at night. Vandegrift, knowing that a large-scale enemy land assault was imminent, concentrated the bulk of his forces among defensive positions along 'Alligator Creek' in the east and south from Kukum to a low range of hills in the west.

The enemy struck the east of the perimeter in force on the night of 20 and 21 August – the Battle of Tenaru River – but were defeated. They attacked again, this time against the south of the perimeter on 13–14 September – the Battle of Bloody Ridge. A Japanese regimental-sized force attempted to capture positions on Lunga Ridge, overlooking the airfield to the south. The attacks were carried out with determination and were a foretaste of what the Americans could expect in the months and years ahead. The Japanese almost broke through the Marine positions but were eventually repulsed with heavy losses.

In September and October both sides built up their forces. By mid-October Vandegrift had 23,000 men on Guadalcanal and the Japanese 20,000 (two divisions of the Seventeenth Army under General Haruyoshi Hyakutake). The fighting would go on until February 1943 when the Japanese evacuated the island. The campaign on the island was the first large-scale Allied victory on land against the Japanese in the war and marked the turning of the tide in the Southeast Pacific.

ABOVE Capturing Gaudalcanal represented the first stage of a plan that would take Allied forces northwest to the Japanese base at Rabaul.

THE BATTLE OF EL ALAMEIN

DATE

....

23 October–
4 November, 1942

SUMMARY

....

The British victory
marked a turning
point in the North
African War.

LOCATION

....

El Alamein, Egypt

The British defeat at Gazala resulted in the Eighth Army retreating east to a position covering the 48km (30 miles) of desert between the coast and the impassable Qattara Depression to the south, where the road and railway line ran through a small Egyptian village called El Alamein. Fortunately for the British, Rommel's Panzer Army Africa was exhausted and in no state to push on into Egypt. It was a stroke of luck but the Eighth Army's new commander, General Bernard Montgomery, was determined to leave nothing to fate or chance when he engaged the Desert Fox.

ALAM HALFA

....

Montgomery began to build up his forces, at the same time establishing a strong position around Alam Halfa that incorporated extensive minefields. The Qattara Depression also meant that Rommel could not use his favoured tactic of an outflanking movement through the open desert. When Rommel did attack at Alam Halfa at the end of August he was repulsed. Now it was the turn of Panzer Army Africa to dig in, his troops deployed behind deep minefields and backed by strong anti-tank gun positions. Both sides began to prepare for the coming battle.

Montgomery resisted calls from London to attack until his army was at full strength. Men and materiel poured into Egypt so that by October 1942 the Eighth Army could muster 1,029 tanks, including 252 of the new Sherman M4 models that outclassed the Panzer III. In contrast Rommel could field only 173 Panzer IIIs, 38 Panzer IVs and 278 largely obsolete Italian tanks. In the air it was a similar story with the Eighth Army being able to call on 530 aircraft to Rommel's 340. Axis forces totalled 100,000 men, the Eighth Army 195,000. Rommel's men suffered a blow to their morale on 23 September when their field marshal, ill and exhausted, flew back to Germany for medical treatment. General Georg Stumme arrived from the Eastern Front to act as deputy commander of Panzer Army Africa in his absence.

Montgomery's plan was simple, bold, and utilised his superiority in artillery, tanks and aircraft. It consisted of two phases. The first, codenamed Operation Lightfoot, would be preceded by a massive artillery bombardment to soften up the enemy. There would be a diversionary assault in the south by 13th Corps while to the north 30th Corps would launch the main British break-in assault to create two corridors through the enemy minefields, through which the tanks of 30th Corps would advance.

OVERWHELMING ROMMEL'S FORCES

The bombardment commenced on the night of 23 and 24 October, 1,000 artillery pieces supported by aircraft hammering Axis positions. It raised British morale and during it Stumme died of a heart attack, but when the British infantry and tanks advanced they soon encountered heavy resistance. It is a testimony to the courage of Axis troops that during the last week of October their extensive minefields successfully slowed the armoured attacks of 30th Corps. In addition, local panzer counterattacks actually defeated some armoured penetrations. However, Panzer Army Africa lacked supplies, with fuel for only 11 days of operations, enough ammunition for only nine days' fighting, and bread rations for just 21 days. The longer the battle went on the greater the likelihood that the panzers would simply run out of supplies.

By 2 November, Montgomery concluded that Axis forces were on the verge of collapse and unleashed the second phase of the battle: Operation Supercharge. The Axis line, thin and under relentless pressure, gave way under the weight of British tanks and infantry. Rommel, who had returned from Germany on 25 October, realised that his position was now untenable and gave the order to retreat.

El Alamein had been a hard-fought battle with 51,000 Axis and 14,000 British casualties. It had not only prevented Egypt and the Middle East falling into Axis hands, it had gone a long way to restoring British military prestige. It was also the turning point of the war in North Africa, which would end in Axis defeat.

AUSTRALIAN FORCES ENTER KOKODA

DATE

....

1 November, 1942

SUMMARY

....

A turning point
in New Guinea saved
Australia from
invasion by Japan.

LOCATION

....

Kokoda, New Guinea

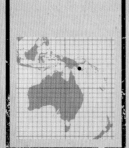

The tropical island of New Guinea became a strategic target for both sides during the Pacific War. For the Japanese, bases in New Guinea would cut Australia off from its lines of communication with the United States. For the Allies it held the key to a southern approach to the Philippines and was crucial to the defence of their southwest Pacific forces. For the soldiers of both sides who fought on the island it was a malaria-infested, sodden, muddy hell.

The Japanese landed on the north coast of the island, at Buna, on 22 July, 1942. The soldiers were Major-General Tomitaro Horii's South Seas Detachment, which had earlier captured Rabaul in New Britain. Horii's objective was Port Moresby on the southern coast. On the map this was a short distance; on the ground it comprised rain, forest, swamps, and the Owen Stanley Mountains. The Japanese troops hacked their way through the thick jungle, brushed aside small units of Australian militia, and began climbing the Owen Stanley Mountains to advance along the Kokoda Trail that ran from Buna to Port Moresby. By August it appeared that the Japanese were on the verge of capturing Port Moresby itself. If that happened it could be used as a springboard for an invasion of Australia.

NO MORE RETREATS

The reality was that the soldiers of the Australian Imperial Force (AIF) and New Guinea Volunteer Rifles had inflicted substantial casualties on the Japanese. Port Moresby had been saved, for the moment. Well aware of the stakes involved, both sides sent reinforcements. The Japanese dispatched 13,000 veterans to the island, the Australians the AIF's 7th Division under Major-General 'Tubby' Allen. The initial Japanese attacks were successful after some hard fighting, the Australians retreating to Ioribaiwa Ridge on the Kokoda Trail in early September. They were determined to make a stand at that place, the soldiers digging in and building strongpoints. There would be no more retreats.

The Japanese launched a series of heavy assaults between 17 and 24 September. Savage fighting erupted as small groups of soldiers battled over a few metres of muddy ground. The Japanese attacks were determined, but they could not dislodge the stubborn Australians from their positions, and they were also losing three times as many casualties as the Diggers. On 26 September, the Japanese, short of supplies and suffering heavily from enemy small-arms fire and air attacks, began to pull back. The Japanese assault on Port Moresby had been stopped by the indomitable spirit of the ordinary Australian soldier.

The 7th Division now launched a counterattack, pushing the enemy back towards Kokoda. On 16 October, the 25th Brigade, now exhausted, was relieved by the veteran 16th Brigade and the advance continued. The Japanese proved adept at defensive tactics and the Australians had to contend with a grim attritional campaign of ambushes and booby traps. The jungle and swamps fragmented units and placed the burden of battle on small squads of drenched and tired men who crawled through the mud searching for well-camouflaged enemy bunkers. When they were discovered they had to be destroyed with grenades and small-arms fire. These tactics were exhausting both physically and mentally, and were not the only problems the Australians had to contend with. The combination of tropical insects and disease was often a greater threat than the Japanese Army.

In such close-quarters fighting, the Japanese inflicted a heavy toll on the Australians, who nevertheless pressed on and entered Kokoda on 1 November. Its fall marked a turning point in the war in the Southwest Pacific.

BELOW After months of savage fighting, Australian forces successfully countered Japanese attacks, eventually arriving in Kokoda in November 1942.

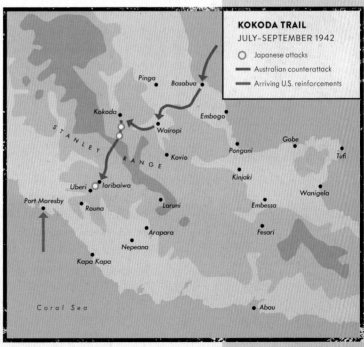

KOKODA TRAIL
JULY–SEPTEMBER 1942

○ Japanese attacks
— Australian counterattack
— Arriving U.S. reinforcements

OPERATION TORCH

DATE

8 November, 1942

SUMMARY

The first Anglo-American amphibious operation of the war secured Vichy North Africa for the Allies and hastened Rommel's defeat.

LOCATION

Vichy North Africa

Winston Churchill had for some time been concerned that the Vichy territories in North Africa – Morocco, Algeria and Tunisia – might fall into German hands and thus prolong the war in North Africa. To prevent this he persuaded President Roosevelt to support an Anglo-American operation to seize the ports of Oran, Casablanca and Algiers. The operation, codenamed Torch, was under the supreme command of General Dwight D. Eisenhower, then commanding American troops in England. Eisenhower had never led soldiers in battle and had never seen action himself but by the end of the war was Supreme Allied Commander.

AN UNWELCOME LIBERATION

Once Vichy Algeria had been secured, Anglo-U.S. forces would drive east to secure Tunisia. It was hoped that the invaders would be seen as liberators from the threat of German occupation, and secret negotiations had been conducted beforehand with local French leaders with this in mind. However, Vichy forces not only resisted, but invited German forces into their territories when Allied troops landed.

French resistance was strong against the Western Task Force's landings. However, the three assault forces made it off the beaches on 8 November and concentrated for an attack on Casablanca on 11 November. The Central Task Force also met heavy resistance during the landings east and west of Oran on 8 November. But two days later Allied troops had captured the city. A frontal naval assault by troops of the Eastern Task Force met with disaster at Algiers but the city was soon surrounded on the landward side and the garrison surrendered on 10 November.

On mainland France Marshal Pétain ordered Vichy forces to continue resisting. A furious Hitler ordered the remainder of 'unoccupied' France to be seized and began sending German troops by air into Tunisia. On 11 November the Allies received a boost when Admiral Jean Darlan, Vichy vice-premier and foreign minister, who had had contact with an Office of Strategic Services (OSS) operative and had agreed to co-operate with

Allied forces, issued an immediate cease-fire order on 11 November (he was in North Africa at the time). Pétain immediately disavowed Darlan's action and many British and Americans were critical of dealing with a fascist and collaborator. But Darlan's order saved thousands of lives and aided Allied chances of winning the race to Tunis. Darlan would be assassinated in December 1942.

In the event the Germans, receiving reinforcements of 1,000 men a day, flown in aircraft that had been withdrawn from the Eastern Front, were able to secure Tunisia because the Allies were unprepared for a major overland operation after securing the Vichy ports in Morocco and Algeria. British troops under the command of Lieutenant-General Kenneth Anderson (which became the British First Army) advanced east in a piecemeal fashion, not helped by mud and rain and a supply line that stretched back 800km (500 miles) to Algiers, which meant reinforcements were slow to arrive at the front.

Allied spearheads advanced to within 32km (20 miles) of Tunis but were pushed back by vigorous German attacks and by the end of the year the First Army was facing the Fifth Panzer Army, commanded by General Jürgen von Arnim, in north-central Tunisia.

THE ANGLO-AMERICAN INVASION FORCE

THE LANDING FORCES

Western Assault Force: Major-General George S. Patton, 35,000 American troops.
Objective: Casablanca in French Morocco.

Central Task Force: Major-General Lloyd R. Fredendall, 18,500 American troops building up to 39,000.
Objective: Oran.

Eastern Task Force: Lieutenant-General K.A.N. Anderson, 20,000 troops in the first wave, half American and half British.
Objective: Algiers.

THE NAVAL TASK FORCES

Western Naval Task Force: All U.S. Navy vessels: three battleships, five carriers, seven cruisers, 38 destroyers, eight fleet minesweepers, five tankers commanded by Rear-Admiral H. Kent Hewitt with an accompanying Assault Force of 91 vessels including 23 'combat loaders' (the same as Landing Ships, Infantry (LSIs)).

Central Naval Task Force: Under Commodore T. H. Troubridge with HMS *Largs*, two carriers, two cruisers, two anti-aircraft ships, 13 destroyers, six corvettes, eight minesweepers and various ancillary craft as well as the landing force.

Eastern Task Force: Under the command of Vice-Admiral Sir Harold Burrough with HMS *Bulolo*, two aircraft carriers, three cruisers, three anti-aircraft ships, a gun monitor, 13 destroyers, three submarines, three sloops, seven minesweepers and seven corvettes, as well as the landing forces.

OPERATION URANUS

DATE

19 November, 1942

SUMMARY

The Soviet operation trapped the German Sixth Army in and around Stalingrad in the southern USSR, and led to a pivotal strategic German defeat on the Eastern Front.

LOCATION

Southern USSR

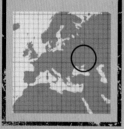

The German army did not have the manpower to launch an offensive across the whole of the Eastern Front in the summer of 1942. So Hitler took the decision that his forces would remain on the defensive in the centre and north while in the south they would attack to capture the oil of the Caucasus region. The assault, codenamed Operation Blue, commenced on 28 June, 1942, when 1.4 million troops and 1,495 armoured fighting vehicles, supported by 1,550 aircraft, smashed through Soviet defences and advanced rapidly towards the River Don.

STALINGRAD

By the last week of August, the German advance into the Caucasus had slowed to a crawl, due not only to overextended supply lines but also Hitler's fixation with the city that bore the name of the Soviet dictator – Stalingrad. During September, 20 Axis divisions, spearheaded by the German Sixth Army and including the Fourth Panzer Army, were locked in a grim battle for control of the city, fighting the Red Army road by road. But the Soviets were merely keeping the Germans occupied as they organised an offensive against the Sixth Army's flanks.

As summer gave way to fall and then winter the flanks of the Sixth and Fourth Panzer armies were protected by the Romanian Third Army (100,000 troops) and the Romanian Fourth Army (70,000 troops). The Soviet High Command, the Stavka, was determined to launch an offensive against these armies that would smash through the Romanians, link up, and trap enemy forces in a giant pocket, which would then be annihilated. The operation, codenamed Uranus, would involve the Southwestern Front (398,000 troops), Don Front (307,000 troops) and Stalingrad Front (429,000 troops). Each front contained hundreds of tanks, thousands of artillery pieces and hundreds of aircraft.

When Uranus was launched on 19 November, Red Army forces crushed anything in their path. The Romanian Third Army suffered 55,000 casualties on 19 November and, when Red Army units linked

LEFT Soviet forces advance at Kalach, trapping the German Sixth Army in Stalingrad. Hitler's insistence that there be no retreat ensured the destruction of Paulus' forces.

up at Kalach on 23 November, the town had ceased to exist. In five days the Red Army had destroyed the flanks protecting Axis forces fighting in Stalingrad, which meant that those forces, commanded by General Friedrich Paulus, were now surrounded. Inside what Hitler titled 'Fortress Stalingrad' were 256,000 German troops, 11,000 Romanians, 100 tanks, 1,800 artillery pieces, 10,000 motor vehicles and 23,000 horses. If allowed to retreat there was a good chance that Paulus' men could have broken through the Soviet ring. But Hitler forbade any withdrawal, assuring Paulus that his troops would be supplied and eventually rescued.

Over the following weeks the Red Army ringed the pocket with troops and artillery while other forces drove west to further isolate the pocket from the German frontline. The *Luftwaffe* tried, and failed, to supply the troops trapped in the pocket and a ground assault, codenamed Winter Storm, failed to reach Stalingrad. Hitler promoted Paulus to field marshal on 30 January, 1943, (no German field marshal had ever surrendered); the next day he surrendered what was left of his army. Only 90,000 filthy, starving members of the Sixth Army were left alive.

The defeat at Stalingrad was a catastrophe of strategic proportions. Not only had the campaign cost the Axis hundreds of thousands of men and hundreds of *Luftwaffe* aircraft, the elite panzer arm had suffered crippling losses. By late January 1943, for example, the German army's total tank strength numbered just 502 operational panzers. The southern sector of the Eastern Front was in danger of collapsing completely.

SCUTTLING THE FRENCH FLEET

DATE

....

27 November, 1942

SUMMARY

....

The French scuttled
their fleet at Toulon
to prevent the ships
falling into the
hands of the Germans.

LOCATION

....

Toulon, France

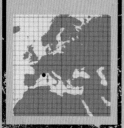

The success of Operation Torch, the Anglo-American landings in Vichy North Africa, had secured Morocco and Algeria for the Allies. But a question mark still hung over the French fleet at Toulon. Three days after the Torch landings Admiral Darlan, who had thrown in his lot with the Allies and who was in North Africa when they landed, sent a message to Admiral de Laborde, commander of the French fleet at Toulon, urging that his ships should come to North Africa immediately. However, in his discussions with Admiral Cunningham (Allied Commander-in-Chief, Mediterranean) Darlan admitted that he was doubtful whether his suggestion would be adopted. First, de Laborde was known to be fanatically anti-British and second, he was able to argue that Darlan's proposal had no backing from the Vichy government, to which he (de Laborde) was responsible. Subsequent events were to prove that Darlan's estimate of his countrymen's reactions was accurate. Although Admiral Auphan, the Minister of Marine at Vichy, supported Darlan, de Laborde's attitude made it impossible for the ships to move until it was too late.

GERMAN FORCES MOVE SOUTH

....

Hitler showed no such dithering, informing the Italians on 9 November that he intended to occupy Vichy France. The next day he informed the Vichy prime minister, Pierre Laval, that German troops would be moving south from German-occupied France on the 11th. They would be doing so to 'defend' Vichy France against an Allied invasion. On 13 November the Führer assured Laval that he would not touch the fleet at Toulon but 12 days later he ordered that the ships should be seized.

French officers at Toulon realised that it was only a matter of time before German troops entered the port and took control of the dozens of warships and submarines at their berths. The Germans had previously issued orders that the ships should have empty fuel tanks to prevent their escape. On 15 November some officers began to lobby their

superiors to flee the port and sail to North Africa (fuel gauges had been tampered with to give the illusion of empty tanks). The vast majority of petty officers and sailors supported this course of action. However, the Vichy authorities would not countenance it and arrested the ringleaders.

On 27 November German troops attacked the port with infantry and tanks. There was a farcical moment at the base's entrance when the Germans were held up by a sentry who denied them entry because they did not have the required paperwork! The delay allowed French crews to prepare their demolition charges. Admiral de Laborde who was on the battleship *Strasbourg* issued orders that the fleet was to be scuttled. The size and layout of the port aided the French because it took German troops an hour to traverse the maze of the dockyard to reach the quays, by which time the French warships were either burning after setting off demolition charges or sinking if they had opened their sea valves. Some ships burned for days afterward.

In total the French scuttled three battleships, seven cruisers, 15 destroyers, 13 torpedo boats, six sloops, 12 submarines and nine patrol boats. The Germans captured only three destroyers and four submarines (five submarines escaped from Toulon).

The French naval High Command had fulfilled the promise it had given to the British in 1940: its ships would never sail with German crews.

THE FRENCH FLEET AT TOULON

In November 1942 Toulon harboured 80 warships divided into three groups.

The high seas forces (under Admiral de Laborde): the battleship *Strasbourg*, three heavy cruisers, two light cruisers, 10 destroyers and three torpedo boats.

The warships subordinated to the Maritime Prefect (Admiral Marquis): the battleship *Provence*, seaplane carrier *Commandant Teste*, six torpedo boats and eight submarines.

Ships with reduced crews as specified in the armistice terms with the Germans: the battleship *Dunkerque*, cruisers *Foch* and *Dunkerque*, eight destroyers, six torpedo boats and 10 submarines.

JAPAN'S OIL DILEMMA

DATE

December 1942

SUMMARY

Oil was the Achilles' heel that fatally weakened Japan's ability to wage a modern war against the allies.

LOCATION

Japan

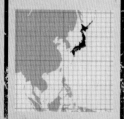

At the beginning of World War II Japan possessed a modern army, air force and navy, all of which contributed to a series of staggering victories in the first six months of the Pacific War. But aircraft, motor vehicles and warships are all dependent on one thing: oil. To power its war machine Japan had to import 90 percent of its oil, having very few domestic wells (the wells at Akita, Niigata and Nutsu produced around 2.7 million barrels of oil a year).

The United States was the world's major producer of oil and, before the war, was Japan's principal supplier. Clearly this source would dry up if Japan attacked Pearl Harbour, but Tokyo reasoned that the riches of the Southern Resource Area, specifically the oil fields of the Dutch East Indies, would enable Japan to maintain a 'Pacific Wall' against the Allies to bring about a negotiated peace. By mid-1942 Japan dominated the Western Pacific and East Asia but the huge area that had been conquered created major problems that Tokyo had no answer to.

INSUFFICIENT SUPPLIES

The Dutch East Indies possessed the largest oil reserves in East Asia, but they had been sabotaged before their capture and the Japanese were frustrated by the time it took to restore them to full production. Matters were not helped when the U.S. submarine *Grenadier* sank the liner *Taiyo Maru* in May 1942 en route to the Dutch East Indies. The ship was carrying 1,000 specialists in oil production and petroleum engineers of the Japanese oil industry, 700 of whom died as a result of the incident.

But even if the oil fields of the Dutch East Indies had been producing anticipated levels of output it would not have been enough for the navy, which required 1.6 million barrels of oil a month to operate over the vast distances of the Southern Resource Area. Oil had to be shipped in tankers over great distances from oil fields in East Asia to refineries in Japan, which required fuel for the tankers and the ships that acted as their escorts.

LEFT The scale of Japan's imperial ambitions was not matched by the resources available, and attempts to conquer oil-rich lands proved a logistical and military bridge too far.

PEAK OIL

That the Americans had cracked Japanese naval codes meant that U.S. submarines could prey on enemy transport routes, with dire results for oil deliveries. Oil imports reached a peak in the first quarter of 1943 but thereafter declined. Japanese imports fell from 1.75 million barrels of oil per month in August 1943 to 360,000 barrels a month in July 1944.

But even if the United States Navy had not initiated a highly effective blockade campaign the Japanese navy would have still struggled to obtain the fuel it required. In the first quarter of 1942, for example, around 217,424 tonnes (214,000 tons) of crude oil was being delivered to Japan. However, at the same time the Japanese navy was consuming 309,880 tonnes (305,000 tons) of fuel oil a month. Fuel consumption was greatly increased by the Midway operation, which consumed more fuel than the Japanese navy had ever used in an entire year of peacetime operations.

The U.S. submarine attacks on the flow of oil to Japan were critical in destroying Tokyo's ability to wage war (the Japanese had not even anticipated that U.S. submarines might prey on their oil tankers travelling from the East Indies to Japan). After Midway future naval campaigns had to take into account the availability of fuel and potential fuel usage. Those ships that had not been sunk simply ran out of fuel. And not only warships: allocations of fuel to Japan's fishing fleet were drastically cut throughout the war.

THE ATOMIC AGE BEGINS

DATE
....
2 December, 1942

SUMMARY
....
Physicists in Chicago created the world's first controlled, self-sustaining nuclear chain reaction.

LOCATION
....
Chicago, USA

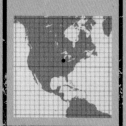

While millions of men in uniform faced each other across the globe a small group of physicists in Chicago achieved the first nuclear chain reaction. It was a key step in the Manhattan Project to develop the atomic bomb. A chain reaction is a process whereby neutrons released in fission produce an additional fission in at least one further nucleus. This nucleus in turn produces neutrons to enable the process to repeat. The process can be controlled, as in nuclear power, or uncontrolled, as in nuclear weapons.

PLUTONIUM-239
....

Italian-born Enrico Fermi and his colleagues at the University of Chicago built a 'pile' that resembled a flattened sphere 7.5m (25ft) in diameter containing 386 tonnes (380 tons) of graphite blocks, 6 tonnes (6 tons) of uranium metal and 40.6 tonnes (40 tons) of uranium oxide as fuel. This pile – Chicago Pile-1 – became the prototype for several large nuclear reactors. It was discovered that the radioactive element plutonium was created in nuclear reactors when uranium atoms absorbed neutrons.

Uranium occurs in slightly differing forms known as isotopes. The isotopes differ from each other in the number of neutrons (uncharged particles) in the nucleus. Uranium-235 (U-235) is the isotope that can be most readily split, yielding a lot of energy. However, Plutonium-239 has a higher spontaneous fission rate (the probability per second that a given atom will fission spontaneously, without an external intervention).

RIGHT Enrico Fermi, the Italian physicist driven into the arms of the Americans by the racist ideology of Mussolini's fascisti.

The bomb dropped on Hiroshima in 1945, 'Little Boy', comprised a gun that fired one mass of uranium-235 at another mass of uranium-235 to produce a supercritical mass. Once the two pieces of uranium were brought together the initiator introduced a burst of neutrons to begin the chain reaction. 'Fat Man', the bomb dropped on Nagasaki, was a plutonium bomb that used explosive charges to compress a sphere of plutonium rapidly to a density that would cause it to go critical and produce a nuclear explosion.

To produce these two bombs and the one that was tested in July 1945 required a huge amount of time and resources. The Manhattan Project began in late 1941 and was originally fairly small-scale. But following the first nuclear chain reaction at the University of Chicago in December 1942 it rapidly expanded. Nuclear facilities were built at Oak Ridge, Tennessee, and Handford, Washington. The main assembly plant for the production of the atomic bomb was built at Los Alamos, New Mexico, where the brilliant physicist Robert Oppenheimer was director. Los Alamos had a workforce of 3,000 and in total the Manhattan Project employed 120,000 people, though the majority of them did not know the true nature of the work they were engaged in. Secrecy was all-important and only a select few knew about the atomic bomb's development (they did not include Vice-President Truman, who learned of the Manhattan Project only when he became president in April 1945).

ABOVE An illustration of Chicago Pile-1, the prototype for the nuclear reactor that would produce fissile material for atomic weapons.

Eyewitness

ENRICO FERMI HAD THIS TO SAY OF HIS SUCCESS IN DECEMBER 1942:

'One might be led to question whether the scientists acted wisely in presenting the statesmen of the world with this appalling problem. Actually there was no choice. Once basic knowledge is acquired, any attempt at preventing its fruition would be as futile as hoping to stop the earth from revolving around the sun.'

BATTLE OF THE BARENTS SEA

DATE

31 December, 1942

SUMMARY

The battle resulted
in a furious Hitler
scrapping Germany's
surface fleet.

LOCATION

Barents Sea,
Arctic Ocean

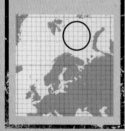

In the final days of 1942 the heavy cruiser *Admiral Hipper*, pocket battleship *Lützow*, and six destroyers were ordered from their base in northern Norway to intercept and destroy Convoy JW-51B that was sailing from Scotland to Murmansk. The convoy was escorted by six British destroyers and a shadowing cruiser escort: Force R. The 14 merchantmen of the convoy were carrying tanks, aircraft, fighters, fuel and supplies for the Russians.

SO MUCH OLD IRON

JW-51B was spotted by *U-354* on 30 December and on the same day Admiral Oskar Kummetz, commanding the naval squadron at Altenfjord, was ordered to intercept the convoy. Hitler took a keen interest in the operation codenamed Rainbow, hoping it would change his view of the surface fleet. That very day he had stated: 'Our own navy is but a copy of the British – and a poor one at that. The warships are not in operational readiness; they are lying idle in the fjords, utterly useless like so much old iron.'

Kummetz's plan was simple: *Hipper* and three destroyers would attack first from the north to draw off the convoy's escorts, after which Lützow and the other three destroyers would attack the merchant ships from the south. The Battle of Barents Sea began at 09:15 hours on 31 December, when the destroyers with *Hipper* sighted the convoy and opened fire. But Captain Sherbrooke, the commander of the convoy's destroyer escort, kept his ships between them and *Hipper*.

Half an hour later two of Sherbrooke's ships simulated torpedo attacks, causing the *Hipper* to turn away from the convoy. At 10:19 hours the *Hipper* returned and crippled HMS *Onslow* but failed to sink the destroyer HMS *Orwell* in her way.

Kummetz's plan had worked as hoped, with all the escorts being drawn away from the convoy, but though *Lützow* closed in from the south she did not attack. *Hipper*, meanwhile, approached the convoy

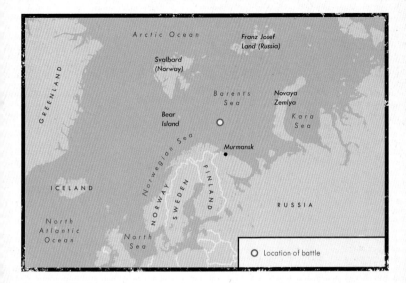

LEFT The Battle of the Barents Sea took place some 150 miles off the north coast of Norway, where convoy JW-51B was heading towards the Russian city of Murmansk.

for a fifth time but again turned away for fear of torpedoes. At 11:33 hours two British cruisers of Force R arrived and opened fire on *Hipper*, which retired. Kummetz broke off the action and ordered a retreat to Altenfjord. Operation Rainbow had been a total failure.

SENT TO SCRAP

A furious Hitler raged the next day that the surface fleet was useless and was nothing more than a breeding ground for revolution. He therefore announced that he was doing away with these 'useless ships'. At a stroke he disposed of the battleship *Tirpitz* (which would be reprieved), the pocket battleships *Lützow* and *Admiral Scheer*, the aged battleships *Schleswig-Holstein* and *Schlesien*, the battle cruisers *Scharnhorst* (which would also be reprieved) and *Gneisenau*, the heavy cruisers *Hipper* and *Prinz Eugen* and the light cruisers *Leipzig*, *Köln*, *Nürnberg* and *Emden*. Their crews would be put to other uses and the steel yielded after scrapping would be used for U-boat construction.

The head of the German navy, Admiral Erich Raeder (who pointed out to the Führer that it was his own policy of not allowing the big ships to take any risks that had led to the Rainbow fiasco), resigned in protest and was replaced by the commander of the U-boat arm, Admiral Karl Dönitz. Thus in a fit of pique did Hitler scrap his surface fleet and give the Allies a bloodless victory. As Admiral Raeder correctly stated: 'It will be viewed by the Allies as a sign of weakness'.

This was the year the Axis powers lost the strategic initiative in Europe, and Japan was thrown onto the defensive in the Pacific. Having suffered defeat at Stalingrad, only the genius of Erich von Manstein was able to prevent the total collapse of the southern sector of the Eastern Front in early 1943. But the summer witnessed a series of heavy Axis defeats, indicating that Germany and Italy would eventually lose the war. The Axis war effort came to an end in North Africa, when an entire army group was captured by the Allies. Sicily and mainland Italy were invaded, resulting in the overthrow of Mussolini. In the Atlantic, the Allies finally defeated the U-boat menace, and on the Eastern Front the Red Army won a major victory at Kursk, which crippled Germany's panzer arm.

In the Pacific, the Americans continued their bloody island-hopping campaign against Japan by conquering the Gilbert Islands.

1943

THE CASABLANCA CONFERENCE

DATE

14–24 January, 1943

SUMMARY

The Allied conference decided strategy for 1943 and 1944 and demanded unconditional surrender of the Axis powers.

LOCATION

Casablanca, Morocco

The Casablanca Conference took place just two months after the Operation Torch landings in French North Africa in November 1942. At this meeting, U.S. President Roosevelt and British Prime Minister Churchill focused on co-ordinating Allied military strategy against the Axis powers over the course of the coming year. Stalin was invited to attend but the Soviet dictator was unwilling to travel while the epic struggle at Stalingrad was still raging.

The British and American leaders resolved to concentrate their efforts against Germany in the hopes of drawing German forces away from the Eastern Front, and to increase shipments of supplies to the Soviet Union. While they would begin concentrating forces in England in preparation for an eventual invasion of northern France, they decided to first concentrate their efforts in the Mediterranean by launching an invasion of Sicily and the Italian mainland designed to knock Italy out of the war. This was particularly pleasing to Churchill because it would make the Mediterranean line of communications more secure, including Malta and the Suez Canal.

SICILY

The choice of Sicily made sense militarily because Italian forces had already demonstrated that they were ill equipped, poorly led and suffering from low morale. A blow against Sicily and the Italian mainland stood a good chance of knocking Italy out of the war. This would lead to either the Allies quickly occupying all the country or, more likely, the Germans committing substantial numbers of troops to the Italian peninsula to fight them.

Among the American delegation Chief of Staff General George Marshall put forward the case for a cross-Channel invasion in 1943 in order to deliver a mortal blow to Nazi Germany. It was a tempting prospect but at the time the Allies did not have sufficient numbers of landing craft and troops in Britain. In any case large numbers of

veteran troops were already in North Africa and so the logistics of getting them to Sicily were simple compared to transporting them to Britain and then to the Continent.

The leaders also agreed to strengthen their strategic bombing campaign against Germany.

UNCONDITIONAL SURRENDER

In the Pacific, the two leaders agreed on a military effort to eject Japan from Papua New Guinea and to open up new supply lines to China through Japanese-occupied Burma. The Anglo-American Combined Chiefs of Staff also authorised the concept of a drive through the Central Pacific, specifically against the Japanese-occupied Gilbert Islands, Marshall Islands and Caroline Islands. The major Japanese base at Rabaul would be neutralised by air and naval action rather than direct assault.

On the final day of the Conference, President Roosevelt announced that he and Churchill had decided that the only way to ensure postwar peace was to adopt a policy of unconditional surrender. With hindsight this can be seen as a mistake as it forced the Germans to continue fighting, as they had no alternative. *Wehrmacht* General Friedrich Wilhelm von Mellenthin had this to say of the policy of unconditional surrender: 'The Churchill–Roosevelt demand for "Unconditional Surrender" gave us no hope from the West, while the men fighting on the Eastern Front were well aware of the horrible fate which would befall Germany if the Red hordes broke into our country'.

HEAVY WATER SABOTAGE

DATE

28 February,
1943

SUMMARY

The daring raid that
damaged the Nazis'
efforts to develop
an atomic bomb.

LOCATION

Rjukan, Norway

Before World War II Germany was a leading nation in the field of nuclear research and when the Nazis came to power they accelerated the programme to develop an atomic bomb. It was fortunate for the Allies and indeed mankind as a whole that Nazi racial policies led to the brilliant physicist Albert Einstein seeking refuge in the United States in 1933. Nevertheless the Germans continued with their research, which received a boost in 1941 when the *Wehrmacht* conquered Norway.

The Germans took possession of the Norsk-Hydro power station at Vemork, to the west of Rjukan in Telemark County, a remote mountainous area deep in a long valley at the foot of Telemark's tallest mountain, Mount Gausta, in southern Norway. At the time the plant was the only industrial-scale production facility in Europe capable of producing heavy water for the German atomic programme (heavy water was used to slow down nuclear reactions during testing). The power station was built of reinforced concrete and nestled against the cliff, with its critical processing machinery located in the basement. Its location and fortress-like nature made it almost impregnable from both ground and air attack.

CODENAME GROUSE

The British decided that the plant had to be sabotaged to halt the supply of heavy water to Germany. The first effort by the Special Operations Executive (SOE), codenamed Freshman, was launched in late 1942. The mission was a failure, with the glider-borne troops never getting near the plant before being killed or captured. However, an advance team of four Norwegians had landed near the plant before the others arrived under the codename Grouse. It was decided that they should remain in Norway until a second operation could be mounted to destroy the plant. The four men, all of them born in Rjukan, managed to survive the winter months living off the land and their own sparse rations. But they also managed to reconnoiter the area around the plant and work out the best access and extraction routes.

GROUSE MEETS GUNNERSIDE

....

The second SOE operation, codenamed Gunnerside, consisted of six Norwegians under the command of Lieutenant Joachim Rønneberg. Their training was extremely thorough and included a scale-model replica of the Vemork plant itself. The team parachuted into Norway on 16 February, 1943, but due to bad weather it was a week before they rendezvoused with the Grouse team. Like the Grouse team the Gunnerside party was made up of men who were predominantly from the local area and who were familiar with the terrain.

Fully briefed by the Grouse team about German guard routines the combined team traversed the steep terrain, infiltrated the plant unseen, set their charges, and left without firing a shot. The subsequent explosion destroyed the heavy water production facility. The team itself withdrew to their mountain base and then began the long retreat to Sweden by ski, covering the 400km (250-mile) journey in 14 days. All made it to safety. A British rifle had been intentionally left at the plant so the Germans would not retaliate against Norwegian civilians.

Operation Gunnerside not only showed what a small group with specialised training could do, it was also a major setback for the Nazis' nuclear programme.

BELOW The location of the Norsk-Hydro power station meant that a covert operation was the only viable option.

BATTLE OF KHARKOV

DATE

14 March, 1943

SUMMARY

The German counter-offensive saved the entire southern sector of the Eastern Front from collapse.

LOCATION

Ukraine, USSR

As the disaster at Stalingrad was unfolding the Red Army pushed west in a series of offensives that ruptured the German front. On 11 February Hitler ordered German forces in Kharkov to hold the encircled city at all costs. The German Führer, determined to hold every inch of Soviet territory, became obsessed with Kharkov and paid little attention to Red Army armoured spearheads threatening Dnepropetrovsk, Krasnograd and Pavlograd. Two Soviet Fronts – Southwestern and Voronezh – were threatening to conquer the whole of Ukraine.

DISOBEYING THE FÜHRER

The defence of Kharkov had been given to the newly formed SS Panzer Corps under the command of SS-Obergruppenführer Paul Hausser. The corps was made up of four elite SS panzer divisions, which, if they stayed in the city, would be surrounded and another Stalingrad would be the result. So Hausser disobeyed Hitler and pulled his men out. The Führer flew into a rage but the commander of Army Group Don, Field Marshal Erich von Manstein, persuaded him that it was all part of a plan to lure the Red Army into a trap.

Stalin interpreted the abandonment of Kharkov as a sign that Hitler was conducting a strategic withdrawal behind the River Dnieper. So the Soviet dictator ordered his forces to continue their offensive westwards. It was to prove a costly mistake.

Manstein organised a series of counterattacks throughout February using the SS Panzer Corps and armoured units of the

RIGHT Erich von Manstein assured Hitler that, by withdrawing from Kharkov, Soviet forces would be lured into a trap.

Fourth Panzer Army being brought up from the Caucasus. By the end of the month these counterattacks had destroyed 615 Red Army tanks, 354 artillery pieces and 69 anti-tank guns, killed 23,000 Red Army personnel and captured 9,000 more. The first phase of Manstein's plan was complete; the next phase involved retaking Kharkov itself.

THE PANZERS CLOSE IN

ABOVE German panzers roll through Kharkov in March 1943. The process of clearing Soviet troops from the city was fraught with difficulty.

Red Army units, over-extended and running low on supplies and ammunition, were now trapped between two pincers as SS Panzer Corps and 48th Panzer Corps closed in on Kharkov. By 11 March Waffen-SS units were entering the city from the north against dogged Red Army resistance. The city had to be taken road by road. SS Tiger tanks were used as mobile pillboxes, parking on road corners and blasting apartment blocks containing enemy troops. It was slow, bloody work because every city block had to be cleared of Red Army snipers, dug-in anti-tank guns and hidden T-34 tanks. The Soviet soldiers were joined by thousands of Kharkov's citizens who did not wish to live under Nazi rule again. During the street fighting 1,000 Waffen-SS soldiers were killed and thousands more Red Army troops and many more civilians died.

On 14 March the battle for Kharkov was over and the city was once again in German hands. In the following days, Waffen-SS and German army armoured units recaptured Belgorod to the north as Red Army forces withdrew east. Inside Kharkov, meanwhile, Gestapo and SS Einsatzgruppen men with mobile gas chambers instigated reprisal actions, murdering up to 10,000 men, women and children.

The Germans claimed that the Kharkov counteroffensive had cost the Red Army 50,000 dead, 19,594 taken prisoner, and 1,140 tanks and 3,000 artillery pieces destroyed. The SS Panzer Corps had also suffered considerable losses: 11,500 killed or wounded.

In the final days of March the temperature began to rise and snow began to give way to mud that made all movement off roads impossible. Manstein had saved the southern sector of the Eastern Front from disaster but to the north the Red Army remained in control of a huge salient that extended more than 80km (50 miles) westwards into German-held territory. In the centre of the salient was the city of Kursk.

THE WARSAW GHETTO UPRISING

DATE

....

19 April, 1943

SUMMARY

....

The Jews of the
Warsaw Ghetto rose
up against their
Nazi oppressors
in an act that
stunned the SS.

LOCATION

....

Warsaw, Poland

The Warsaw Ghetto was the largest of some 800 ghettos the Nazis established in the Central Government. It was entirely under the control of the Nazis, though the SS did set up a Council of Jewish Elders to administer it and a Jewish police force to enforce law and order and undertake the SS's work. The ghetto itself was divided into two sections: the 'Big Ghetto' in the north and the 'Little Ghetto' in the south, divided by a large wooden bridge over Chłodna Street. The latter was initially regarded as a better place to live than the larger, grossly overcrowded former. But the SS controlled the supply of food to the whole ghetto and soon the conditions for the 500,000 inhabitants were intolerable. Even from its establishment in 1939 disease and starvation were ever-present.

AN UNDERGROUND ARMY

As the war dragged on and more and more Jews were crammed into the ghetto thousands began to die. In July 1942 a new horror was visited on the inhabitants of the ghetto when the Germans began deporting 6,000 Jews a day to the death camp at Treblinka. Word soon spread that transportation out of the ghetto meant only one thing: death. In response the Jews set up an underground resistance group: *Zydowska Organizacja Bojowa* (ZOB) – Jewish Fighting Organisation. Made up of no more than 750 men and women fighters, it was armed with a motley collection of captured pistols, rifles and homemade Molotov cocktails. But the ZOB had created a maze of underground bases and storerooms and used the city's sewers as lines of communication.

The first the Nazis learned of the ZOB was on 18 January, 1943, when a section ambushed German troops who had entered the ghetto, killing a number over several days of combat. German reprisals were savage and often random, public hangings and shootings in the ghetto becoming a daily occurrence. But even using terror the Germans felt that the ghetto was a hotbed of 'corruption and revolt'. *SS-Reichsführer* Heinrich Himmler therefore announced on 19 April that the ghetto was to be emptied of its residents in honour of Hitler's birthday the following day. On the same day the uprising began.

A BRUTAL RESPONSE

There were an estimated 56,000 Jews left in the ghetto and the man Himmler gave the task to remove them (in other words, to kill them) was the SS and Police Chief in Warsaw, Jürgen Stroop. With just over 2,000 men drawn from training battalions, security police and army engineers, Stroop's men used explosives and flamethrowers to battle the poorly armed insurgents.

Stroop sent daily reports of the fighting to Himmler, listing how many Jews he had killed. It took him longer than expected, the fighters of the ZOB putting up fanatical resistance from their makeshift strongpoints. By the end of April Stroop estimated that he had taken or killed 37,359 Jews but resistance continued. He boasted: 'The longer the resistance lasted the tougher the men of the Waffen-SS, police and *Wehrmacht* became. They fulfilled their duty indefatigably in faithful comradeship, and stood together as models and examples of soldiers. Their duty hours often lasted from early morning until late at night.'

Organised resistance in the Warsaw Ghetto ended on 16 May. The buildings were either on fire or piles of rubble and all 56,000 Jews had either been killed or captured (those captured were sent to death camps). But the fact that the Jews of the Warsaw Ghetto had risen up was an inspiration to those battling Nazism on the European mainland.

It is immensely satisfying to report that after the war Stroop was captured by the Poles and hanged on the site of the former ghetto in July 1952.

BELOW Civilians are forced out of hiding by German forces. The photo was included in one of Stroop's regular reports to Himmler.

OPERATION MINCEMEAT

DATE

30 April, 1943

SUMMARY

One of the greatest deception exercises of World War II, which convinced the Germans that the Allies would land in Greece and Sardinia instead of Sicily.

LOCATION

Huelva, Spain

Originally codenamed Trojan Horse, Operation Mincemeat was a plan devised by British naval intelligence and MI5 to deceive the Germans into believing that the planned Allied landings in southern Europe would take place in Greece and Sardinia rather than the intended target of Sicily.

GLYNDWR MICHAEL

The plan had been devised in 1942 by Flight Lieutenant Charles Cholmondeley of MI5 and Lieutenant Commander Ewen Montagu of naval intelligence, who proposed to plant a corpse carrying false papers to mislead the Germans regarding Allied plans in the Mediterranean theatre. In January 1943 a suicide by a 34-year-old man, Glyndwr Michael, provided a suitable corpse for Mincemeat. In early February, XX Committee (a British intelligence co-ordinating committee created in January 1941 to supervise the management of MI5's double agents and give approval to information being passed to the enemy) was informed that a suitable corpse had become available and approved the operation. The corpse was dressed in the uniform of a Royal Marines major and given the false identity of Major Martin. Attached to the corpse by a chain was a briefcase containing forged documents.

Much preparation had gone into making Major William Martin a convincing figure. One officer wore his uniform every day before it was placed on the corpse, to give it a worn look. Great thought had gone into the contents of Martin's wallet, which included a photograph of his fake fiancée (who was actually an MI5 secretary). Martin's pockets contained angry letters from creditors and a bill from his tailor. In his briefcase was a fake letter from Lieutenant-General Archibald Nye, Vice-Chief of the Imperial General Staff, to General Harold Alexander, head of the Near East Command, hinting that the Allies were planning to attack Greece and Sardinia.

The body, packed with dry ice, was driven from London to Holy Loch, Scotland, on 17 April. The next day it was placed aboard the submarine HMS *Seraph*, which sailed for the southern coast of Spain. On 30 April the body was released into the sea and it washed up on the coast near the town of Huelva.

TAKING THE BAIT

···

Spanish fishermen discovered the body and handed it over to the authorities. Soon German agents became aware of the corpse and its briefcase. The head of German intelligence in Madrid, Major Karl-Erich Kühlenthal, convinced that the documents were genuine, personally flew them to Berlin with a report testifying to their significance. Fortunately for the British he embellished his reports greatly and also relied heavily on one of his Spanish assets, Juan Pujol García, who was actually a double agent working for the British.

The British had another stroke of luck when the documents arrived in Berlin where Alexis Baron von Roenne, a top intelligence analyst, vouched for their authenticity. But Roenne disliked Hitler intensely and seems to have been engaged in a one-man campaign to sabotage the Nazi war effort. A conversation with the Spanish coroner who examined the corpse would have compromised the entire operation. For example, the dated papers in Martin's pockets showed that he had been in the water for five days but the corpse was far too decomposed to have been in the sea for less than a week. But Germany's spies informed Berlin that something false was actually true and Hitler acted on it.

The Führer was already fixated on the idea of an Allied landing in Greece so he was ready to believe the deception in any case. He might have moved the panzer division from Sicily to Greece anyway. What Mincemeat did was to convince him that he was right (not particularly difficult when it came to the Führer). Sardinia was also reinforced with troops, which meant that the Axis garrison on Sicily was not as strong as it should have been when the Allies launched their invasion in July 1943.

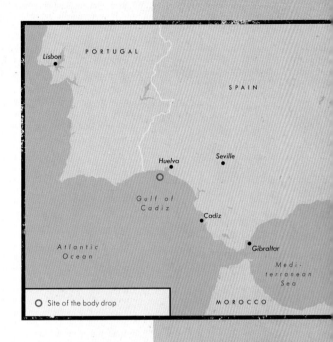

ABOVE Major Martin was dropped into the Mediterranean Sea just off the Spanish coast near Huelva and left to drift ashore. But despite the meticulous preparation, it is debatable whether Mincemeat would have been successful without the acquiescence of key Nazi officials.

Map labels: PORTUGAL, Lisbon, SPAIN, Huelva, Seville, Gulf of Cadiz, Cadiz, Atlantic Ocean, Gibraltar, Mediterranean Sea, MOROCCO

○ Site of the body drop

AXIS COLLAPSE IN NORTH AFRICA

DATE
....
12 May, 1943

SUMMARY
....
The surrender of
Axis forces in North
Africa cost Germany
and Italy an entire
army group, losses
the faltering Third
Reich in particular
could not afford.

LOCATION
....
Tunisia, North Africa

Rommel's defeat at El Alamein in November 1942 occasioned a
great retreat by his depleted Army Group Africa, through Tripolitania,
abandoning Tripoli, and at the end of January 1943 halting at the
defensive line of the old French Mareth Line fortifications on the
Libya–Tunisia border. To the west the Germans had managed to halt
Anglo-American forces that had landed in Vichy North Africa in
November 1943, so that by mid-December 1942 Axis forces had
managed to consolidate their defensive positions held by the newly
formed Fifth Panzer Army.

Thanks to reinforcements being flown into Tunisia and the arrival of
the new Tiger heavy tank, the Fifth Panzer Army was able to establish
a front in western Tunisia that snaked south to link up with Rommel's
troops, now designated the German–Italian Panzer Army. On paper
these formations looked impressive but the reality was that they were
both understrength. Von Arnim's Fifth Panzer Army, for example, had
only one Italian and three German divisions in January 1943 to resist
General Anderson's British First Army.

ALLIED STRENGTH IN DEPTH

....

Nevertheless, Rommel believed that Axis forces could exploit their
unenviable position of being sandwiched between the Eighth Army
in the east and the First Army in the west. He hoped to do this by
concentrating Axis combat power at a single point to inflict a major
defeat on the widely spread Allied forces. It was a tactically sound plan
but did not take into account the Allied ability to speedily reinforce their
frontline units. Rommel struck American forces between 14 and 22
February in the Kasserine Pass area of western Tunisia. U.S. forces
buckled in the face of the armoured and infantry attack, with Axis
forces advancing 96km (60 miles). Rommel inflicted 10,000 casualties
on the Allies for the loss of only 2,000, and yet his enemy was able to
rush in reserves of tanks and infantry to plug the gap and Rommel had

insufficient reserves to exploit his victory. Aside from alarming the Americans Kasserine Pass did not alter the strategic position.

It was the same at Medenine in early March when Rommel launched an assault against the Eighth Army facing the Mareth Line. The Germans assembled three panzer divisions (160 tanks in total), 200 artillery pieces, and 10,000 infantry to break through British positions. However, Montgomery, forewarned of the impending attack by Ultra intercepts, deployed 400 tanks, 350 artillery pieces and 470 anti-tank guns to blunt the German assault. The plan worked and the losses suffered at Medenine (52 panzers knocked out for no British tank losses) meant that Axis forces were unable to withstand renewed British attacks in late March and early April that broke through the Mareth Line.

ABOVE British Crusader tanks in El Hamma, Tunisia. Such was the Allies' material strength that tanks destroyed in combat were quickly replaced.

MATERIAL ADVANTAGE

In addition to enjoying overwhelming superiority in air power, troops and equipment, the Allies could also call on almost unlimited supplies, in stark contrast to their Axis adversaries. Between January and April 1943 the Germans created an 'air bridge' to supply Axis forces in North Africa with reinforcements, food and ammunition (Allied control of the Mediterranean meant that Axis cargo vessels were unable to make the journey to North Africa). But it was all to no avail.

Hitler clung on to the fantasy that Axis forces could hold on to their precarious bridgehead in Tunisia for a few more months to tie down Allied forces. But in May Allied forces pierced the Axis perimeter in Tunisia, U.S. and British aircraft roaming the skies at will (the *Luftwaffe* was in the process of withdrawing to Sicily). Allied units entered the capital Tunis on 7 May, prompting Axis troops to begin surrendering in droves. By 12 May the war in North Africa was over. A staggering 275,000 German and Italian troops entered captivity. Hitler had lost an entire army group in Tunisia – Germany's next greatest military disaster after Stalingrad. On the southern flank of the Third Reich the fighting would soon move to Sicily.

THE TRIDENT CONFERENCE

DATE

12–25 May, 1943

SUMMARY

The Anglo-U.S. conference ratified strategy in Europe and the Pacific, but also indicated that the United States was now the dominant partner in the relationship.

LOCATION

Washington, D.C., USA

On the same day that Axis forces surrendered in North Africa, President Roosevelt, Prime Minister Churchill and the Combined Chiefs of Staff began a conference in Washington to determine future strategy in Europe and the Pacific. Things had developed very favourably for the Allies since the Casablanca Conference in January: Axis forces had suffered two major defeats at Stalingrad, and in North Africa and in the Pacific the Americans were now on the offensive. But Trident revealed some strains in the Anglo-American relationship regarding strategy and also indicated that the United States, with its vast industrial and military resources, was becoming the dominant partner in the Allied alliance.

REACHING A COMPROMISE

In Washington Roosevelt queried an Italian operation after the conquest of Sicily, which had been agreed at Casablanca. He and his planning staff had little enthusiasm for an Italian campaign at the expense of a cross-Channel invasion of France. U.S. Chief of Staff General George Marshall in particular was worried that committing ground forces to Italy would result in Allied troops fighting on the Italian mainland for the remainder of 1943 and all of 1944. He believed this would prolong the war in Europe and delay the defeat of Japan.

Churchill, though, was adamant that an invasion of the Italian mainland would knock Italy out of the war and divert German troops away from the Eastern Front. In the end a compromise was reached whereby the British agreed to a target date of 1 May, 1944, for a cross-Channel invasion, codenamed Overlord, and the Americans agreed to post-Sicily operations against Italy. There was also agreement on a Combined Bomber Offensive aimed at destroying and disrupting the German 'military, industrial and economic system'. This would involve critically undermining the morale of the German people and whittling down *Luftwaffe* fighter strength.

In the European theatre of operations (ETO) the British and Americans were more or less equal partners but in the Pacific it was a different story. At the conference the U.S. Joint Chiefs of Staff submitted 'The Strategic Plan for the Defeat of Japan', which became a cornerstone of Pacific strategy for the remainder of 1943 and for 1944 (see box). It not only did nothing to reassure the British that the United States might devote too large a portion of its resources to the defeat of Japan before the Third Reich could be destroyed, it also showed how Britain had declined in power and influence in the Pacific. For example, at the conference it was agreed not to attempt to reconquer all of Burma (which was beyond British capabilities) but to try to occupy north Burma only. The limited ground offensive would include the construction of a new road from India to join with the old Burma Road inside China.

Admiral Ernest J. King, U.S. Chief of Naval Operations, outlined the operations U.S. forces hoped to carry out in the Pacific in 1943–44, which again illustrated the resources the Americans could call upon. King considered a decisive action against the Japanese fleet and the seizure of the Mariana Islands as prime requirements for ultimate victory in the Pacific.

AMERICAN HEGEMONY IN THE PACIFIC

The Trident Conference laid down the strategy for the conduct of the war against Japan, which would include U.S., British and Chinese forces. The latter two, however, would be supporting partners only. The war against Japan was divided into six phases:

- The British, assisted by the U.S. and Chinese Nationalists, would attempt to retake Hong Kong.
- The Americans would retake the Philippines.
- During the campaign against Hong Kong, the Nationalist Chinese, assisted by U.S. forces, would enter the northern reaches of the South China Sea.
- The three nations would prepare an overwhelming air offensive against Japan from bases in China.
- The mounting of the air offensive.
- The invasion of Japan itself.

THE ALLIES STRIKE A BLOW IN THE ATLANTIC

DATE

24 May, 1943

SUMMARY

The decisive month in the Battle of the Atlantic which signalled the ultimate defeat of Germany's U-boat fleet.

LOCATION

Atlantic Ocean

On 24 May, 1943, Admiral Karl Dönitz, the head of the *Kriegsmarine*, temporarily withdrew his U-boat fleet from the Atlantic following heavy losses against Allied convoys. For Dönitz it was a heavy defeat and signalled that he was losing the Battle of the Atlantic. His U-boats would return to the Atlantic but would never regain ascendancy against growing numbers of Allied merchant ships, convoy escorts and anti-submarine aircraft.

ZONES OF RESPONSIBILITY

'Black May', as it would be called, was the culmination of a number of developments that together brought about a reversal of fortune in the war against the U-boats. First was the change in strategy agreed at the Atlantic Convoy Conference held in Washington in March, which divided up the Atlantic into zones of responsibility. The Royal Canadian Navy was to protect the northerly routes, south of Greenland, the Royal Navy was to guard the eastern convoy routes and the U.S. Navy was to protect the southerly convoys. In the same month the first five Royal Navy support groups were available for operations in the North Atlantic. Each group had a number of destroyers and corvettes, the ships being equipped with radar, sonar and effective anti-submarine weapons such as depth charges and Hedgehog forward-firing projectiles.

The aircraft carriers HMS *Archer* and USS *Bogue* were also ready for action in March 1943, which meant that the Atlantic 'air gap' could finally be closed. In addition, the entry into service of very long-range aircraft with the U.S., Canadian and British air forces meant Allied air cover was further extended from the shores of North America and Britain. These naval patrol aircraft – B-24 Liberator, Catalina and B-17 Flying Fortress – were fitted with radar and Leigh lights and became powerful weapons against surfaced submarines, especially in the Bay of Biscay. Crucially, by early 1943 fully mobilised U.S. shipyards were producing large numbers of escort and merchant ships. Finally, the Allies had cracked the U-boat Enigma ciphers.

SHIFTING FORTUNES

··

With these advantages the war against the
U-boats began to gradually tilt in the Allies'
favour. In March 1943, 90 British, Allied and
neutral merchant ships, a total of 546,608
tonnes (538,000 tons), were sunk in the
Atlantic for the loss of 12 U-boats. In April
the number of merchant ships sunk in the
Atlantic had dropped to 40, a total of
245,872 tonnes (242,000 tons), for the loss
of 14 U-boats. In this month Dönitz had
240 U-boats operational, over half of them
on passage through or on patrol in the
North Atlantic.

But it was the convoy battles in May that
broke the back of the U-boat fleet in the
Atlantic. A total of 15 convoys sailed from the
United States – 622 merchantmen in all.
They were guarded by seven British and five
Canadian convoy groups, six British and one
U.S. escort groups and three escort carriers
(HMS *Biter*, HMS *Archer* and USS *Boque*, with each carrier
deploying between 15 and 20 aircraft). In their efforts to get close to
the merchantmen the U-boats suffered heavy losses at the hands of
the warships and escort carriers. Eleven of the convoys completed
their journey unscathed, the other four losing a total of 19 ships. But
40 U-boats were lost, 25 percent of Dönitz's operational strength at
the time.

Convoy ONS-5 (46 merchantmen and 22 escorts) was attacked by no
less than four 'wolfpacks' between 28 April and 6 May. The submarines
sank 13 ships, the last time a convoy would lose a high number of vessels.
But eight U-boats were lost and a further seven suffered severe battle
damage and had to limp home. That May 1943 was a turning point is
illustrated by the ratio of tonnage sunk for U-boats lost. Against ONS-5
the ratio was less than 9144 tonnes (9,000 tons) per U-boat. A year
earlier the figure had been 101,600 tonnes (100,000 tons) for every
U-boat sunk.

ABOVE By May 1943,
Karl Dönitz (centre) was
facing a crisis. In that month
alone, a quarter of the
U-boat fleet was lost.

RUSSIAN PARTISANS DEFY THE AXIS FORCES

DATE

June 1943

SUMMARY

On the eve of the
Battle of Kursk
Soviet partisans
were causing serious
problems for the
Wehrmacht in the
occupied areas of
the western USSR.

LOCATION

German-occupied
Russia

The vast expanse of the Soviet Union had come as a nasty shock to the invading German troops in June 1941, but the huge forests and great distances between urban centres was ideal terrain in which partisan groups could operate. The partisan war would become a problem that the Germans would be unable to solve, fuelled as it was by Nazi racial policies that viewed ordinary Russians as 'subhumans'.

ALL MEANS POSSIBLE

In July 1941 the Soviet Central Committee gave orders for underground Communist Party committees to be established in the occupied lands. These bodies were to use all means possible to disrupt enemy operations, including attacks on ammunition and fuel supply lines. By the spring of 1942 the partisans had set up large camps in remote forests and had established radio communications with the Partisan Movement Headquarters in Moscow. Some partisan groups numbered 2,000 though most, operating near small towns, were only 20–30 strong. To support them the Soviet Air Force regularly dropped food, ammunition, explosives and medicines to the partisan camps.

By mid-1943 the Soviets had around 1,200 partisan groups operating behind German lines and controlling vast areas of territory, especially in the Belorussian forests and swamps and in northern Ukraine. By this date partisans in Belorussia had killed around 300,000 Axis personnel (not all frontline soldiers; many killed were local collaborators and low-grade police and military personnel), caused 3,000 train accidents, destroyed 1,200 tanks and other armoured vehicles, burnt 4,000 trucks and blown up around 900 depots. Senior Nazi and *Wehrmacht* officers had vastly underestimated the impact that partisans would have on the war effort. Anti-partisan operations were invariably crude and brutal and resulted in the local population becoming further alienated from the occupiers. To fight the 'shadow army' of partisans, which numbered around 140,000 in mid-1943, the Germans were forced to devote more and more units to anti-guerrilla operations. In the spring, for example, they deployed up to 100,000 soldiers and police to clear the Bryansk Forest of partisans but the results were negligible. Though the Germans often killed many partisans and the local villagers who supported them, many partisans were able to evade capture and move to another region where they reassembled. This frustrated German commanders who resorted to shooting civilians out of hand as reprisals for partisan attacks. Thus in May and June 1943, German troops shot 5,000 suspects, including many women and children, during the anti-partisan Operation Cottbus in the Minsk, Vitebsk and Vileika districts.

ABOVE Partisan fighters could readily make themselves indistinguishable from civilians, which prompted Germany to enact brutal reprisals on noncombatant populations.

The partisans undertook important work during the so-called War of the Rails in the spring, summer and autumn of 1943 when they launched over 2,500 attacks on railway lines and bridges in an effort to weaken German forces preparing for the Kursk offensive. The result was 44 bridges, 298 locomotives and 1,223 railway carriages destroyed in June and July. The War of the Rails continued after the battle to assist Red Army units advancing west.

PARTISANS IN YUGOSLAVIA

Following the conquest of Yugoslavia and Greece in 1941 the Germans left only two divisions in the Balkans, the bulk of the garrison duty falling on 38 Italian divisions. Yugoslavia was divided between Germany and Italy, with the fascist Ustashi regime controlling most of Croatia and Bosnia. Resistance to Axis rule was at first weak and fragmented but eventually the partisans under Marshal Tito became the largest group, their activities sucking in more and more Axis troops into Yugoslavia to deal with them. No less than five major offensives were launched against Tito's guerrillas between September 1941 and June 1943, all of them failures. By 1944 the Germans had 700,000 soldiers (admittedly not all of them frontline units) in the Balkans vainly trying to destroy the partisan movement.

THE POINTBLANK DIRECTIVE

DATE

14 June, 1943

SUMMARY

The Anglo-U.S. directive took the Combined Bomber Offensive to a new level in the war against Germany's industries.

LOCATION

Western Europe

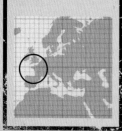

Operation Pointblank put German fighter aircraft at the top of the Allied target list, both to draw away *Luftwaffe* fighter aircraft from other fronts and to degrade enemy fighter strength and fighter-production capacity to such an extent that it would not be an impediment to the planned 1944 cross-Channel invasion.

The RAF would bomb cities and industrial areas by night to destroy aircraft production factories in the target areas. The United States Air Army Force (USAAF) would bomb airfields and factories by day to destroy as many enemy airfields as possible and to further cripple fighter production. The highest priority was given to fighter assembly plants, aircraft engine factories and ball-bearing manufacturers.

RIGHT B-17 Flying Fortress heavy bombers of the USAAF on a bombing raid over Dresden in November 1943.

A COSTLY SUCCESS

The United States Strategic Bombing Survey, which began in 1945, estimated that 18,000 aircraft of all types were denied the *Luftwaffe* between July 1943 and December 1944 as a result of Pointblank. The intensive bombing campaign also diverted around half the *Luftwaffe's* fighter force to anti-bomber operations. In 1943 alone the *Luftwaffe* was forced to withdraw 180 single-engine fighters from the Eastern Front and 120 from the Mediterranean to combat Allied bombers.

But Pointblank exacted a heavy toll on bomber crews, especially General Ira Eaker's Eighth Air Force flying from bases in England. On 17 August, 1943, the Eighth Air Force mounted a raid against the ball-bearing factories at Schweinfurt. The town was a target because Allied planners believed that the German aviation industry consumed an average of 2.4 million ball bearings a month and Schweinfurt accounted for more than 40 percent of ball-bearing production. Enemy flak and fighters shot down 60 of the 315 heavy bombers that took part in the raid.

Worse was to follow on 14 October, 1943, when Eaker's bombers mounted a second raid against the Schweinfurt factories. Some 60 of the 291 bombers were lost with a further 138 suffering casualties or damage. These losses meant that throughout the summer and autumn of 1943 Eighth Army bomber crews were experiencing a monthly attrition rate of 30 percent, while *Luftwaffe* fighter pilots were dying at a rate less than half that of the Americans. Such losses, which included highly trained crews, were unsustainable, thus the Americans sped up the development of what would prove the answer: long-range fighters.

Nevertheless, by 1944 Pointblank was seriously degrading not only German aircraft production but also the entire war economy.

TARGETS OF THE POINTBLANK DIRECTIVE

The directive identified 19 vital German industries (and the number of targets associated with them) which if destroyed would stagnate the German war machine. The industries and number of associated targets were:

- Single-engine fighter aircraft: 22 targets
- Ball bearings: 10 targets
- Petroleum products: 39 targets
- Grinding wheels and crude abrasives: 10 targets
- Nonferrous metals: 13 targets
- Synthetic rubber and rubber tyres: 12 targets
- Submarine construction plants and bases: 27 targets
- Military transport vehicles: seven targets
- Transportation (rail, barge and surface roads): no specific number
- Coking plants: 89 targets
- Iron and steel works: 14 targets
- Machine tools: 12 targets
- Electrical power: 55 targets
- Electrical equipment: 16 targets
- Optical precision instruments: three targets
- Chemicals: not thought to be vulnerable to air attack when the directive was issued because of their dispersal
- Food: 21 targets
- Nitrogen: 21 targets
- Anti-aircraft and anti-tank artillery: not thought to be vulnerable to air attack when the directive was issued

THE BATTLE OF KURSK

DATE

5–13 July, 1943

SUMMARY

The battle marked the last great German offensive on the Eastern Front and signalled that the Soviets would defeat the Nazi invaders.

LOCATION

Central USSR

The Kursk salient was a tempting target for the Germans in the summer of 1943, Hitler's generals convincing the Führer that by destroying it the *Wehrmacht* would regain the initiative on the Eastern Front. Codenamed Citadel, a major effort was mounted to rebuild the panzer arm for the forthcoming offensive. The attack was continually delayed to allow the new Panther tank and Ferdinand assault gun to take part in the battle. The Soviets had been warned of the impending attack by British intelligence and their own spies inside the *Wehrmacht* (the Red Orchestra), so the Red Army commander in the Kursk salient, Georgi Zhukov, advised the building of intricate defence lines so the Germans would grind to a halt in trying to breach them. Stalin agreed and for the first time a battle would be fought on the Soviets' terms.

The longer Hitler delayed Operation Citadel the more time the Red Army had to prepare its defences. When the battle began on 5 July the length of the Red Army frontline in the Kursk salient was 190km (110 miles), behind which were deployed 20,000 artillery pieces and mortars, 6,000 anti-tank guns and hundreds of Katyusha rocket launchers. Over a million Red Army soldiers had laid 2,700 anti-personnel and 2,400 anti-tank mines every 1.6km (1 mile).

DUAL ATTACK

The German plan was for two pincers to attack simultaneously at the base of the salient and link up to cut off the huge numbers of troops in the bulge. In the north was the Ninth Army under the command of Colonel-General Model (335,000 men, 590 tanks and 424 assault guns); in the south was the Fourth Panzer Army, commanded by Colonel-General Hermann Hoth, and Army Detachment Kempf, commanded by General Werner Kempf (combined total 350,000 men, 1,269 tanks and 245 assault guns).

The Germans attacked on 5 July and immediately ran into enemy minefields and anti-tank guns. The Ninth Army advanced 8km (6 miles)

Eyewitness

PRIOR TO KURSK, HEINZ GUDERIAN HAD BEEN APPOINTED INSPECTOR GENERAL OF PANZER FORCES AND HIS COMMENTS ON THE BATTLE SUMMED UP THE CATASTROPHIC RESULT.

'By the failure of Citadel we had suffered a decisive defeat. The armoured formations, reformed and re-equipped with so much effort, had lost heavily both in men and equipment and would now be unemployable for a long time to come.

Needless to say the Russians exploited their victory to the full. There were to be no more periods of quiet on the Eastern Front. From now on the enemy was in undisputed possession of the initiative.'

and suffered 20 percent tank and assault-gun losses and nearly 20,000 casualties. In the south they did better, advancing 20km (16 miles). Over the next six days the Germans continued to grind forwards but failed to breach the Red Army's defence lines, incurring high losses in tanks, assault guns and men. Soviet losses were higher but Zhukov's tactics were working.

By 11 July, though, it appeared that the Fourth Panzer Army would break through Soviet defences in the south, near the town of Prokhorovka.

On 12 July a massive tank battle took place around the town, the 500 tanks of the Soviet Fifth Guards Tank Army striking the panzers of II SS Panzer Corps and forcing them back. But the cost was high, the Red Army losing 192 tanks during the day, a poor return for knocking out 30 German panzers. However, the attack had stopped the German advance in its tracks (the advance of the Ninth Army had been stopped on 11 July).

On 13 July Hitler called off Operation Citadel, alarmed by a new Soviet offensive to the north of the Kursk salient and another in the far south. And Allied forces had landed on Sicily on 10 July.

Losses had been high on both sides. The Red Army had suffered over 177,000 casualties, the Germans nearly 50,000. The panzer arm, having been carefully rebuilt prior to Citadel, had been decimated, the Germans losing 1,612 tanks damaged and 323 irreparable losses. Red Army losses in armoured fighting vehicles amounted to 1,614.

THE INVASION OF SICILY

DATE

10 July, 1943

SUMMARY

The short campaign secured Sicily for the Allies and prompted the overthrow of Italian dictator Benito Mussolini.

LOCATION

Sicily, Italy

Following their victory in North Africa and the strategy agreed at the Casablanca Conference, the British and Americans prepared to invade the island of Sicily. Operation Husky, the codename for the invasion, was under the supreme leadership of General Dwight D. Eisenhower, with General Sir Harold Alexander being his deputy and in command of Allied land forces during the campaign. Alexander's Fifteenth Army Group comprised Lieutenant-General George S. Patton's U.S. Seventh Army and General Sir Bernard Montgomery's British Eighth Army.

THE EIGHTH ARMY LANDS

The landings, the first large-scale amphibious assault in the European theatre, were launched on 10 July. The Eighth Army landed from the Pachino Peninsula to just south of the port of Syracuse, while the Seventh Army landed in the Gulf of Gela. The strategic objective of the campaign was the port of Messina in the northeastern corner of the island. Allied forces landed along the island's southeastern coastline because of the preponderance of favourable beaches, ports, and airfields.

On paper the island's defences and garrison were formidable. Some 200,000 Italian troops of the Sixth Army, commanded by General Alfredo Guzzoni, defended the island but were poorly equipped and trained and their morale was brittle. The best Axis troops on the island were those of the German 15th Panzergrenadier Division and the Hermann Göring Panzer Division – a total of 30,000 men (the German 1st Parachute Division would also arrive on the island days after the invasion).

From the beginning opposition from Italian units was patchy at best and on the first day the Eighth Army secured Syracuse and was on its way to Augusta. Thereafter progress slowed in the face of adverse terrain and resistance from the 1st Parachute Division. In the American sector it was a similar story, the commitment by Guzzoni of the Hermann Göring Division slowing the advance of Patton's Seventh Army, but only temporarily.

By 24 July Patton's men had secured the entire western half of Sicily, capturing 53,000 Italian soldiers and 400 vehicles for the loss of 272 men. Italian morale and inclination to fight, fragile at best, collapsed completely the next day when Benito Mussolini was deposed and replaced by Marshal Pietro Badoglio. Guzzoni was still talking of making a stand along the so-called Etna Line in the island's northeast corner but his men were now deserting. The German High Command decided to withdraw from the island. General Hans Hube, commander of the newly formed XIV Panzer Corps, was placed in command of Axis forces on Sicily and ordered to evacuate them across the Strait of Messina.

A TASTE OF THINGS TO COME

The evacuation was a textbook example of how to conduct a withdrawal in the face of a superior enemy and was a foretaste of what the Allies could expect when they crossed to the Italian mainland. Under the cover of massed flak guns 40,000 German troops, 9,975 vehicles, 47 tanks, 94 pieces of artillery, and 17,272 tonnes (17,000 tons) of ammunition were ferried to the mainland.

Operation Husky had been a relatively easy campaign. By the time the German evacuation was complete on 17 August, less than six weeks after the invasion, 29,000 Axis soldiers were dead and a further 140,000 prisoner. The Allies had suffered 31,000 killed, wounded or missing. The success on Sicily led the Allies to believe that an invasion of the Italian mainland would have similar results. This view was greatly mistaken. Nevertheless, Husky provided important lessons in how to prepare and conduct a large-scale amphibious operation, lessons that would bear fruit in the planning of Operation Overlord in 1944. Husky also demonstrated the imperative of having aerial superiority over the landing sites and enemy airfields. On 10 July Allied aircraft flew 1,092 sorties to protect the landing beaches and ships offshore, and at the same time bombers attacked Axis airfields to restrict enemy sorties. By the middle of July the *Luftwaffe* had only 25 aircraft on Sicily. By the end of the month the Allies had no less than 40 squadrons on the island.

ABOVE British troops disembark onto a Sicilian beach. Operation Husky provided invaluable experience of large-scale amphibious invasion.

MUSSOLINI OVERTHROWN

DATE

25 July, 1943

SUMMARY

After 21 years in power Italian fascist dictator Benito Mussolini was deposed by his own Fascist Grand Council and arrested. Italy was now out of the Axis.

LOCATION

Rome, Italy

Italy's participation in World War II was a disaster for the country and its people. Notwithstanding the promises of Mussolini that the Mediterranean Sea would become an 'Italian lake', Italian forces had suffered successive defeats in North Africa and Greece. In early July 1943 the Allies landed on Italian soil itself – Sicily – as a prelude to an amphibious invasion of the mainland.

By 1943 the Italian armed forces were demoralised, poorly equipped and even worse led. The people had also grown weary of the war, demonstrations against the war beginning at the Fiat plant in Turin in March 1943, resulting in nearly 50,000 taking part. When the Allies invaded Sicily on 10 July Hitler hastily convened a meeting with Mussolini 10 days later. Mussolini had intended to explain to the Führer Italy's desperate situation and its need for an armistice, but Hitler informed the Duce that he was proposing a German command in Italy under Mussolini, to which the Italian armies would be subordinate. In effect it amounted to the total military control of Italy by the Germans.

THE FASCIST GRAND COUNCIL

At a subsequent meeting of the Italy's Fascist Grand Council, Mussolini mentioned nothing about an armistice. Instead, the Council insisted that removing the Duce was the only way to put an end to Italy's suffering. It had not met since December 1939, when it had opted for neutrality in the European war, but given the grave situation that was

ABOVE RIGHT Italy's experiment in Fascism, led by the incompetent Benito Mussolini, was devastating for the country.

Eyewitness

THE BRITISH PRIME MINISTER SUMMED UP ITALY'S FASCIST LEADER THUS:

'Thus ended Mussolini's 21-years' dictatorship in Italy, during which he had raised the Italian people from the Bolshevism into which they might have sunk in 1919 to a position in Europe such as Italy had never held before.

His fatal mistake was the declaration of war on France and Great Britain following Hitler's victories in June 1940. Had he not done this he could well have maintained Italy in a balancing position, courted and rewarded by both sides and deriving an unusual wealth and prosperity from the struggles of other countries. Even when the issue of the war became certain, Mussolini would have been welcomed by the Allies. He had much to give to shorten its course.

Instead he took the wrong turning. He never understood the strength of Britain, nor the long-enduring qualities of island resistance and seapower. Thus he marched to ruin.'

---

unfolding on Sicily Mussolini had little choice but to agree. The council was convened for 24 July. The proposal put before its members was that supreme command of the armed forces should revert to King Victor Emmanuel (from whom it had been taken by Mussolini in 1940). The meeting began in the afternoon and went on into the early hours of the next day when Mussolini stated that handing over military powers to the king would mean his retirement from politics. The motion was carried 19 to 11.

The council stated that Mussolini himself should inform the king of the decision it had taken, which he did later on 25 July. The Duce was further humiliated when the king informed him that Marshal Badoglio would form a government to succeed him and after the meeting the dictator was arrested. Italian Fascism had come to an end.

The Badoglio government lasted six weeks, after which German forces occupied the country and its members fled south to Allied-controlled territory. Mussolini was eventually rescued by German commandos in a daring operation on 12 September, thereafter being established by Hitler as the head of a fascist puppet state in northern Italy.

THE INVASION OF ITALY

DATE

3–9 September, 1943

SUMMARY

British and U.S. troops landed in southern Italy expecting a relatively easy campaign, but the Germans reacted quickly to blunt the Allied strike.

LOCATION

Southern Italy

Buoyed by the speedy and relatively bloodless victory on Sicily, Allied planners began preparing for an amphibious invasion of the Italian mainland, which was authorised by General Eisenhower on 16 August, 1943. The British Eighth Army would land across from the Strait of Messina between 1 and 4 September in an operation codenamed Baytown, to tie down enemy forces that might interfere with the assault by the U.S. Fifth Army further north. The American operation, codenamed Avalanche, would take place on 9 September in the Salerno area.

But the Allies had underestimated the German response. With the Italians wavering, Hitler appointed Field Marshal Albert Kesselring Commander-in-Chief South, responsible for defending southern Italy. To do so he had General Heinrich von Vietinghoff's German Tenth Army and the unreliable Italian Seventh Army. The latter withdrew when the Eighth Army landed on 3 September and the Italian Badoglio government signed a secret armistice agreement the same day (the Italians formally surrendered to the Allies on 8 September). The Germans, already in position, moved quickly to disarm their former allies.

DRIVING THE PANZERS BACK

The Allies, as they had on Sicily, possessed overwhelming air and naval supremacy but wherever they landed they would encounter shallow beaches overlooked by mountains. The Allies had hoped that there would be light or no resistance to the landings but when General Mark Clark's U.S. Fifth Army landed on 9 September the 16th Panzer Division immediately engaged it, with its artillery on the high ground overlooking the beaches. Allied warships and aircraft reduced the division to 35 operational tanks by nightfall, forcing its commander to withdraw the division inland.

On 10 and 11 September, Vietinghoff rushed more units to the Salerno area so that Clark's men were facing six enemy divisions. A German attack on 13 September nearly reached the sea but intense Allied naval and air attacks over the following days forced the enemy back.

Baytown went more smoothly and by 14 September the Eighth Army was advancing along Italy's eastern coast. By the end of September the Allies had 190,000 troops ashore and were advancing north. In response Kesselring established a number of defence lines that not only halted the Allied advance but also turned the war in Italy into a grim battle of attrition. The Gustav and Gothic lines in particular made a lasting impression on the Allied soldiers who had to breach them.

ABOVE An African-American division of U.S. Army engineers clears mines from a beach at Viareggio, Italy. The Germans had made extensive defensive preparations ahead of the Allied invasion.

USING THE TERRAIN

The Germans never had the men or resources in Italy to turn their defensive lines into anything resembling the Maginot Line in France, but by making use of the hilly terrain and by sighting artillery and anti-tank guns, machine guns and mines expertly they exacted a heavy toll on Allied units. German strongpoints of artillery, mortars and machine-gun nests, surrounded by mines positioned on high points, were able to dominate the battlefield. A favoured tactic was to position them along river lines so overlapping fields of fire covered the whole front. German engineers blew up dozens of bridges as they withdrew north, which meant Allied engineers had to rebuild them. This further slowed the advance.

The first defensive position was the Barbara Line, a hastily built number of strongpoints along the River Volturno, 40km (25 miles) north of Naples. The second line, the Bernhard Line, extended east from the coast to Monte Camino, Monte Maggiore and Monte Sammucro. The strongest of the three, the Gustav Line, was 19.2km (12 miles) north of the Bernhard Line and anchored on Monte Cassino and the Garigliano and Rapido rivers.

It was not until mid-January 1944 that the Allies had broken through the first two defence lines and were facing the Gustav Line. It would take another five months of hard fighting before they would breach this line of interlocking bunkers and fortifications. The 'soft underbelly' of Europe was proving a very tough nut to crack.

U.S. FORCES LAND ON THE GILBERT ISLANDS

DATE
....
20 November, 1943

SUMMARY
....
The American conquest of the Gilbert Islands involved one of the fiercest battles of the Pacific War, on the small island of Betio in Tarawa Atoll.

LOCATION
....
Gilbert Islands, central Pacific

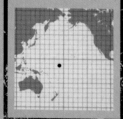

One of the results of the Trident Conference was an agreement to intensify the war against Japan, which entailed attacking the Marshall Islands in the central Pacific while simultaneously continuing the offensive against the Japanese base at Rabaul. But the U.S. Central Pacific campaign would open not with an assault on the Marshalls but an attack on the Gilbert Islands.

The Marshalls group consisted of 32 atolls and separate islands, arranged in two parallel chains over a distance of 555km (350 miles). The Japanese had administered them since World War I and Tokyo had embarked on a programme of their fortification in 1940. The staff of Admiral Chester Nimitz, Commander-in-Chief, Pacific Ocean Areas, therefore believed it was more logical to assault the Gilbert Islands first, a group of 16 islands and atolls southeast of the Marshalls. The Japanese had occupied the Gilberts since December 1941, so it was felt that they were more lightly defended, an assumption that was very wide of the mark.

THE FIRST AMPHIBIOUS ASSAULT

....

The assault on the Gilberts, codenamed Operation Galvanic, was the first large-scale amphibious assault in the Pacific War and provided the Americans with some hard-learned lessons. Nimitz established the U.S. Fifth Fleet, under Admiral Raymond A. Spruance, to invade the Gilberts and undertake subsequent operations in the central Pacific region. Not every island and atoll would be taken; small garrisons would be bypassed and starved into surrender when the Americans closed their supply lines. The troops assigned to capture the Gilberts were part of U.S. Marine Major-General Holland M. Smith's V Amphibious Corps: the battle-tested 2nd Marine Division and the 'green' U.S. Army 27th Infantry Division. The Marines were tasked with taking Tarawa Atoll; the 27th Infantry Division would capture Makin Atoll.

On 20 November the first wave of 6,500 U.S. Army troops landed on Butaritari Island following a naval bombardment. The Americans quickly learned that air and naval bombardments did not necessarily kill all the defenders, because the 800 Japanese naval infantry defending Butaritari emerged from cover and manned their defensive positions. They also learned that Japanese soldiers would often fight to the death rather than surrender and every inch of an island had to be painstakingly cleared.

A SINGLE JAPANESE SURVIVOR

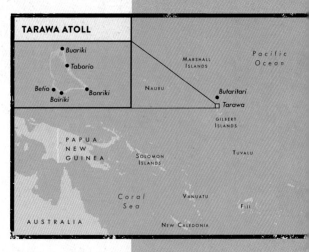

It took three days of heavy fighting before Makin was secured, during which the U.S. Army suffered 218 casualties, 64 of them fatalities. Only one Japanese soldier survived, along with 105 Korean labourers. The U.S. Navy lost 43 killed and 19 wounded on board the battleship USS *Mississippi* when a turret exploded and 644 ratings killed when the escort carrier USS *Liscome Bay* was sunk.

On 20 November the 2nd Marine Division assaulted the beaches of Betio Island in Tarawa Atoll. Rear-Admiral Keiji Shibasaki's Japanese garrison comprised 3,000 naval infantry and 600 Korean labourers, who had built a maze of solidly constructed bunkers dug into the coral and protected by log barriers and barbed wire. There was also a reef offshore that enhanced the Japanese defences.

The island was subjected to a massive naval bombardment but many of the shells, fired at a flat trajectory, glanced off the bunkers. The first wave of amphibious tractors traversed the reef and landed on the island but the following landing craft got stuck on the coral, forcing the Marines to wade ashore in chest-deep water while being raked by enemy machine-gun fire. Nevertheless the Marines pressed on and by dusk on 20 November, 3,500 had established a narrow bridgehead on the island 270m (300 yards) deep. Casualties had been high: 1,500 Marines had been killed or wounded.

On the second day the Marines brought artillery and a few tanks ashore and cleared the western end of Betio. On 22 November a Japanese counterattack was halted. The next day the Marines pushed on, reaching the eastern tip of the island and killing 4,500 Japanese in the process. Betio was secure. Fewer than 150 of the enemy surrendered, most of them Korean labourers. The 2nd Marine Division had lost almost 1,000 dead and 2,000 wounded. The Gilberts had been taken at a high cost.

ABOVE The Gilbert Islands was a first step in driving the Japanese back towards their home islands and provided a steep learning curve: U.S. commanders made important changes to subsequent amphibious landings.

LONG-RANGE FIGHTER ESCORTS ARE INTRODUCED

DATE

1 December, 1943

SUMMARY

The first operational sortie of the North American P-51 Mustang, a fighter that changed the course of the air war over Europe.

LOCATION

Western Europe

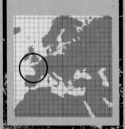

The U.S. 354th Fighter Group arrived in England from America in November 1943. Its equipment and personnel were assigned to Boxted operational sortie in the European theatre of operations (ETO). They took off at 14:29 hours, flew over Belgium and the Pas de Calais before touching down at 15:49 hours, one aircraft having sustained flak damage. There was nothing remarkable about the mission aside from its being conducted by North American P-51B Mustang fighters, aircraft that would single-handedly transform the air war over Europe.

WAITING TO STRIKE

United States Army Air Force (USAAF) daylight bomber raids in the ETO had often incurred heavy losses in both aircraft and crews. The bombers did have fighter escorts but they did not have the range to offer protection for the whole journey. The farthest extent was the city of Aachen, just inside Germany's western border, at which point the fighters had to turn back. *Luftwaffe* pilots were well aware of the Republic P-47 Thunderbolt and Lockheed P-38 Lightning escort fighters and simply waited for them to turn for home before attacking the now vulnerable bombers with Messerschmitt Bf-109 and Focke-Wulf Fw-190 fighters. The Americans believed that grouping bombers together so they could bring all their defensive armament to bear on enemy fighters would solve the problem. It did not.

The answer lay in the P-51 Mustang, though at first the aircraft did not appear to be suitable for the task. Fitted with an Allison powerplant engine it gave mediocre performance, but when equipped with a British Rolls-Royce Merlin engine, as used in Spitfire fighters, its performance increased tremendously. For example, a Mustang powered by a Merlin had a speed of 705km/h (441mph) at 9,144m (30,000ft), 160km/h (100mph) faster than earlier Mustang models. The Merlin-equipped Mustang became the Mk III in RAF service and the P-51B and P-51C in USAAF service.

Eyewitness

U.S. PILOT WILLIAM LYONS FLEW THE P-51D
ON ESCORT MISSIONS IN THE ETO.

'There are no gauges for the two 110-gallon [416-litre]
external wing tanks. Pilots have to estimate their use-up
rates during each mission. My method is to run off each
external tank, switching them every 15 minutes on the way
to the target—to keep from flying right- or left-wing
heavy—and use all the gas I can from the two externals
before drawing on the internal tanks. The internal tanks
are strictly for combat and getting home. Before combat, I
must jettison both externals and switch to an internal tank,
so that the Mustang can compete with Messerschmitt Me-109s
or Focke-Wulf Fw-190s. With external tanks still attached,
the P-51 is slower and less manoeuvrable, a sitting duck.'

Production of the re-engined Mustang was ramped up and the first
P-51s began arriving at Eighth Army Air Force bases in England at
the end of 1943. The powerful Merlin was not the only reason the
Mustang was an outstanding aircraft. Its laminar wings, aerodynamic
'smoothing', and armament made it a formidable opponent, but the
addition of two 567-litre (150-gallon) external drop tanks meant it
could fly as far as 4,160km (2,600 miles) without the need to refuel.
This gave it the range to escort U.S. bombers all the way to a target
and back. Not only that, the Mustang could also engage the enemy and
shoot him out of the sky in the process. The definitive version of the
Mustang was the P-51D, which had a 'teardrop' canopy and an
armament of six 12.7mm air-cooled machine guns.

By the time of the first USAAF heavy bomber strike against Berlin
in March 1944 there were 175 P-51s in the ETO. When the war ended in
May 1945 Mustangs had destroyed 4,950 enemy aircraft, making them
the highest-scoring U.S. fighter in the ETO. In all 15,469 P-51s had
been built by 1946. The Truman Senate War Investigating Committee
(formed in 1941 to identify and rectify problems in U.S. war production)
in 1944 described the P-51 Mustang as 'the most aerodynamically
perfect pursuit plane in existence'.

The growing industrial and military might of the USA provided the resources for the Allied nations to wage a war of attrition against both Germany and Japan throughout 1944, while on the Eastern Front the colossus that was the Red Army literally ground down the German army and its eastern European allies. Germany itself was pounded night and day by massed fleets of Allied bombers, and in the Pacific, Japan was slowly being strangled by a U.S. naval blockade. American ships and aircraft also inflicted a number of crippling defeats on Japan's armed forces, in the Marshall Islands, in the Philippine Sea, and at Leyte Gulf.

In Europe, the second front became a reality with the D-Day landings, and on the Eastern Front the Red Army destroyed Army Group Centre during its Operation Bagration. Seeing the devastation that was engulfing their country, a group of German officers tried to assassinate Hitler. Their failure ensured that the war in Europe would continue.

1944

OPERATION CARPETBAGGER

DATE
....
January 1944

SUMMARY
....
Air drops to
Resistance fighters
in German-occupied
Europe formed an
integral part of
preparations for
the D-Day landings.

LOCATION
....
Western Europe

Under the control of the Office of Strategic Services (OSS), Operation Carpetbagger was a mission beginning in January 1944 to deliver supplies to Resistance groups in enemy-occupied territory, to deliver personnel to liaise with and organise Resistance groups, and occasionally to evacuate personnel back to Britain. It formed part of Allied preparations for the D-Day landings that would take place in the summer of 1944.

THE LIBERATORS

To drop the supplies the OSS used B-24 Liberator four-engine bombers of the 801st Bombardment Group (the aircraft chosen because of their long range and spacious fuselage), flying from Harrington, a former RAF base in Northamptonshire (when the unit received additional squadrons in August 1944, it was redesignated the 492nd Bombardment Group). The aircraft flew at night, avoiding contact with the enemy when possible because the priority was to deliver the cargoes they were carrying. These included 'Joes' (agents), supply containers, propaganda leaflets and passengers. Agents would board an aircraft wearing civilian clothes and would be padded with latex foam to cushion their landing. An 80-year-old woman made one parachute drop from a Carpetbagger B-24.

Altitude rarely exceeded 2,134m (7,000ft) for flights, dropping to 610m (2,000ft) or lower when approaching the target in an effort to evade radar detection. The majority of Carpetbagger operations were made when the moon was out to make the ground visible to the aircraft's navigator and bombardier. Non-moon flights were made with the use of special navigation equipment, such as the 'Rebecca' airborne transceiver, S-Phone two-way radio system and radio altimeter. When dropping containers the aircraft descended to an altitude of 122–183m (400–600ft) and reduced speed to 208km/h (130mph) or less to minimise the chances of the containers being smashed when they hit the ground.

ABOVE Those B-24 Liberators used in Operation Carpetbagger were repurposed and painted black as an anti-detection measure.

NIGHT FLIGHTS

....

Under guidance from RAF personnel the B-24s were modified for nighttime drops. The ball turret was removed and replaced with a hole lined with smooth metal, through which agents and supplies not in containers were dropped. When not in use the hole was covered by a circular plywood door. The B-24s were also painted black to evade enemy searchlights. By mid-June 1944 the 801st Bombardment Group had 54 B-24s modified for Carpetbagger missions and eventually 80 B-24s were modified for Carpetbagger work. In addition, the group also flew Douglas A-26 Invaders, Douglas C-47 Dakotas and British de Havilland Mosquitoes on Carpetbagger missions.

Beginning in January 1944 the USAAF dropped supplies to Resistance groups in France, Norway, Belgium and Holland in the run-up to D-Day and after. The busiest month was July 1944 when B-24s dropped 4680 containers, 2,909 packages, 1,378 bundles of leaflets (to disguise what they were really doing) and 62 agents to Resistance groups that were now supporting Allied forces ashore after D-Day.

Flights to support French, Dutch and Belgian groups ended in September 1944 when large areas of those countries had been liberated. Beginning in January 1945 there were supply drops to groups operating in Norway and Denmark, countries still under Nazi occupation.

By the end of the war the Carpetbaggers had completed 1,860 missions, delivering over 20,000 containers, 11,000 packages and 1,000 airborne troops to aid Resistance forces in enemy territory. The price paid was 25 Liberators lost, eight so badly damaged that they were withdrawn from service, and 208 aircrew killed. But the airdrops allowed the French Resistance to disrupt German units and movements prior to D-Day.

THE GUSTAV LINE IS BREACHED

DATE

January–May 1944

SUMMARY

The savage battle to pierce the German Gustav Line required no less than four Allied offensives and five months of bitter fighting before it succeeded.

LOCATION

Central Italy

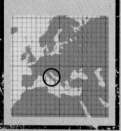

In January 1944 U.S. troops landed behind German lines at Anzio and the U.S. Fifth Army was ordered to link up with the beachhead. Doing so meant breaching the German Gustav Line, which lay along the Garigliano and Rapido rivers. The British Eighth Army, commanded by Lieutenant-General Sir Oliver Leese, would support the operation by crossing the River Sangro and capturing Pescara. In the centre of the Gustav Line lay the monastery of Monte Cassino, which would enter military folklore.

OPERATIONS BEGIN

The first Allied assault began on 17 January, the attacks failing to dislodge German troops from the heights of the Liri Valley that lay beyond the rivers. By 26 January, however, U.S. and Free French units had gained a precarious foothold on the northeastern slopes of Monte Cassino, on top of which was a Benedictine monastery.

The second attempt to breach the Gustav Line was undertaken by the New Zealand Corps, commanded by Lieutenant-General Sir Bernard Freyberg. German troops had been spotted in the monastery so Allied bombers pounded it, reducing it to rubble, into which German paratroopers infiltrated. The Allied attack commenced on 15 February, Freyberg's men suffering heavy casualties. Although they took part of the town of Cassino their high losses meant the offensive stalled.

The terrain over which the two sides were fighting was a defender's dream. Monte Cassino itself dominated the surrounding countryside and looked down on the town of Cassino. But the Germans occupied other high points, such as Castle Hill behind the town, on top of which was Point 193. Then there was Point 435 on the slopes of Monte Cassino itself, Point 593 1km (⅗ mile) to the northwest, and Point 445 further north.

For the third assault Freyberg's men had massive air and artillery support. The aerial bombardment began on the morning of 15 March and was followed by an artillery barrage that fired 200,000 shells on the

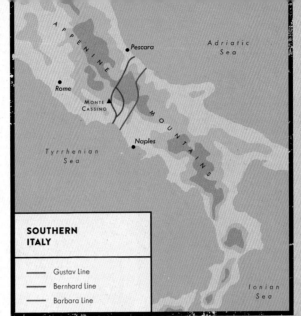

town and on Monte Cassino. Then the New Zealand troops and tanks attacked, the 2nd New Zealand Division taking Point 193 and the 4th Indian Division advancing to within 400m (1,300ft) of the monastery itself. But once again German paratroopers inflicted high casualties on Allied units, with the result that the offensive was halted on 22 March.

THE FOURTH OFFENSIVE

....

The New Zealand Corps, exhausted, was withdrawn. The fourth offensive against the Gustav Line involved the British Eighth Army and U.S. Fifth Army, the troops of General Anders' Polish II Corps being given the task of taking Monte Cassino itself. Preceded by the customary air and artillery bombardments, the offensive began on 11 May, 1944. While the Poles and German paratroopers engaged in a savage battle the British XIII Corps severed the line of communications with Monte Cassino on 17 May by reaching the Via Casilina. Simultaneously French and U.S. units had finally managed to breach the Gustav Line north and south of Cassino. The German Tenth Army, under relentless Allied air and ground attacks, had lost 40 percent of its combat strength in three days. Kesselring, the German commander-in-chief, therefore gave orders on 17 May that the entire Cassino front was to be evacuated.

The battle for the Cassino sector in May 1944 had cost the Germans 25,000 men, while the Poles had lost 1,000 killed in the fighting for Monte Cassino alone. The losses on both sides during the battles for the Gustav Line amounted to 200,000 killed and wounded. As Major Rudolf Böhmler, German 1st Parachute Division, stated: 'One must appreciate that the fighting at Cassino was mountain warfare; and in mountain warfare the inevitable rule is that whoever is master of the hill is master of the valley'.

ABOVE The Gustav Line, the most heavily fortified of the defensive lines, took Allied forces five months to breach.

OPERATION FLINTLOCK

DATE

31 January—
24 February, 1944

SUMMARY

The U.S. conquest of
the Marshall Islands
put into practice
lessons learned at
Tarawa and brought
the war ever closer
to the Japanese
home islands.

LOCATION

Marshall Islands

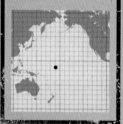

The Marshall Islands formed part of the outer perimeter of the Japanese Empire and as such had to be taken as part of the American drive towards the Philippines and the Japanese home islands. At their heart was Kwajalein Atoll, which was the U.S. objective. Admiral Nimitz also agreed to the seizure of the lightly held Majuro Atoll to provide an anchorage to allow the fleet to get closer to Kwajalein.

LESSONS LEARNED

For the assault on the Marshalls, codenamed Operation Flintlock, Nimitz assembled overwhelming firepower. Admiral Raymond Spruance commanded the U.S. Fifth Fleet, Admiral Richmond Turner the Expeditionary Force, and Lieutenant-General Holland Smith the Expeditionary Troops, who would make the island assaults. The troops were from the 4th Marine Division, the U.S. Army's 7th Infantry Division, and a battalion from the U.S. Army's 27th Infantry Division. The plan was for the 7th Infantry Division to assault Kwajalein Island; the Marines would land on the islands of Roi and Namur, and the 27th Infantry's battalion would take Majuro.

After the bloodbath at Tarawa the Americans used Operation Flintlock to test new tactics and equipment for island assaults to minimise casualties. In addition to the usual heavy aerial and naval bombardments to 'soften up' the enemy, at Kwajalein, Roi and Namur U.S. troops would seize nearby inlets before the landings to set up field artillery to support the beach assaults. Armoured amphibious tractors – LVT(A)s – armed with 37mm cannon would form part of the assault waves and would also ferry supplies and ammunition to the beaches. The new amphibious truck, the DUKW, would also be used for this purpose.

The Japanese withdrew their troops from Majuro before the Americans arrived but the other objectives were strongly defended. There were 2,000 troops and 1,000 labourers on Roi and Namur and 1,750 soldiers and 5,000 labourers on Kwajalein.

The American assault began on 31 January, the operation on Kwajalein going largely as planned. Two U.S. battleships positioned 1,800m (2,000 yards) offshore pounded Japanese defences before the assault went in. The U.S. troops were fiercely opposed once ashore but fanatical Japanese infantry charges were defeated by heavy firepower. The majority of the garrison was wiped out at the cost of 173 killed and 793 U.S. wounded. The price of taking Roi and Namur was higher – 313 dead and 502 wounded – but of the defenders fewer than 100 survived to become prisoners of war.

CATCHPOLE

Nimitz then looked to the next objective: the massive natural anchorage of Eniwetok Atoll in the westernmost Marshall Islands. Once again a combined assault force of U.S. Marines and U.S. Army soldiers would attack the three main islands in the atoll: Eniwetok, Parry and Engbi. The Japanese garrisons were relatively small – 300 on Parry and Engbi and 600 on Eniwetok – but they put up the usual fanatical resistance. However, U.S. tactics and firepower meant there was only one outcome: the assaults began on 17 February and were over by the 24th.

Capturing these islands, codenamed Catchpole, cost the Marines 254 dead and 555 wounded and the U.S. Army 94 dead and 311 wounded. Only 66 of the Japanese defenders of Eniwetok remained alive after the fighting. As soon as Eniwetok was in U.S. hands engineers began to construct an airstrip from which long-range bombers such as the B-24 could operate. The home islands were getting nearer.

Parallel to the Marshall operations was an attack on the major Japanese naval base at Truk, 1241km (776 miles) southwest of Eniwetok, by 500 aircraft of Vice-Admiral Marc Mitscher's Task Force 58. On 17 and 18 February his carrier aircraft put the Japanese airfields out of action, shot down two-thirds of the defending fighters (270 aircraft), and sank 194,056 tonnes (191,000 tons) of shipping. It was another devastating defeat for the Japanese.

ABOVE U.S. forces unload supplies onto the beach at Kwajalein after the initial assault had established a beachhead.

THE BATTLE FOR KOHIMA AND IMPHAL

DATE

7 March, 1944

SUMMARY

The abortive Japanese offensive in northern Burma marked the beginning of the Allied reconquest of the country.

LOCATION

Northern Burma

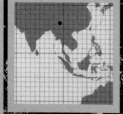

By the end of 1943 the Japanese were aware that the British Fourteenth Army was nearing the end of its preparations to launch an invasion of Burma from India. To forestall this the commander of the Japanese Burma Area Army, General Masakazu Kawabe, decided that the Fifteenth Army should launch a limited offensive to capture the British forward supply base at Imphal.

The Japanese plan involved the 33rd Division cutting off the 17th Indian Division at Tiddim and forcing the British to commit their reserves to rescue it. At the same time the 31st and 15th Divisions would cross the River Chindwin further north and capture the towns of Kohima and Imphal. The latter had to be captured quickly because the mountainous terrain and dense jungle that covered much of the area of operations meant that it would be impossible to supply the divisions attacking the British.

OPERATION U-GO

Operation U-Go, the codename of the Japanese offensive, began on 7 March with assaults to cut the Tiddim–Imphal road. The 85,000 men of the Fifteenth Army made good progress. The Japanese cut the Tiddim road on 14 March as the British IV Corps began to concentrate around Imphal. The next day the Japanese 15th and 31st Divisions crossed the River Chindwin and advanced to cut the Imphal–Kohima road. Japanese troops displayed their customary fanatical courage and tenacity and by 29 March had cut the road, signalling the start of the siege of Imphal. But the Japanese had made a fatal error because they gambled on capturing British stores after a brief campaign. But Imphal did not fall.

As the siege went on IV Corps received reinforcements flown in by the RAF. When the battle had ended the RAF had flown in 18,824 tons of supplies and 12,561 troops and evacuated 13,000 casualties and 43,000 noncombatants. But the Japanese had no aerial supply and by

May their food supplies were running out
– without captured supplies the threat of
starvation was very real. By 4 April the
British IV Corps was concentrated
around Imphal and its commander,
General Geoffrey Scoones, could now
begin a battle of attrition against the
Japanese.

Further north on the same day the
Japanese reached Kohima and quickly
established strong defensive positions
around the now cut-off town. The British
launched a series of desperate attempts
to relieve the besieged garrison. The
fighting was at close quarters and intense
and throughout May the British 33rd
Corps launched a series of attacks, many
of which were repulsed. However, as at
Imphal Japanese supply problems meant
troops were running out of ammunition and food (according to Japanese
plans Imphal should have fallen and the troops at Kohima would be
receiving captured British supplies).

On 31 May what was left of the Japanese 31st Division began to
withdraw from Kohima. The Battle of Kohima ended on 3 June and 33rd
Corps prepared to advance towards Imphal. Troops of the British 2nd
Division reached the defenders on 22 June, though bitter fighting
continued around the town. Indeed, the struggle would continue until
18 July when the Japanese High Command called off the offensive.

The Fifteenth Army had suffered 53,000 dead or wounded and British
casualties totalled 17,000. Imphal and Kohima had been major Japanese
defeats and made the reconquest of Burma by the British possible.
The ordeal of the Fifteenth Army was not over, however, as the war
correspondent Shizuo Maruyama reported: 'We had no ammunition,
no clothes, no food, no guns … the men were barefoot and ragged, and
threw away everything except canes to help them walk. At Kohima we
were starved and then crushed.'

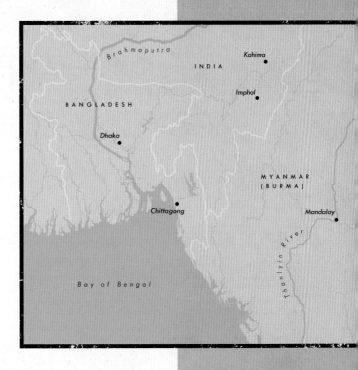

ABOVE Japanese forces
moved to cut the route
between Imphal and Kohima
before taking both. The lack
of a supply route to their
troops allowed Allied forces
simply to bide their time and
wait for the enemy to run out
of food and munitions.

OPERATION ICHIGO

MOVING INTO WESTERN CHINA

DATE

19 April–
31 December, 1944

SUMMARY

The Japanese
campaign mortally
wounded the Chinese
Nationalists and
paved the way
for the Chinese
Communists to assume
power in China after
the war.

LOCATION

Western China

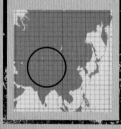

By early 1944 the Japanese were suffering major defeats in the Pacific but in China the Japanese Imperial Army was undefeated after seven years of the Sino-Japanese War. In the spring of 1944, partly as a result of American victories in the Pacific, General Yasuji Okamura's China Expeditionary Army began preparations to launch a major offensive into western China. The Japanese occupied the eastern third of the country and controlled all the country's ports and main railways and roads. The offensive, codenamed Operation Ichigo, would be the largest military operation in the history of the Japanese Imperial Army and was designed to open a north–south corridor from Korea to Indochina, thus providing an overland alternative to the sea lanes that were now the domain of Allied submarines, warships and aircraft. The Japanese also wished to weaken Chiang's Nationalist Army and capture the 12 airfields that were being used by the U.S. Fourteenth Air Force in Nationalist territory.

After seven years of fighting the Japanese, Chiang Kai-shek's Nationalist government was in dire straits despite huge amounts of American Lend–Lease aid that flowed into the country. President Roosevelt sent advisers, who discovered that the Nationalist government and army were riddled with incompetence and corruption. Lacking modern weaponry and bereft of tanks and aircraft, Chiang's armies were always inferior to their Japanese opponents.

Some 500,000 Japanese troops were committed to Ichigo, which began on 19 April in Henan Province. The Nationalists had 34 divisions in the area

RIGHT Chiang Kai-shek photographed in 1940. By 1944, his Nationalist forces, indeed the government itself, was at the point of collapse.

but they disintegrated in the face of the Japanese onslaught. Within a month the Japanese had captured Luoyang and cleared the railway corridor between Peking (Beijing) and Wuhan. The offensive then struck into Hunan Province, the largest rice-producing area in China and the economic heartland of Chiang's government. This was a deliberate plan by the Japanese to destroy crops and worsen the Nationalist food situation. When Nationalist soldiers fled before the Japanese, local peasants, tired of the corruption of Chiang's officials, disarmed and shot them before welcoming the Japanese as liberators.

ABOVE The Imperial Japanese Army making inroads on their way towards Luoyang.

The city of Changsha fell to the Japanese on 18 June and Ichigo then expanded into Guangxi Province in September, capturing Guilin, Liuzhou and Nanning, all sites of U.S. airbases. The southeastern thrust of Ichigo, designed to open the Hengyang–Guangzhou rail link, had been completed by October and the final phase of the offensive, to secure the rail link to Nanning and south to the border of Indochina, had been completed by the end of the year.

A FATAL BLOW

Operation Ichigo had mortally wounded the Nationalist cause in China. The army, the foundation of Nationalist power, had been shattered: by the end of the Japanese offensive 750,000 Nationalist soldiers had been either killed, rendered combat-ineffective, or had deserted. In addition to the loss in manpower the Nationalists lost a quarter of their factories, Guilin was burned to the ground, and Changsha, the largest city in Hunan Province, was left a depopulated ruin. The Japanese are estimated to have suffered 100,000 casualties during Ichigo, many of their units outrunning their supply lines and having to plunder the land they were moving through.

The real winner of Operation Ichigo was the Chinese Communist Party, which took no part in the fighting. But with the Nationalists politically, militarily and economically broken and the Japanese still the hated invaders and occupiers, it was Mao's Communists who became the natural leaders of the Chinese people. From their northern powerbase they increased their strength and influence. In 1937 the Communists had 40,000 troops; by 1945 this figure had increased to one million regulars and two million militia.

U.S. FORCES LAND ON OMAHA BEACH

DATE

....

6 June, 1944

SUMMARY

....

The Western Allies
opened a second
front in Europe to
hasten the defeat
of Nazi Germany.

LOCATION

....

Normandy, France

Operation Overlord, the Allied invasion of Normandy in the summer of 1944, was a logistical triumph. For the amphibious invasion of France the Allies intended to land 50,000 men in the initial assault drawn from five divisions, and afterward two million men would be shipped to France. Some 138 major warships were used in the landings, with 221 smaller combatants, over 1,000 minesweepers and auxiliary vessels, 4,000 landing ships or craft, 805 merchant ships, 59 blockships and 300 other small craft. In the air 11,000 aircraft (fighters, bombers, transports and gliders) ensured total Allied air superiority. And yet in the final analysis the battle would be won by ordinary soldiers storming ashore to secure the landing beaches and objectives further inland. Victory was not certain, especially on Omaha Beach.

STORMING THE GERMAN FORTRESS

....

Omaha was the only significant beach between the British and Canadian beaches (Gold, Juno and Sword) and the American beach of Utah. It had to be taken to ensure a continuous beachhead but it was a defender's dream. The wide, gently curving beach was 6.4km (4 miles) long and overlooked by cliffs, with only four exits through them. In these gaps were 35 pillboxes filled with German infantry armed with rifles, machine guns and grenades. Along the top of the cliffs were 85 machine-gun posts, while the defenders could also call upon anti-tank guns, artillery and rocket launchers. The Germans had also positioned mined steel obstacles in the water and mines and barbed wire along the shingle bank.

The initial assault was made by two Regimental Combat Teams, made up from the 16th Regiment of the U.S. 1st Infantry Division and the 116th Infantry Regiment of the U.S. 29th Infantry Division. The amphibious assault began at 05:40 hours, the rough seas making the approach to the beach arduous for those on the landing craft. Of the 32 DD amphibious tanks of the 741st Tank Battalion, 30 were sunk immediatley, drowning their crews. The infantry in the landing craft were on their own.

SLAUGHTER ON THE BEACH

Of the nine infantry companies that landed in the first wave, three were decimated by machine-gun fire. Company A, 1st Battalion of the 116th Infantry, landed at 06:30 hours and had 91 killed and almost as many men wounded in the space of a few minutes. Less than 20 men got across the beach. Soon hundreds of soldiers were trapped between the cliffs and the sea, unable to move under murderous enemy fire. At 07:30 hours the second group of assault troops came in at five separate points but fared no better. By noon General Omar Bradley, commander of the U.S. First Army, was considering ordering the evacuation of Omaha but then received a radio report that 'troops formerly pinned down on beaches now advancing up heights behind'. This amazing change in fortunes was due to the raw courage of the U.S. soldiers on Omaha and the officers who led them. In small groups they left the safety of the beach wall or obstacles to charge forward. Crucial to their success were the combat engineers of the U.S. Army's demolition teams who had the task of clearing obstacles. By nightfall over 40 percent of the assault engineers on Omaha were dead or wounded.

The quality of leadership on Omaha was excellent, epitomised by Colonel Taylor of the 16th Infantry Regiment who declared before leading an attack: 'The only people on this beach are the dead and those who are going to die ... now let's get the hell out of here!'

By 15:00 hours the troops on Omaha were fighting their way inland and during the night more infantry and 17 tanks were landed to reinforce the men now digging in on the heights above the beach. Over 3,000 U.S. soldiers had been killed or wounded taking Omaha but it and the other beaches were secure. The Allies had their bridgehead and in the days following were able to expand it, the Germans being unable to counter the vast Allied material superiority. The invasion had succeeded.

THE AIR WAR OVER NORMANDY

DATE

6 June–22 August,
1944

SUMMARY

The air support
provided by U.S. and
British aircraft
during the Normandy
campaign condemned
the German army
to defeat.

LOCATION

Normandy, France

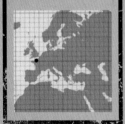

Air superiority was crucial not only to the success of the D-Day
landings but also the subsequent campaign in Normandy in 1944.
Not only did Allied aircraft support the advances of troops, they also
inflicted heavy losses on the German army, losses it could ill afford.
The support of ground forces was the task of the U.S. Ninth Air Force
and the British 2nd Tactical Air Force. Both formations were made up
of fighters, fighter-bombers, light and medium bombers, and transport
aircraft. On June 6, 1944, Major-General Lewis Brereton's Ninth Air
Force possessed 810 fighters, of which 585 were P-47 Thunderbolts.
Air Marshal Sir Arthur Coningham's 2nd Tactical Air Force numbered
1,348 aircraft, including 20 squadrons of Hawker Typhoons. By
comparison *Luftflotte* 3, deployed to defeat the Allies in Normandy,
had just over 800 aircraft in total.

THE THUNDERBOLT

The P-47 Thunderbolt was ideally suited to ground-support operations,
having a sturdy airframe to absorb the battle damage that was
inevitable when conducting low-level attacks. Armed with eight
12.7mm machine guns it could also carry up to 1,136kg (2,500lb) of
externally mounted ordnance. The RAF's Hawker Typhoon was armed
with four 20mm cannon plus underwing rockets. The RAF operated the
so-called 'cabrank system' whereby a group of fighter-bombers, usually
four Typhoons but sometimes an entire squadron, circled a specific
point just behind the front, available to attack a target as soon as a
forward controller on the ground called for support. The availability of
almost immediate air support not only wore down German units, it also
boosted the morale of Allied troops. Once the Americans had launched
their breakout operation, codenamed Cobra, in July 1944, dedicated
flights of close-support aircraft escorted advances by armoured combat
command task forces. In the advancing armoured columns fighter-
bomber pilots were placed in command tanks equipped with air–ground

radios to co-ordinate air attacks.

From June 6 British and American fighter-bombers played an important part in the campaign. On D-Day itself RAF Typhoons mounted continuous attacks on the vehicles of the 21st Panzer Division, the nearest German armoured unit to the invasion beaches. As a result only six tanks and a handful of infantry made it to the coast and proved no threat to the invasion forces. During Operation Cobra more than 400 armoured cover missions were flown. And afterward U.S. ground-support aircraft continued to support ground forces. On 29 July, for example, the P-47 squadrons of the 50th Fighter Group destroyed 46 enemy tanks, over 80 other vehicles, eight horse-drawn guns and killed an estimated 50 German soldiers.

The power of ground-attack aircraft was brutally displayed during the battles in August 1944 when Allied troops had surrounded 20 German divisions in a pocket around Falaise. As the pocket was closed the 2nd Tactical Air Force averaged 1,200 sorties a day, strafing German columns at will with rockets, machine-gun and cannon fire, and bombs. By the time resistance in the pocket ceased on 22 August, 10,000 German soldiers were dead and 50,000 had surrendered. Material losses included 567 tanks, 950 artillery pieces and 7,700 vehicles. To all intents and purposes the German Seventh Army and Fifth Panzer Army had ceased to exist. As had *Luftflotte* 3, which in France lost 931 aircraft on operations against overwhelming Allied aerial superiority.

With the *Luftwaffe* largely absent from the skies in 1944, Allied close-support aircraft were able to roam at will, with inevitable results. From D-Day to the end of the war, for example, P-47 units alone were responsible for the destruction of 86,000 railway carriages, 9,000 locomotives, 6,000 armoured fighting vehicles and 68,000 trucks.

Eyewitness

SERGEANT ERICH BRAUN, 2ND PANZER DIVISION, WAS ON THE RECEIVING END OF RAF TYPHOON FIREPOWER WHEN HIS UNIT WAS TRAPPED IN THE FALAISE POCKET IN AUGUST 1944.

'Anyone dying on top of those rolling steel coffins was just pitched overboard, so that a living man could take his place. The never-ending detonations, soldiers waving at us, begging for help — the dead, their faces still screwed up in agony, huddled everywhere in trenches and shelters — the officers and men who had lost their nerve, burning vehicles from which piercing screams could be heard and men, driven crazy, crying, shouting, swearing, laughing hysterically — and horses, some still harnessed to wagons, screaming terribly, trying to escape the slaughter on the stumps of their hind legs.'

THE BATTLE OF THE PHILIPPINE SEA

DATE

19–20 June, 1944

SUMMARY

The carrier battle destroyed Japanese naval aviation in the Pacific.

LOCATION

The Philippine Sea

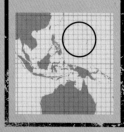

The Japanese High Command saw in the U.S. invasion of the Marianas an opportunity to instigate a decisive engagement against the U.S. Navy in the Pacific. The Japanese were correct in believing that the battle would be decisive, though not in the manner they envisaged. By mid-1944 the U.S. armed forces in the Pacific had become a colossus in terms of resources, manpower and technology, as the Imperial Japanese Navy was to discover to its cost.

OPERATION A-GO

The Japanese plan to destroy the U.S. fleet (Task Force 58) off the Marianas was codenamed Operation A-Go. The 1st Mobile Fleet, commanded by Vice-Admiral Jisaburo Ozawa, earmarked for the operation was a formidable force: the large carriers *Taiho*, *Shokaku* and *Zuikaku*, five smaller carriers, five battleships, including the huge *Yamato* and *Musashi*, 13 cruisers, 27 destroyers and 450 carrier aircraft. But this was not 1941 and many of the pilots were poorly trained and inexperienced. Unfortunately for Ozawa, Vice-Admiral Marc Mitscher's Task Force 58, thanks to the Allies' increasing material wealth, was both larger and more formidable, with 15 carriers, seven fast battleships, 10 cruisers, 60 destroyers, and 902 aircraft operated by well-trained crews.

On 19 June Ozawa's scout aircraft spotted the U.S. fleet, allowing him to dispatch his first wave of aircraft before Mitscher. By the end of the day he would launch 374 aircraft; 130 would return. The aircraft were detected by U.S. radar and

RIGHT U.S. Navy pilot Alexander Vraciu shot down six Japanese aircraft in a single sortie during the Battle of the Philippine Sea.

intercepted by U.S. airmen flying the new, powerfully armed Grumman F6F Hellcat fighter. The result was the 'Great Marianas Turkey Shoot' as the American fliers shot their opponents out of the sky. While his aircraft were being decimated, two of Ozawa's carriers, *Taiho* and *Shokaku*, were sunk by U.S. submarines.

EARLY WARNING

Despite his discomfiture on the day before, on 20 June Ozawa was determined to continue the fight, but his fleet was spotted by U.S. scout aircraft during the afternoon. It was now Mitscher's turn to strike first. Because his ships were close to the Marianas his aircraft would be operating at their maximum range but the prize was worth the risk. He had dispatched 226 aircraft against the Japanese fleet before intelligence reached him that the enemy ships were 440km (275 miles) from Task Force 58, 96km (60 miles) further west than originally reported. Mitscher held back his second wave but the first wave was now already in the air. He did not recall them.

The U.S. aircraft arrived over the 1st Mobile Fleet at 18:30 hours. In the ensuing action as the light faded the carrier *Hiyo* was fatally damaged and two oilers sunk. Four other carriers were damaged plus the battleship *Haruna*, the cruiser *Maya*, the destroyer *Shigure*, and another oiler. In addition, 80 Japanese aircraft were shot down over the 1st Mobile Fleet. Ozawa had started the battle with 473 aircraft; at the end he had only 47 left.

On the return journey in the dark many U.S. aircraft began to go down, some due to damage but most because their fuel had run out. Mitscher ordered his fleet to turn on their lights and searchlights to guide the aircraft back but even so 84 aircraft were lost. After the battle the admiral was criticised for being too defensive in his deployment and keeping his fleet too close to the Marianas instead of moving aggressively towards Ozawa. This would have undoubtedly saved many American aircraft having to ditch in the sea after the battle on 20 June. But in the space of two days Mitscher had not only won a great victory, he had also destroyed the Japanese Imperial Navy's carrier aviation arm.

ABOVE Despite the realisation that many of his aircraft would run out of fuel, Vice-Admiral Mitscher did not recall the first wave. In doing so, he struck a decisive blow in the battle.

OPERATION BAGRATION

DATE

22 June, 1944

SUMMARY

The Soviet offensive destroyed Army Group Centre and brought the Red Army to the gates of Warsaw and the borders of the Third Reich itself.

LOCATION

Central USSR

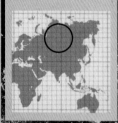

At the beginning of June 1944 the Red Army had liberated the Ukraine, lifted the siege of Leningrad and pushed German armies back towards the Soviet border. There were 1.5 million German troops on the Eastern Front facing 52 armies and 5.5 million Red Army troops. The Soviet High Command – *Stavka* – identified Army Group Centre, which occupied a large enemy salient that extended into the east, as the main target of its summer offensive, codenamed Bagration.

To destroy the German salient the *Stavka* assembled 2.5 million troops, 5,200 tanks, 31,000 artillery pieces, 2,300 Katyusha rocket launchers, 70,000 motor vehicles and 5,300 aircraft. Army Group Centre contained 580,000 troops, 9,500 artillery pieces, 900 tanks and 775 aircraft. Most German units were understrength, ill equipped, and had shaky morale after almost continuous retreats since July 1943. In contrast Red Army units were well equipped, armed, and, at long last, well led.

EARLY GAINS

Bagration opened on 22 June preceded by massive air and artillery strikes, and immediately made rapid gains. German units were obliterated in the face of the Soviet onslaught. Vitebsk fell on 25 June and Minsk on 3 July, in the process trapping 100,000 troops of the Fourth Panzer Army. Five days later the army had been destroyed, 60,000 soldiers being killed and the rest being captured. By the end of July the Red Army was on Polish soil and was seemingly unstoppable. But the great victories were bought at a high price. By 31 July, the midpoint of Bagration, the Red Army had incurred the following casualties during the offensive: 1st Baltic Front, 41,000 killed and 125,000 wounded; 1st Belorussian Front, 65,000 killed and 215,000 wounded; 2nd Belorussian Front, 26,000 killed and 90,000 wounded; and 3rd Belorussian Front, 45,000 killed and 155,000 wounded.

LEFT July 1944. German prisoners of war are marched through Moscow on their way to POW camps.

THE RED ARMY MARCHES ON

As the offensive continued it began to affect other sectors of the Eastern Front, and not to Germany's advantage. At the beginning of August the Finns, themselves under Red Army attack, began to seek ways to escape Berlin's clutches and agreed a cease-fire with Moscow on 25 August. In the Baltic Hitler refused to sanction the retreat of Army Group North, with the result that it was cut off in the Courland Pocket (there to remain until the end of the war). In the south the Soviet Lvov–Sandomir Offensive opened on 13 July against Army Group North Ukraine (German and Hungarian divisions). On 20 August the Jassy–Kishinev Offensive began when the Soviet 2nd and 3rd Ukrainian Fronts launched a blistering attack on Romanian and German divisions. The Axis units crumbled and on 31 August the Red Army occupied Bucharest and then advanced west over the Carpathian Mountains into Hungary and south into Bulgaria. These offensives would lead to Germany's Axis allies – Bulgaria, Hungary and Romania – deserting the Nazi cause.

In addition to losing its Axis allies Berlin also suffered huge losses in manpower and materiel, losses that it could not afford. Between 1 June and 30 November the *Wehrmacht* lost 903,000 men on the Eastern Front. The Red Army was positioned to conquer the remainder of Poland, Hungary and Austria in a single campaign. The Red Army had also lost hundreds of thousands of men and in an effort to reduce manpower losses its High Command introduced doctrine that made more use of artillery, armour and air power in assaults. Soviet units halted to rest and recuperate in preparation for the great 1945 offensive that would be launched against Berlin itself.

THE ARSENAL OF DEMOCRACY EMERGES

DATE

July 1944

SUMMARY

The United States became the power-house of Allied armies, air forces and navies in World War II, producing more war material than any other nation in the world.

LOCATION

USA

In a speech in December 1940 President Roosevelt made a call to arms to support the Allied nations in their fight against Nazi Germany. He implored Americans to stand up as the 'arsenal of democracy'. It was a call that his people answered with gusto. The transformation of the United States from a peacetime economy to a wartime superpower was staggering in its scope and intensity.

ECONOMIC TRANSFORMATION

In 1939 the United States Army numbered fewer than 200,000 men and the U.S. Marines less than 20,000. Many of those troops went on manoeuvres using broomsticks to simulate rifles and trucks to simulate tanks. But America possessed the means to convert its civilian-based industry into a mighty war economy. As soon as the United States entered the war the government's War Production Board immediately halted car production. The U.S. automobile industry employed over 500,000 workers spread across 44 states, with a further seven million people indirectly employed in the industry. By this measure the automotive industry became a major component of the war economy, producing more than 50 percent of all aircraft engines, 33 percent of all machine guns, 80 percent of all tanks and tank parts, one-half the diesel engines and 100 percent of the trucks the U.S. Army used.

The conversion to a wartime economy was in no way a smooth process but after Pearl Harbour the majority of the population was behind the Roosevelt administration, which allowed government directives regarding war work to be implemented with ease. The Department of the Treasury, for example, was able to collect huge sums by extending income tax to almost all working Americans, thus generating funds to finance the war. The American government took in $45 billion in 1945, compared to $8.7 billion in 1941. With the increase in production came a rise in employment. By 1945 the percentage of the labour force in employment was 98.1, with millions of women working in factories.

A GIANT IS BORN

....

Massive conversion of the
industrial base and generous
government funding for infrastructure
construction ensured that the
United States was able to churn
out a prodigious amount of tanks,
ships, aircraft and armaments.
In addition, and crucially, the
American homeland was beyond the
range of enemy bombers. The scale
of production was impressive. In
1943, for example, the United States
manufactured 29,500 tanks, more
in one year than Germany produced
in the entire war. In every category
the United States outproduced its
enemies (and often its allies). The United States produced 97,810
bombers during the war, against Germany's 18,235, and 99,950 fighters
to Germany's 53,727.

ABOVE By the end of the
war, women were a significant
part of the U.S. workforce,
adding to the manufacturing
boom the country enjoyed.

The capacity of the war economy was demonstrated by the building of
the so-called Liberty ships, the merchantmen constructed by shipyards.
Each ship was 135m (441ft) long and 17m (56ft) wide and comprised
250,000 parts that were prefabricated throughout the country in
255-tonne (250-ton) sections and welded together in an average of
45 days. Some 2,710 were completed during the war, allowing the war
materiel produced in U.S. factories to be shipped to the front in North
Africa, Europe and the Pacific (each Liberty ship could carry 2,840
jeeps, 440 tanks or 230 million rounds of rifle ammunition).

In the Pacific the United States outproduced the Japanese in ships
and submarines, giving the U.S. Navy a crucial strategic advantage in
the war. American shipyards built 22 aircraft carriers to Japan's 16; 349
destroyers to the Japan's 63; and 1,337 submarines to Japan's 167.

THE JULY BOMB PLOT

DATE

....

20 July, 1944

SUMMARY

....

The failure of the
assassination attempt
on Hitler ensured
that Germany and
the German people
would face another
10 months of
total war.

LOCATION

....

Berlin, Germany

By July 1944 it was apparent that Nazi Germany would lose the war. The Western Allies had landed in Normandy, and on the Eastern Front the Red Army was making huge advances after opening its summer offensive. To a small group of officers in the German armed forces the removal of Hitler had become a matter of urgency if a negotiated peace was to be achieved. The man who would lead the assassination attempt in July 1944 was Colonel Claus von Stauffenberg, a conservative monarchist who had lost an eye and half of his left hand while fighting in North Africa in 1943. By 1944 he had become deeply disillusioned with Hitler and believed the Führer to be the Antichrist.

VALKYRIE

....

Stauffenberg quickly made contact with anti-Hitler groups through his cousin Count Peter Yorck von Wartenburg and took personal charge of the conspiracy against the Führer. His efforts were given a boost when he was appointed chief of staff to General Friedrich Fromm, commander of the Home Army. This gave him access to conferences at Hitler's various headquarters and Stauffenberg would be the man who would plant a bomb in one such conference to kill Hitler, after which the Home Army would take control of Berlin and other major cities, neutralise Nazi institutions, and proclaim a new government headed by General Ludwig Beck and the ex-Mayor of Leipzig, Carl Goerdeler. The plan was codenamed Valkyrie.

RIGHT Claus von Stauffenberg's promotion gave him access to meetings of Hitler's inner circle.

On 20 July Stauffenberg took a time bomb in his briefcase into a wooden hut at Hitler's East Prussian headquarters at Rastenburg – 'Wolf's Lair'. He placed the briefcase on the floor close to Hitler and then excused himself on the grounds that he had to receive an important telephone call. After he had left the hut Colonel Heinz Brandt moved the briefcase with his leg to make more room and in doing so saved Hitler's life.

The bomb exploded at 12:42 hours, causing the roof to collapse. Stauffenberg observed the explosion from a distance and believed that Hitler had been killed. He then left the compound and flew to Berlin to put Operation Valkyrie in motion. But when he arrived at Bendlerstrasse in Berlin, the proposed centre of the coup, he was shocked to discover that nothing had been done. This was because General Friedrich Olbricht, deputy commander of the Home Army, had heard that Hitler was still alive. His duplicitous commander Fromm now decided to support the Führer and, worse, the wounded Hitler managed to speak to Major Otto Remer, commander of the Berlin Guard Battalion that the conspirators had earmarked to spearhead their rebellion. But now Remer began to crush the revolt.

ABOVE Given the extent of the destruction in the 'Wolf's Lair', it is unsurprising that Stauffenberg believed the Führer to be dead.

RETRIBUTION

Fromm speedily arrested the conspirators and had them shot, including Stauffenberg. General Beck botched a suicide attempt and got a sergeant to finish him off. He was one of the lucky ones. In the days and weeks afterward Nazi retribution got into full swing, all those implicated in the plot being rounded up and subjected to show trials in the People's Court, presided over by the fanatical Nazi Roland Freisler. Stauffenberg's wife and brothers, their children, cousins, aunts and uncles were all taken into custody. Eventually 5,000 people would be executed and 10,000 sent to concentration camps. Field Marshal Rommel, associated with the Bomb Plot, was forced to commit suicide to save his family from retributions (Fromm's double-dealing did not save him: he was arrested, tried, and executed in March 1945).

The failure of the Bomb Plot removed the last possibility of a negotiated end to the war. The fate of the German people was now tied to that of Hitler in a futile war against an unbeatable enemy. Destruction and ruin would be the only outcome.

THE BLOCKADE OF JAPAN

DATE

August 1944

SUMMARY

The U.S. Navy's submarine campaign in the Pacific helped to bring Japan's war effort to its knees and hastened victory in the Pacific War.

LOCATION

Pacific Ocean

The USA's great sea and land victories against Japan in the Pacific War have quite rightly earned their place in military history but the U.S. Navy's submarine campaign against Japanese shipping also warrants praise for its role in decimating the enemy's war-making potential. And when U.S. forces took Guam in August 1944, U.S. submarines based there and on Saipan imposed an almost total naval blockade of Japan.

From the very beginning of the Pacific War President Roosevelt had authorised 'unrestricted submarine warfare' against Japan. The U.S. Navy's prewar War Plan Orange assumed that Japan could be forced to surrender through naval blockade and aerial bombardment. Although incorrect, Japan was brought to its knees by the naval blockade.

TEETHING TROUBLES

At first the U.S. submarine campaign was haphazard and yielded poor results. From 1942 the submarines operated under one of two commands: Commander Submarine Force, Pacific Fleet (commanded after January 1943 by Vice-Admiral Charles A. Lockwood at Pearl Harbour), and Commander Submarines, Southwest Pacific, commanded by Rear-Admiral Ralph W. Christie, at Perth-Fremantle, Australia. The submarines based at Pearl Harbour operated in the East China Sea, close to the Japanese home islands, and off the Marshall, Mariana, Palau and Caroline Islands. Those based at Perth roamed the South China Sea, the Celebes Sea and the Java Sea.

At first the submarines encountered a number of problems, tactical and material, but they were solved quickly. As soon as the Americans realised that the Japanese war economy was extremely vulnerable to submarine attacks, they changed their tactics accordingly. Japan's seizure of the oil-rich Dutch East Indies had secured for Tokyo a reliable source of oil, but the vast ocean distances between that oil source and the home islands made Japan vulnerable to blockade. Thus in late 1943 the U.S. Navy made oil tankers the top-priority targets for its subs.

A SIGNIFICANT IMPACT

....

The results were impressive, with the navy's submarines drastically reducing the flow of oil to Japan. Oil imports fell from 1.75 million barrels per month in August 1943 to 360,000 barrels per month in July 1944. During the last 15 months of the war the ratio of gas successfully shipped from the southern regions to Japan averaged nine percent.

It was not only tankers carrying oil that were sent to the bottom. The submarine attacks severely restricted other imports. Bauxite imports declined 88 percent between the summer and autumn of 1944 and in 1945 pig-iron imports fell 89 percent, raw cotton and wool 91 percent, fats and oils 92 percent, iron ore 95 percent, fodder 99 percent, and raw rubber 100 percent. The reduction of bauxite imports by 508,000 tonnes (500,000 tons) from Indonesia and Malaya resulted in a 70 percent drop in aluminium production in 1944, which had a disastrous effect on aircraft production. By the spring of 1945, for example, the Japanese were using wood in the manufacture of aircraft.

The submarine campaign also had an adverse effect on the Japanese navy, with 30 percent of its losses inflicted by submarines. In addition, damage inflicted on warships by submarines required resources to repair it, which were diverted from construction. As a result the Japanese navy spent 12 percent of its construction budget on ship repairs in 1943 and 1944, a figure that increased to 34 percent in 1945.

Japan's merchant marine lost 8.2 million tonnes (8.1 million tons) of shipping during the war, with submarines accounting for 4.97 million tonnes (4.9 million tons). And the drastic fall in iron imports proved fatal to Japan's ability to replace lost ships.

The price of success was high for U.S. submarine crews: of the 288 U.S. Navy submarines deployed during the war 48 were lost in the Pacific.

ABOVE USS *Bowfin*, now part of an eponymous museum at Pearl Harbour, was involved in operations upholding the blockade.

THE DESERTION OF HITLER'S AXIS ALLIES

DATE

August–September 1944

SUMMARY

The defection of Berlin's eastern European allies deprived Germany of hundreds of thousands of troops and also brought the Red Army closer to the Reich's frontiers.

LOCATION

Eastern Europe

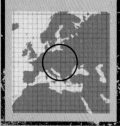

Hungary, Romania and Bulgaria had been enthusiastic members of the Axis alliance, all of them signing the Tripartite Pact. They all reaped economic and military benefits from Berlin's friendship, especially during the early war years. The German defeat at Stalingrad in 1943, however, marked a turning point in their relations with Nazi Germany. The subsequent Red Army victories and retreat of Axis forces meant two things: that Soviet troops would soon be approaching their borders, and that Germany would probably lose the war on the Eastern Front.

HUNGARY MOVES FIRST

By late 1943 the Red Army was approaching the borders of Hungary and so its leader, Admiral Horthy, tried to broker a peace deal with the Soviets. Tentative approaches had been made in late 1943 using the Vatican and other intermediaries. Berlin was aware of Hungary's wavering support and Hitler ordered the occupation of the country in March 1944. Horthy, however, continued to maintain contact with Moscow and on 15 October, 1944, he dismissed the pro-German cabinet and announced that he had signed an armistice with the Soviet Union. The next day Horthy was seized by German troops and the pro-Nazi Arrow Cross regime was installed as the new Hungarian government.

It was the approach of the Red Army in 1944 that motivated Bulgaria's Premier Dobri Bozhilov to increase the pace of negotiations with the Western Allies, while at the same time avoiding German occupation. Bulgaria had been in the curious position of never having declared war on the Soviet Union, though that did not prevent the Red Army invading the country. In the event the discussions with the Western Allies failed and on 8 September, 1944, Premier Konstantin Muraviev was forced to declare war on Germany because the Red Army was then on Bulgarian soil.

ROMANIA SWITCHES SIDES

The most important of Germany's eastern European allies was Romania because of its Ploesti oil fields, which were crucial to the Nazi war effort. Romania itself contributed a lot to the war on the Eastern Front and suffered accordingly: around 300,000 Romanian soldiers were killed fighting the Red Army. In late 1943, seeing the dire strategic situation facing the Axis powers, Romanian dictator Ion Antonescu was using his ambassador to Turkey, Alexandru Cretzianu, as an intermediary with the Western Allies to find a way out of the war. Parallel to his efforts were the manoeuvrings of King Michael and royalist army officers who formed a National Democratic Bloc with the same aim.

On 20 August, 1944, the Red Army launched its Jassy–Kishinev Offensive in Romania, which shattered the Romanian units of Army Group South Ukraine. Two days later the Romanians deposed Antonescu and placed him under arrest (he would be hanged in Moscow in 1946). King Michael took his place and ordered all Romanian units to stop fighting and surrender to the Soviets or disband and go home. Unfortunately Romania's ordeal was not over because its armed forces were taken over by the Soviets and compelled to fight against the Germans. Their former enemies treated them appallingly and of the 538,000 Romanians that fought the Axis until May 1945 over 160,000 became casualties. The Red Army occupied the Ploesti oil fields on 30 August.

At the Second Moscow Conference that began on 9 October, 1944, Churchill and Stalin discussed Soviet influence in a postwar eastern Europe. The exercise was largely academic because the Red Army already occupied most of the region. Soviet control of eastern Europe would not end until the 1980s.

BELOW By January 1944 Soviet tanks were already on the roads of Minsk.

THE WARSAW UPRISING

DATE

1 August–
2 October, 1944

SUMMARY

The rising of the
Polish Home Army was
intended as the first
step in the libera-
tion of Poland, but
they were betrayed
by Stalin, who wished
to see a Communist
postwar Poland.

LOCATION

Warsaw, Poland

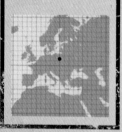

At the end of July, 1944, Red Army spearheads reached the River Vistula and neared the eastern suburbs of Warsaw. Convinced that the Soviets would assist them if they rose up against the German garrison, the Commander-in-Chief of the Polish Home Army, General Tadeusz Komorowski, issued orders to assault German positions in the city. He did this with the support of the Polish government-in-exile in London in order to greet the liberating Red Army as hosts and 'masters in our own house'. But Stalin had no interest in the London Poles and the Western-backed insurgents, having the puppet Committee of National Liberation in the wings to rule a postwar Poland.

The Home Army comprised 40,000 male and female fighters and had enough weapons to equip a quarter of them. It had ammunition for seven days of fighting but fresh supplies were expected to be supplemented by those captured from the enemy. The German garrison also numbered 40,000 but was better armed and could call on artillery and air support.

THE FIGHTBACK

At 17:00 hours on 1 August, the uprising began, it becoming clear immediately that the Poles lacked the assault weapons required to breach pillboxes and other reinforced concrete defences. The next day SS chief Heinrich Himmler appointed *SS-Obergruppenführer* Erich von dem Bach-Zelewski as commander of all German units assigned to crush the rising. They were an unsavoury collection of thugs, criminals, sadists and Russians fighting for the Germans.

Despite Himmler rushing troops to the city, by 5 August the Home Army controlled three-fifths of Warsaw, though split into three areas. In the south Mokotow and Czerniakow; the city centre and Powisle; and in the north the Old Town and Zoliborz. The Germans originally intended to raze the whole city to the ground but Polish and German pockets were so intermingled that they decided to launch counterattacks to meticulously wipe out enemy pockets. Artillery and aircraft supported these assaults, the latter dropping incendiary and fragmentation bombs that caused many fires.

GERMAN BRUTALITY

....

The Poles, ill equipped and outgunned, fought bravely but firepower began to tell and across the Vistula the Red Army and its aircraft made no attempt to aid them. On 12 August the Germans began their assault to capture the Old Town, the Poles being forced to evacuate the district on 30 August. As they retook parts of the city the Germans murdered prisoners, civilians and the wounded, the SS raping nuns and nurses before executing them. The city centre came under heavy attack on 8 September and two days later Red Army units actually reached the east bank of the Vistula. Despite frantic appeals from the Poles, however, they made no attempt to link up with the Home Army.

Overwhelming German firepower had forced the Poles away from the river by 23 September and on the 27th they retook Mokotow. On the 30th the Poles in Zoliborz, facing a hopeless situation, were ordered by Home Army headquarters to surrender. The Poles still fighting were now facing shortages of food, ammunition, medicines and water. With no hope of aid Komorowski surrendered on 2 October. Threats issued by the British and Americans made the Germans recognise the Poles as prisoners of war but the population of Warsaw was not so lucky.

The brave, hopeless Warsaw Rising resulted in 15,200 insurgents being killed, 5,000 wounded and 15,000 taken prisoner. The Germans lost 16,000 dead, 9,000 wounded and 2,000 captured (1,000 of whom were killed). Some 200,000 of Warsaw's civilian population were killed, 700,000 were expelled from the city and 55,000 were sent to concentration camps. Hitler ordered the destruction of Warsaw, resulting in the razing of 85 percent of the buildings on the western bank of the Vistula.

ABOVE Soldiers of the Polish Home Army fight through the rubble of Warsaw in August 1944.

OPERATION MARKET GARDEN

DATE

17 September, 1944

SUMMARY

Montgomery's audacious plan to end the war in 1944 ended in failure and high Allied losses.

LOCATION

Arnhem, Holland

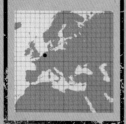

Following the rapid Allied advances in France in July and August 1944 the pace slowed as German resistance stiffened and American and British armies suffered fuel and supply shortages. Nevertheless, they had aircraft and Field Marshal Sir Bernard Montgomery was determined to use this superiority to launch an audacious operation that, if it succeeded, would end the war in 1944.

His plan, codenamed Operation Market Garden, involved using three divisions of airborne troops to capture the bridges at Eindhoven, Grave, Nijmegen and Arnhem (spanning the Maas, Waal and Nederrijn rivers). The German Siegfried Line would then be outflanked, the British Second Army would be able to thrust into Germany itself, and the war would be considerably shortened. Despite harbouring doubts, the supreme Allied commander, General Eisenhower, gave his approval.

A PROMISING START

Market Garden was launched in excellent weather, the 1,545 aircraft and 478 gliders carrying the men of the First Allied Airborne Army encountering little flak as they made their way from England to Holland. As soon as the paratroopers began exiting their aircraft, the tanks of the British 30th Corps would advance to link up with them at Eindhoven, Nijmegen, and the farthest bridge (which would prove to be a bridge too far) at Arnhem.

The first part of the operation went well, the U.S. 101st Airborne Division capturing the bridges at Eindhoven and the U.S. 82nd Airborne Division capturing the Maas and Maas–Waal canal bridges but encountering heavy resistance at Nijmegen. At Arnhem, however, a disaster was unfolding.

The commander of the British 1st Airborne Division, Major-General Robert Urquhart, decided to commit his division in three separate lifts over three days to the west of Arnhem (due to heavy German flak defences around the town). The first lift consisted of the 1st, 2nd

and 3rd Parachute Battalions of the 1st Airborne Brigade. On
17 September the 2nd Battalion reached the main bridge over the
Nederrijn at Arnhem and occupied the northern side. But an attempt
to secure the southern side was repulsed by the enemy. That enemy was
not, as Allied intelligence had suggested, demoralised enemy units
but elements of **II SS Panzer Corps** that were
refitting in the area.

FORTUNES CHANGE

On 18 September the 1st and 3rd Parachute
Battalions were involved in heavy street fighting
in the west of Arnhem and the 4th Parachute
Brigade (the second airborne lift) was virtually
wiped out the next day. By 19 September,
therefore, the 2nd Parachute Battalion was
dangerously isolated in Arnhem and being
assaulted by SS troops and panzers. The
remainder of the 1st Airborne Division
concentrated around Oosterbeek. By this date
Allied tanks were only 16km (10 miles) away but
Urquhart's men had suffered crippling losses.

On 20 September the 82nd Airborne Division
and 30th Corps captured the bridge at Nijmegen
in a combined assault. But at Arnhem the men of
the 2nd Parachute Battalion, short of food,
ammunition and backup, were nearing the end.
The *Waffen-SS* panzers halted the tanks of the British Guards Armoured
Division at Elst, a short distance from Arnhem, on 21 September.
What was left of the 2nd Parachute Battalion surrendered at **09:00** hours
on the same day. At **17:15** hours on 21 September, two battalions of
Polish paratroopers dropped south of the Nederrijn but could not get
supplies across the river to relieve Urquhart's beleaguered men, who
were now being assaulted by SS troops on all sides.

On 25 September Montgomery ordered a withdrawal. For the British
1st Airborne Division it had been a costly failure; only 2,163 of
Urquhart's 10,000 men reached safety on 27 September.

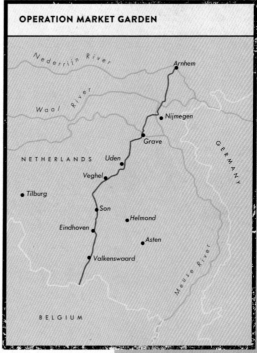

OPERATION MARKET GARDEN

ABOVE Despite some
scepticism, Montgomery was
given the green light to target
bridges in Eindhoven, Grave,
Nijmegen and Arnhem. British
tanks supported the airborne
troops from a starting position
in Belgium (the route is
shown in red).

197

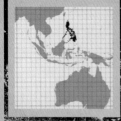

DATE
....
10 October–
25 December, 1944

SUMMARY
....
General Douglas
MacArthur fulfilled
his long-cherished
dream of returning
to the Philippines,
and in doing so
inflicted a major
strategic defeat
on the Japanese.

LOCATION
....
The Philippines

ABOVE RIGHT General
MacArthur making a triumphant
return to the Philippines alongside
President Sergio Omeña.

THE LEYTE LANDINGS

In the autumn of 1944 General Douglas MacArthur, Commander of the
Southwest Pacific Area, having secured northern New Guinea and
the Solomons in 1943, was ready to fulfill his dream of returning to the
Philippines. With the American war economy in full swing he could call
on huge resources to retake the Philippines. The actual assault on Leyte
would be undertaken by Lieutenant-General Walter Krueger's U.S.
Sixth Army (200,000 men), while also under MacArthur's command was
the U.S. Seventh Fleet (Vice-Admiral Thomas C. Kinkaid). Numbering
over 700 vessels the fleet was divided into three units: Task Force 77
(Kinkaid), Task Force 78 (Rear-Admiral Daniel E. Barbey) and Task
Force 79 (Vice-Admiral Theodore S. Wilkinson). The task of the Seventh
Fleet was to get the troops ashore and support them once on land.
In addition, though not under MacArthur's command, was the U.S.
Third Fleet under Admiral William F. Halsey, the mission of which
was to cover the entire Leyte operation.

The Japanese Army was totally inadequate to mount a defence against
such a vast expeditionary force. The overall command of forces in the
Southwest Pacific was the responsibility of Field Marshal Hisaichi
Terauchi and the main commander in the Philippines was General
Tomoyuki Yamashita, 'The Tiger of Malaya'. But on Leyte itself the only
troops available were Lieutenant-General Shiro Makino's 16th Division
(20,000 men).

MACARTHUR RETURNS

....

Between 10 and 13 October aircraft of the Third Fleet attacked Japanese bases on Luzon, Formosa, and the Ryukyus as cover for the Leyte landings, destroying 600 enemy aircraft. On 17 October the battle for Leyte opened when U.S. Army Rangers landed on several small islands protecting Leyte Gulf. Two days later ships of the Seventh Fleet began pounding Leyte as U.S. carrier aircraft swarmed over the island. On the morning of 20 October, four U.S. divisions stormed ashore near Dulag and Tacloban, the Japanese opposition sporadic and uncoordinated. About four hours after the initial landings MacArthur, accompanied by members of his staff and Philippine president Sergio Osmeña, waded ashore, an image that has since entered military folklore. With Japanese snipers still shooting at the beach MacArthur spoke into a hastily arranged microphone, declaring: 'People of the Philippines, I have returned'.

As U.S. Army troops pushed inland Japanese resistance stiffened but by the 26th Makino's division had been reduced to 5,000 men. Both sides rushed in reinforcements but the Americans were always able to maintain a five-to-one advantage in ground troops, and overhead the Americans maintained total air superiority. By early December the Japanese troops had over 60,000 soldiers on Leyte and against a U.S. advance that was slow due to the unending wet jungle and mud, they were able to build strong defences. But in the face of American firepower they were only able to slow the Sixth Army's advance, not halt it.

On 25 December the Americans captured the town of Palompon, signalling the end of major fighting on Leyte. Control of mopping-up operations was turned over to the U.S. Eighth Army (though 'mopping up' was to be a long and costly business for U.S. and Filipino troops and would last until 5 May, 1945). Leyte cost the Americans 3,500 dead and 12,000 wounded, which paled beside Japanese losses of 60,000 men.

There would follow hard, costly fighting on Luzon in 1945 but the fall of Leyte signalled that it was only a matter of time before the rest of the Philippines would follow. For Japan time was running out in the Pacific. Tokyo was losing soldiers, ships and aircraft at an alarming rate, losses that it could not replace in the face of an American military colossus.

THE BATTLE OF LEYTE GULF

DATE

23–25 October, 1944

SUMMARY

The greatest battle
in naval history was
a crippling defeat
for the Imperial
Japanese navy.

LOCATION

Philippine Sea

Despite the fall of the Marianas the Japanese High Command believed that victory could still be achieved in the Pacific, and devised a plan to bring about a 'decisive battle against the Americans in the Pacific'. That plan was Operation Sho-I, which would inflict a crushing defeat on the U.S. Navy off the Philippines.

HIGH STAKES

....

The Japanese assembled a strong force for the operation, which had to succeed, as there would be no replacements if it did not. From Singapore sailed Vice-Admiral Takeo Kurita's 1st Striking Force: five battleships (including *Musashi* and *Yamato*), 10 heavy cruisers, two light cruisers and 15 destroyers. From Formosa came Vice-Admiral Kiyohide Shima's 2nd Striking Force: two heavy cruisers, one light cruiser and seven destroyers. Vice-Admiral Jisaburo Ozawa's Main Force sailed from Japanese waters and contained four aircraft carriers (a total of only 116 aircraft), two battleships converted to launch aircraft, three light cruisers and eight destroyers. The 4th Group under Vice-Admiral Shoji Nishimura (part of the 1st Striking Force until 22 October) contained two battleships, one heavy cruiser and four destroyers.

It was a large fleet but Sho-I was overly complicated. Thus while Shima decoyed Halsey's U.S. Third Fleet to the north, Kurita would sail through the San Bernardino Strait north of Leyte, and Nishimura would advance through the Surigao Strait to the south. The Japanese would meet in Leyte Gulf, crush the U.S. transports landing troops on Leyte, and then destroy Halsey's fleet. Unfortunately the plan started to unravel almost as soon as it was put into operation.

The Japanese fleets set off for Leyte on 20 October and on the 23rd the submarine USS *Darter* sank the cruiser *Atago*, Admiral Kurita's flagship. The heavy cruiser *Takao* was damaged by torpedoes and had to retire to Brunei. The submarine USS *Dace* sank the cruiser *Maya* and although the *Darter* had to run aground and was subsequently scuttled, by 23 October the Americans were aware that the Japanese Imperial Navy was approaching Leyte. The next day, on the morning of 24 October, Halsey's search aircraft detected Kurita's ships but then Japanese aircraft from Luzon attacked and sank the light carrier USS *Princeton* and damaged the cruiser USS *Birmingham*. While this was happening 250 U.S. aircraft pounced on Japanese ships as they steamed through the Sibuyan Sea, sinking the *Musashi* and damaging a heavy cruiser. Thus ended the Battle of the Sibuyan Sea, the first part of the Battle of Leyte Gulf.

Halsey sailed north to attack the Japanese carriers, leaving the San Bernardino Strait open. Meanwhile, Nishimura's force was spotted by aircraft of the U.S. Seventh Fleet heading for the Surigao Strait, prompting Rear-Admiral Kinkaid to draw up a force of six battleships, four heavy and four light cruisers, 28 destroyers and 39 patrol boats across the neck of the strait.

On 25 October this fleet sank the Japanese battleships *Fuso* and *Yamashiro*, three destroyers and one heavy cruiser in the Battle of Surigao Strait in the second part of the Battle of Leyte Gulf. Over the next few days U.S. aircraft attacked Nishimura's remaining vessels. Of his seven ships only one would survive. Shima, following, managed to escape with two of his cruisers and four destroyers.

ABOVE USS *Princeton* burns after being hit by Japanese dive bombers and torpedoes.

KURITA STRIKES

To the north, Kurita's ships entered the Philippine Sea on 25 October, running straight into Rear-Admiral Clifton Sprague's 'Taffy 3': six escort carriers, three destroyers and four destroyer escorts. With overwhelming firepower at his disposal Kurita ordered his ships to attack. The result was the sinking of the destroyers USS *Hoel*, USS *Johnston* and USS *Samuel B. Roberts*, and the carrier USS *Gambier Bay*. But Kurita, rattled by constant air attacks, recalled his ships north, thus ending the Battle of Samar. On the same day Halsey engaged the Japanese carriers at the Battle of Cape Engaño. U.S. carrier aircraft proved devastating, sinking the heavy carrier *Zuikaku* and three other light carriers.

Thus ended the Battle of Leyte Gulf, a clash that resulted in the Imperial Japanese navy losing 26 ships to the Americans' six. Japan's naval capacity had all but disappeared.

OPERATION WATCH ON THE RHINE

DATE

....

16 December, 1944–
16 January, 1945

SUMMARY

....

The failed Ardennes
Offensive that used
up Nazi Germany's
last military
reserves.

LOCATION

....

Belgium

By the autumn of 1944, in the West the Germans had been pushed back to the borders of the Reich itself. However, the *Wehrmacht* fought fiercely and were excellently led, and the Allies were experiencing problems with their supply lines. This prompted Hitler to dream up a daring offensive in the West – Operation Watch on the Rhine. As in 1940, German forces would sweep through the Ardennes, destroying all Allied forces north of the line Antwerp–Brussels–Bastogne in Belgium, thus forcing the Western powers to sue for peace.

A LAST THROW OF THE DICE

To achieve these grandiose aims the German army marshalled its last reserves of tanks, ammunition and fuel along the Belgium border. Three armies would undertake the offensive: Sixth SS Panzer Army (General Sepp Dietrich), Fifth Panzer Army (General Hasso von Manteuffel) and Seventh Army (General Erich Brandenberger). In total Watch on the Rhine involved 500,000 troops, 9,000 artillery pieces and 1,500 tanks. The Germans had built up these forces in great secrecy and hoped to take advantage of the weather conditions – fog, rain and snow – to facilitate their advance.

The offensive opened on 16 December and achieved complete tactical and strategic surprise, two U.S. divisions being shattered. But from the start the Germans encountered difficulties. The forest roads began to deteriorate due to being pounded by hundreds of tracked vehicles and huge traffic jams held up the advance. In addition, the U.S. 101st Airborne Division, commanded by Brigadier-General Anthony C. McAuliffe at Bastogne, held up the Fifth Panzer Army's progress. To the north, despite a determined defence of St. Vith by the U.S. 7th Armored Division, the Sixth SS Panzer Army moved forward between 19 and 22 December as the Germans created a large bulge in the Allied line.

Field Marshal Model, commander of Army Group B, wanted to shift the weight of the German offensive to Manteuffel's Fifth Panzer Army further south but the Führer, perhaps thinking of the recent revolt against him by some army officers, was determined that his *Waffen-SS* should strike the decisive blow. But even as Hitler was dreaming of SS advances, by 22 December General George Patton's U.S. Third Army was attacking towards beleaguered Bastogne. German tanks were now running out of fuel and grinding to a halt near the River Meuse where they were struck by U.S. and British counterattacks on 25–26 December. And on the 26th Patton's tanks punched through the German perimeter to reach Bastogne. Worse for the Germans, the weather now began to clear to allow Allied aircraft to attack their supply trains west of St. Vith.

BASTOGNE OBSESSION

Hitler became obsessed with Bastogne and ordered it to be taken, regardless of cost, with the result that between 26 December and 2 January a furious battle raged around the town. But had the Führer torn himself away from micro-managing this battle he would have realised that Watch on the Rhine had already failed. In an effort to disrupt Allied air support the *Luftwaffe* launched its last great offensive in the West: 800 aircraft striking airfields in Belgium, France and Holland. The *Luftwaffe* destroyed 156 aircraft but also suffered significant losses and the Allied air offensive continued uninterrupted.

ABOVE Hitler and his commanders' attempt to redeem the parlous situation in western Europe was doomed to fail in the face of the Allies' material superiority.

Backed up by air power Allied armies began to eliminate the German 'bulge' between 3 and 16 January, 1945, and pushed SS and army units back to their original start positions. They had suffered 120,000 dead, wounded, or missing and lost 800 tanks and assault guns and 6,000 other vehicles. The *Luftwaffe* had also lost 1,600 aircraft in December and January. Allied losses (mostly U.S.) totalled 7,000 killed, 33,400 wounded, 21,000 captured or missing, and 730 tanks. The difference was that the Allies could easily make up these losses whereas for Germany there were no reserves left.

The failure of Hitler's Ardennes Offensive at
the beginning of the year used up Germany's last
reserves. But it would take another four months of
fighting and hundreds of thousands of casualties
before World War II in Europe came to an end, leaving
a continent in ruins and millions of its inhabitants
dead. The fate of postwar Europe had been decided at
the Yalta Conference in February, where it became
apparent that the unity of those fighting Nazi
Germany would rapidly disappear once Hitler and his
regime had been destroyed. Stalin was determined to
create a Soviet-controlled eastern Europe, which
would include Poland. Thus Britain was forced to
abandon the very country that it had gone to war
in the first place to defend.

In the Pacific, the Americans scored hard-won
victories at Iwo Jima and Okinawa, and U.S. long-range
bombers reduced Japanese towns and cities to charred
ruins. But it was the dropping of atomic bombs on
Hiroshima and Nagasaki that would eventually force
Tokyo to surrender and bring World War II to an end.

1945

THE YALTA CONFERENCE

DATE

4–11 February, 1945

SUMMARY

The conference of
the 'Big Three'
decided the map
of postwar Europe.

LOCATION

Crimea, USSR

With the war in Europe nearing its end the leaders of the three
main Allied powers – Joseph Stalin, Winston Churchill and F. D.
Roosevelt – met at Yalta to decide the map of postwar Europe. Already
cracks were beginning to appear in the Allied alliance, cracks that the
wily Stalin was determined to exploit. With the Red Army in possession
of large parts of eastern Europe the Soviet leader held the upper hand
in his negotiations with the U.S. and British leaders. To make matters
worse Roosevelt believed that he knew how to handle Stalin but in fact
the opposite was true. In addition, the Americans were reluctant to
take a strong line with the Soviet dictator because they wanted to
bring Stalin into the war against the Japanese in the Far East.

THE SOVIET BLOC TAKES SHAPE

Stalin was determined to exact heavy reparations from a defeated
Germany, which meant removing all the country's industry and wealth
and shipping it east. In addition, Stalin insisted that Poland should be
absorbed into the Soviet sphere of influence with the establishment of
a strong, communist government in Warsaw, effectively becoming a
buffer state between the Soviet Union and a dismembered Germany
(which would be split into British, Soviet, French and American zones
of occupation). This was a bitter blow for Churchill as Britain had
declared war on Germany in 1939 to defend Polish territorial integrity.
But now, nearly six years later, he was powerless to prevent Poland
becoming a Soviet client state.

For his part a terminally ill President Roosevelt got what he
wanted at Yalta: an agreement regarding the establishment of the
United Nations and a promise from Stalin that the Red Army would
enter the war in the Far East against the Japanese. In return the
Soviets would be granted a sphere of influence in Manchuria
following Japan's surrender. This included the southern portion of
Sakhalin, a lease at Port Arthur (now Lüshunkou), a share in the

operation of the Manchurian railways, and the Kurile Islands.

Roosevelt also revealed that the capture of Berlin was not a prime U.S. objective, thus ensuring that the Red Army would be the first to reach Hitler's capital. Roosevelt was satisfied by Stalin's vow to allow free and democratic elections in eastern Europe, failing to see that Soviet-sponsored Communist parties were already in control of the state apparatus in the region.

ABOVE For the U.S. president (centre of front row), military needs took priority over political concerns as negotiations opened with the Soviets.

Stalin also wanted the return of all those Russians who had been working or fighting for the Germans, and Churchill and Roosevelt were also keen that all nationalities should return to their native lands. They thus unwittingly sanctioned the deaths of millions of Soviet and Baltic citizens (the Baltic states once more became part of the Soviet Union). Soviet citizens in British and American hands would be repatriated to the Soviet Union 'irrespective of whether the individuals desire to return to Russia or not'.

Eyewitness

AFTER THE CONFERENCE CHURCHILL ACCURATELY FORESAW THE COLD WAR OF THE POSTWAR WORLD, AS HE INFORMED STALIN.

'There is not much comfort in looking to a future where you and the countries you dominate, plus the communist parties in many other states, are drawn up on one side, and those who rally to the English-speaking states and their associates or dominions are on the other. It is quite obvious that their quarrel would tear the world to pieces and that all of us leading men on either side who had anything to do with that would be shamed before history.'

THE BATTLE OF IWO JIMA

DATE

19 February–
25 March, 1945

SUMMARY

In one of the
bloodiest battles of
the Pacific War, U.S.
Marines captured the
island of Iwo Jima as
the Americans edged
ever closer to Japan.

LOCATION

Bonin Islands,
Pacific Ocean

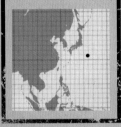

As the Pacific War neared its end the island of Iwo Jima assumed a strategic importance because it is only 1,222km (760 miles) from Tokyo flying from the Mariana Islands (there were two airfields on the island and another uncompleted one). The scene was set for one of the bloodiest battles of the Pacific War.

The man in charge of capturing the island was Admiral Raymond A. Spruance whose V Amphibious Corps would assault the island. The corps comprised: 4th Marine Division (Major-General Clifton B. Cates), 5th Marine Division (Major-General Keller E. Rockey) and 3rd Marine Division (Major-General Graves B. Erskine), a total of 70,000 Marines.

Lieutenant-General Tadamichi Kuribayashi commanded the island's 20,000 garrison and had embarked upon an intensive fortification programme before the Americans arrived, turning the island into a warren of pillboxes and strongpoints.

STORMING THE GARRISON

The assault was carried out with its customary thoroughness, B-24 and B-29 heavy bombers 'softening up' the Japanese before Spruance's ships pounded the island's defences between 16 and 18 February. On 19 February, following a 30-minute naval bombardment, the Marines' landing craft went in. By this stage of the war the Americans had become adept at amphibious landings and within 15 minutes four waves of Marines had landed on the island, each man carrying 32–48kg (80–120lb) of equipment. As the Marines scrambled up the embankment of black volcanic sand they came under intense enemy fire but troops, artillery, tanks and supplies continued to pour ashore. During the day almost 30,000 Marines landed on Iwo Jima, though more than 2,500 were killed or wounded.

On 20 February the Marines cut the island in half, the 4th Marine Division and 27th Marine Regiment, 5th Marine Division, fighting their way to the northeast, onto the central plateau and towards airfields

No. 2 and No. 3. At the same time the men of the 28th Marine Regiment, 5th Marine Division, attacked towards Mount Suribachi in the south. Tanks mounting cannon and flamethrowers attacked the pillboxes defending the approaches to the mountain and on 23 February soldiers of the 28th Regiment hoisted the American flag on the top of Mount Suribachi. But the capture of the mountain marked the end of just one phase of the battle.

On 24 February the assault on Airfield No. 2 began, preceded by a naval bombardment, artillery barrage and air strike. The men of the 4th and 3rd Marine Divisions advanced and captured the objective after four days of heavy fighting. The 21st Marine Regiment, 3rd Marine Division, then battled its way through to the high ground just south of Airfield No. 3. Against Japanese soldiers ensconced in caves only flamethrowers and explosive charges were effective.

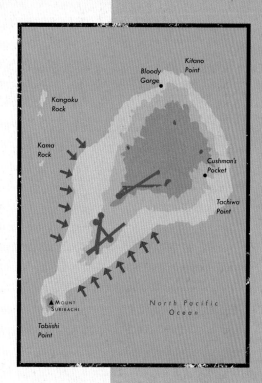

THE MEAT GRINDER

....

As February ended all three Marine divisions fought for possession of a series of strongholds nicknamed the 'Meat Grinder', with good reason. The high points and strongholds required massive firepower and great courage to subdue, the Japanese defenders invariably fighting to the last man. On 8 March the Japanese mounted a night counterattack but had suffered 650 killed by mid-morning on 9 March. The next day the Meat Grinder was captured, signalling the end of organised resistance on Iwo Jima, but not the fighting. There were still isolated Japanese strongpoints holding out, including those nicknamed Cushman's Pocket and Bloody Gorge. Subduing them was a time-consuming and dangerous business.

Fighting on the island finally ended on 25 March, by which time 6,000 Americans had been killed and more than 17,000 wounded. Of the 20,000 defenders only 216 survived to become prisoners of war; the rest died, including Kuribayashi who committed suicide. In U.S. hands Iwo Jima became a base from which P-51 Mustangs could provide fighter escorts for the B-29s flying against Japan, and where damaged bombers could land.

ABOVE American forces, landing on the southern and northern coasts (shown here with red arrows) cut the island in two, with eastern forces pushing towards the airfields (in blue) and western forces towards Mt. Suribachi.

FIRE RAIDS ON JAPAN

DATE
....

March 1945

SUMMARY
....

The strategic
bombing campaign
that burned the
heart out of
Japan's cities.

LOCATION
....

Japan

On 1 November, 1944, a lone B-29 Superfortress heavy bomber flew
over Tokyo and returned safely to its base in the Mariana Islands.
It was the vanguard of huge air fleets that would destroy great swathes
of Japan's cities. The Boeing B-29 was a revolutionary aircraft, having a
range of 6,598km (4,100 miles), a service ceiling of 9,695m (31,808ft)
and having pressurised crew compartments. Because of the B-29 the
U.S. Joint Chiefs of Staff decided that large-scale landings in China
would be unnecessary and that Japan itself could be invaded. To
facilitate this the enemy would be softened up by large numbers of
B-29s based on Pacific islands.

TARGETING JAPAN

On 15 June, 1944, a date that marked the beginning of the strategic
bombing of Japan, B-29s operating from China bombed the Yawata
iron and steel works in southern Japan. On 20 August the bombers
returned to Yawata but the results were disappointing and 18 of the
70 bombers were shot down. The standard of bombing improved when
Brigadier-General Curtis LeMay took over command of the 20th
Bomber Command in China. He believed that bombing alone could
bring about the unconditional surrender of Japan.

In the Marianas, Guam, Saipan and Tinian were developed as B-29
bases for the 21st Bomber Command under Brigadier-General H.S.
Hansell. But daylight bombing was proving disappointing, the crews
finding that bombing from 9,144m (30,000ft) was inaccurate due largely
to the high jet streams over Japan and often fog-covered targets. On
24 November, 1944, for example, 112 B-29s attacked the Musashina
engine factory but only 24 aircraft found the target. In January 1945
LeMay flew to the Marianas to take charge of the 21st Bomber
Command and the recently transferred 20th Bomber Command, both
groups being combined to form the 20th Air Force. By March LeMay
had 300 B-29s but fighter opposition over targets was intense, losses

were substantial, and aircrew morale was falling. The problem was eased with the capture of Iwo Jima in March, which allowed the B-29s to receive fighter escorts: the P-51 Mustang and P-61 'Black Widow', a night fighter armed with eight cannon.

Damage on the ground was still relatively light but that would change dramatically when LeMay changed tactics to low-level incendiary bombing at night. To deliver such attacks the B-29s would be dropping the M-69 firebomb, which weighed 2.72kg (6lb) and was dropped in a cluster of 38 within a container. A time fuse was set to release the bombs from a cluster at a height of 1,524m (5,000ft) and each B-29 carried 37 of the cluster containers.

FIRESTORM

....

The night of 10 March was selected for the first large-scale incendiary raid, against Tokyo. Japan's cities were filled with lightly constructed, highly inflammable wooden houses. The 300 B-29s that attacked Tokyo approached the target at night, making any Kamikaze attacks ineffective,

ABOVE A U.S. Air Force B-29 Superfortress in the skies over Osaka in 1945.

dropped their bombs, and left as the dawn was breaking. They left behind a city gutted by fire, 100,000 killed and another 100,000 injured. Only 14 Superfortresses were lost. During March other fire raids were mounted, against Nagoya (twice), Osaka and Kobe. The devastation was similar to that experienced in Tokyo.

By the end of July 1945, there were nearly 1,000 bombers operating from the Marianas and by the end of the war they had destroyed 170 square km (105 square miles) of Japan's most important industrial centres, in addition to laying waste to dozens of smaller cities. B-29s had launched 34,000 effective sorties in total, dropped 172,720 tonnes (170,000 tons) of bombs, levelled 65 Japanese cities and killed 300,000 people. The cost was 414 B-29s lost and 3,015 crewmen killed, wounded and missing. LeMay's fire raids had burned out the heart of Japan's cities, destroyed her war industries, and mined her sea-lanes and ports.

THE BATTLE OF OKINAWA

DATE

1 April–22 June, 1945

SUMMARY

The island of Okinawa became the scene of bitter fighting when American forces landed to secure a base for the invasion of Japan itself.

LOCATION

Ryukyu Islands, Pacific Ocean

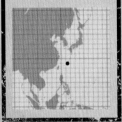

The Island of Okinawa is the largest in the Ryukyu chain, some 96km (60 miles) in length and lying south of Kyushu, one of the Japanese home islands (Okinawa itself is part of Japan). As such its capture would be essential to provide a logistical base for the proposed invasion of Japan. The U.S. plan to take Okinawa, Operation Iceberg, utilised the by now customary huge resources available to American commanders.

THE ALLIED FORCES

Admiral Raymond A. Spruance, in command of Task Force 50, had at his disposal Task Force 58 (Admiral Marc A. Mitscher), the British Carrier Task Force (tasked with neutralising the southern Ryukyus) and the Joint Expeditionary Force (Task Force 51), a joint force of Marine, U.S. army and U.S. navy units that would capture Okinawa. Once ground operations began forces would come under the control of Lieutenant-General Simon Bolivar Buckner's U.S. Tenth Army. In total over 180,000 U.S. army soldiers, Marines and attached naval personnel made up the assault force, supported by 1,500 ships of all types.

The Japanese garrison comprised Lieutenant-General Mitsuru Ushijima's Thirty-Second Army (built around the 24th and 62nd Infantry Divisions) – 77,000 men – plus 20,000 men of the Okinawan Home Guard and 15,000 other Okinawan natives. Ushijima had prepared three defence lines in the southern part of the island, centred on the town of Shuri. His plan was to deny the Americans the use of Okinawa until the Kamikazes and other air and naval units arrived to destroy the invasion fleet. To achieve this aim the Thirty-Second Army was liberally equipped with weapons and ammunition.

On 18–19 March U.S. carrier aircraft struck airfields on Kyushu, destroying over 500 aircraft. Japanese aircraft also struck Task Force 58, four carriers being hit and another, the USS *Franklin*, suffering 724 dead and 260 wounded and being forced to retire to the United States. On 26 March units of the 77th Infantry Division landed on

islands in the Kerama Retto, to
the west of Okinawa, to provide
a safe anchorage and a supply base
for U.S. ships. This was achieved
by 29 March.

EARLY PROGRESS

The main assault commenced on
1 April, U.S. troops meeting little
resistance as they stormed ashore
and captured two airfields located
1.6km (1 mile) inland by nightfall.
Two days later, after consolidating
its beachhead, the Tenth Army

ABOVE Despite recording a
number of successes, including
hitting several U.S. carriers,
the Japanese defences were
unable to prevent Allied
troops landing on Okinawa.

reached Okinawa's east coast, cutting the island in half. On 4 April, 24th
Corps wheeled south and the Marines of III Amphibious Corps advanced
north, but now enemy resistance stiffened. In the south the 7th and 96th
Infantry Divisions ran into the outposts of Ushijima's defence lines and
in the north the Marines suffered 1,200 casualties taking Motobu
Peninsula and Yae-Take Mountain.

By 12 April the Tenth Army had lost its momentum and 24th Corps
had ground to a halt. The 27th Infantry Division reinforced it but only
on 24 April did the corps manage to break through the first Shuri
defence line. Ushijima's tactics were working but then, under pressure
from his officers, he launched a counterattack on 4 May. It was a dismal
failure, 5,000 of the 15,000 men taking part being killed. Two Marine
divisions now reinforced 24th Corps, which launched another offensive
on 6–7 May. Losses were high on both sides but with his position
outflanked Ushijima had no option but to order a withdrawal to his
final defence line. By the end of the month Shuri had been taken by
the 1st Marine Division and 77th Infantry Division but it was not until
22 June that fighting ended on Okinawa. By that date Ushijima had
committed suicide and Buckner had been mortally wounded on 18 June.

There was a high butcher's bill for the conquest of Okinawa: 39,420
U.S. battle casualties and 110,000 Japanese losses (including Okinawan
civilians, some of whom committed suicide rather than fall into
American hands). But the Americans had their springboard for the
invasion of Japan.

THE BATTLE OF BERLIN

The honour of taking Berlin, the 'lair of the fascist beast', was given to Marshal Georgi Zhukov, commander of the 1st Belorussian Front. His front, together with the 2nd Belorussian and 1st Ukrainian Fronts, totalled 2.5 million troops, 41,000 artillery pieces, 6,200 tanks and 7,200 aircraft. Facing them were Army Group Vistula – 200,000 troops, 750 tanks and assault guns and 1,500 artillery pieces – and the northern flank of Army Group Centre: 100,000 troops and 200 tanks and assault guns.

THE BERLIN OFFENSIVE

The Soviet Berlin Offensive began on 16 April, the Red Army suffering heavy casualties at the Battle of the Seelow Heights but forcing the defenders to withdraw nevertheless. By 20 April the artillery of the 1st Belorussian Front was shelling Berlin's eastern suburbs, by which date the Red Army had lost 2,800 tanks in its offensive. But the German defenders, low on ammunition and devoid of air cover, were inexorably pushed back into the city.

By 24 April there was heavy fighting throughout Berlin and on the 28th Soviet troops were just 1.6km (1 mile) from Hitler's bunker below the Chancellery. By the evening they were across the Potsdammer Bridge and fighting in the Ministry of Internal Affairs. The next day the Soviets captured the Moltke Bridge close to the Reichstag, the very centre of

ABOVE RIGHT A soldier raising the Soviet flag over a ruined Berlin: one of the iconic images to emerge from the war.

Nazi rule. Hitler ordered what was left of the garrison of Berlin to fight to the last man. The Führer dictated his political testament on the 29th, stating: 'I die with a joyful heart in the awareness of the immeasurable deeds and achievements of our soldiers at the front, of our women at home, and achievements of our peasants and workers, and the contribution, unique in history, of our youth, which bears my name'.

LAST RITES

....

On 30 April, SS troops were engaged in a vicious room-by-room battle for the Reichstag. In the Führer's bunker, Hitler and his wife Eva Braun committed suicide, the day after their marriage (having both declared that they were of Aryan descent and free of hereditary diseases). On 1 May the Red Army captured the Reichstag, the 5,000 defenders suffering 50 percent casualties. That day propaganda minister Josef Goebbels and his wife Magda ordered an SS orderly to shoot them, having first poisoned their six children. In the power vacuum General Krebs, Chief of the General Staff, asked the Soviets for surrender terms. Stalin was only interested in unconditional surrender so the fighting went on, though large numbers of German soldiers were surrendering anyway, having no ammunition and no hope of relief.

On 1 May Admiral Karl Dönitz, whom Hitler had named as his successor, ordered the utmost resistance in the East in the vain hope that the *Wehrmacht* would hold up the Red Army long enough to allow the British and Americans to occupy more German territory. But in Berlin the battle was already over and General Weidling, commander of the garrison, surrendered. Around 500,000 Germans had been killed and captured in the city and the Red Army had lost 81,000 killed and 272,000 wounded.

Eyewitness
————————

FOR ORDINARY BERLINERS THE BATTLE FOR THE CITY WAS A NIGHTMARE AND THE FIGHTING WAS NOT THE ONLY DANGER. TRAUTE GRIER WAS 14 YEARS OLD WHEN THE RED ARMY TOOK THE CITY.

————————

'When the bombs rained down on Berlin on 28 April, 1945, my mother and I cowered in the bunker of the Karstadt department store in Hermannplatz, in the city's Kreuzberg district.

Suddenly, a pipe burst and within seconds the bunker filled with water. I grabbed my mother and said: "We can drown at home as well." And then we ran — from house to house, fleeing the wheezing Russian Katyusha rockets, which never seemed to end. It was a nightmare. And then the Russian soldiers came. Filled with hatred, they just took whatever they wanted. In our house a woman and her daughter were raped a number of times — this kind of thing happened quite often. If a woman resisted, she was brutally beaten.

Beside constant fear, we were also gripped with hunger. I saw how people literally ate the garbage off the roads and desperately tried to fill their stomachs with potato peels and grass. My mother and I went foraging together. We climbed on the roof of a train and rode out to Schönefeld in the Eastern zone. There we snuck into fields and stole potatoes or turnips, constantly on the lookout to make sure we weren't caught. We had no other choice; we had to eat something'.

ITALY SURRENDERS

In November 1944, following the Allied capture of Bologna, the transfer of troops from Italy to support the Allied advance in southern France brought the Italian campaign to a halt. The Germans now had as many troops in northern Italy as the Allies, though the latter retained overwhelming air superiority. On 13 November, Field Marshal Harold Alexander, commander of the Fifteenth Army Group, issued a proclamation to the Italian partisans that de facto dispersed them for the winter.

AN OPPORTUNITY FOR PEACE

For some Germans in northern Italy the military hiatus appeared to present an opportunity to negotiate a peace with the Allies, chief among them being two senior SS individuals: Eugen Dollmann, one of Himmler's intellectuals who was fluent in Italian and an art historian, and Karl Wolff, senior commander of the SS and police in Italy. Like many senior SS and Germany Army officers they could see that the Third Reich was in its death throes and many began to think of life after it had fallen, especially those who had committed war crimes and might face the wrath of the Allies. Wolff and Dollmann were not in this category but they were both horrified by Hitler's scorched-earth order that cultural and economic resources were to be destroyed as German forces withdrew.

Dollmann and Wolff were appalled at the prospect of Italian culture being destroyed and aghast that the Fiat works outside Turin,

DATE

29 April, 1945

SUMMARY

With the war in Europe nearly over a senior German commander entered talks with the Western Allies to end the war in Italy. The result shortened the war by several weeks and saved thousands of lives.

LOCATION

Caserta, Italy

RIGHT Karl Wolff successfully deceived Heinrich Himmler as he continued negotiations with Dulles regarding surrender in Italy.

one of the most modern industrial plants remaining in Europe, might be blown up. That said they were still SS officers and wished to save Europe from communism and did not believe the Allied insistence on unconditional surrender. What united them and the Allies was a desire to shorten the war as quickly as possible. A series of factors would come together to make this possible in the Italian theatre.

In Switzerland the head of the U.S. Office of Strategic Services (OSS), Allen Dulles, had established contact with several Italian partisan leaders, including Ferruccio Parri, the commander in Lombardy (who had been captured by the Germans). Max Waibel, a Swiss intelligence officer, was on good terms with Dulles and made the American aware that his Swiss masters were eager for the war to end. A large amount of Swiss money was invested in north Italian industry, which would be lost if the Germans destroyed it. In addition, talk of a Nazi Alpine redoubt in the Bavarian and Austrian Alps could affect Switzerland for months if it came about. Thus all parties wished an end to the war in Italy.

SWISS NEGOTIATIONS

At the beginning of March Dollmann met with a subordinate of Dulles, Paul Blum. The talks went well, and Wolff himself travelled to Zurich on 8 March to meet with Dulles. As a sign of his good faith Wolff had arranged the release of Parri and another partisan leader, Usmiani. Dulles, convinced of Wolff's sincerity, informed Alexander of the same.

But SS chief Heinrich Himmler had become aware of Wolff's travels and summoned him to Berlin. On 17 April Himmler confronted Wolff about his dealings with the Allies but his subordinate bluffed his way out of danger by convincing his superior that he had driven a wedge between the Allies and Soviets. Wolff returned to Italy on 19 April and Dulles was ordered to resume negotiations for the German surrender in Italy. They went well and on the morning of 28 April (the day Mussolini was shot) German representatives were flown to Caserta. The next day they signed the document providing for the unconditional surrender of German troops in Italy on 2 May. Wolff himself pleaded with Field Marshal Kesselring, now supreme commander in the south, to support the surrender, especially since Hitler was now dead. The field marshal acquiesced in the early hours of 2 May. Nearly one million men in Italy and Austria laid down their arms in the first German capitulation of the war. The war in Italy was over.

HIROSHIMA

DATE
....
6 August, 1945

SUMMARY
....
Warfare entered the
nuclear age with
the dropping of
the atomic bomb on
the city of Hiro-
shima, an act that
has remained
controversial but
which undoubtedly
hastened the end of
the Pacific War.

LOCATION
....
Hiroshima, Japan

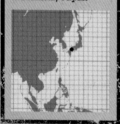

U.S. plans for the invasion of the Japanese home islands – Operation Downfall – estimated that enemy resistance would be more severe than that encountered on Okinawa and in the Marshall, Mariana and Gilbert Islands. Planners believed that the Japanese would resist with an army of two million supported by 8,000 aircraft of all types. Overcoming such determination and resources would cost an estimated one million U.S. casualties in a campaign that would not end until some time in 1946. Fortunately for the Americans they possessed a weapon that might bring about the surrender of Japan without incurring such huge losses: the atomic bomb.

A RAIN OF RUIN

....

In May 1945, U.S. Secretary of War Henry L. Stimson set up a civilian advisory panel to make recommendations concerning the employment of the atomic bomb. The seven-member committee recommended using the bomb as soon as possible with no prior warning. On 16 July the United States successfully detonated the world's first atomic bomb at Oak Ridge, Tennessee. President Truman learned of the successful testing of the bomb while attending the Potsdam Conference in Berlin. Following consultations with his allies – Prime Minister Churchill and Generalissimo Chiang Kai-shek – on 26 July Truman issued an ultimatum for Japan to surrender unconditionally, threatening that if they failed to accept: 'They may expect a rain of ruin from the air, the like of which has never been seen on this earth'. Three days later Prime Minister Kantaro Suzuki rejected the ultimatum.

By this stage of the war many Japanese politicians realised that bombing and starvation could destroy Japan without the need for a foreign invasion, but some of them and militants in the military were determined to fight to the end. Others preferred national suicide to humiliation and the possible execution of the emperor if he fell into Allied hands. The result was the inevitable dropping of atomic bombs on Japan.

LEFT The unprecedented destruction unleashed on Hiroshima (pictured here) and Nagasaki signalled a new threat that would define the Cold War era.

HIROSHIMA

On 11 June, 1945, Colonel Paul W. Tibbets, commander of the 509th Composite Group, arrived at North Field on the island of Tinian. His secret mission was to drop the atomic bomb on Japan, specifically on the city of Hiroshima. The city was chosen because it had been untouched by the fire raids on Japan, which would allow scientists to study the effects of the atomic bomb more easily. Hiroshima also had a high concentration of troops, military bases and military factories.

On 6 August the B-29 'Enola Gay', piloted by Tibbets, took off from Tinian carrying the bomb 'Little Boy'. At 08:15 hours Tibbets dropped the weapon, which detonated at a height of 600m (2,000ft) above the city of Hiroshima with a force of 20,320 tonnes (20,000 tons) of TNT. A massive mushroom-shaped cloud climbed 12km (40,000ft) into the air, which Tibbets and his crew saw 90 minutes later even though they were 576km (360 miles) away. On the ground at Hiroshima 40,000 people were killed instantly, 20,000 others were to die of their wounds or radiation poisoning, and 60,000 others were injured.

The Japanese government, paralysed by the enormity of what had happened, refused to surrender, so 'Fat Man' was dropped on the city of Nagasaki on 9 August. It was now clear that the Americans possessed a weapon that could obliterate entire cities with a single strike and that continuation of the war would result in the destruction of Japan itself. There was no option but to surrender. Despite the attempt of a group of fanatical army officers to shoot those advocating peace, Emperor Hirohito intervened to announce a cease-fire that was broadcast on 15 August. The Pacific War was over.

OPERATION AUGUST STORM

DATE

....

8–20 August, 1945

SUMMARY

....

The Soviet offensive in Manchuria was indicative of growing mistrust between the Western Allies and Moscow that heralded the beginning of the Cold War.

LOCATION

....

Manchuria, China

In accordance with agreements made at Yalta, Stalin authorised a Red Army offensive against Japanese-controlled Manchuria three months after the end of the war in Europe. The dropping of the atomic bombs on Japan on 6 and 9 August had changed the strategic situation in the Far East, however. President Truman no longer needed Soviet intervention in the region to bring about the Japanese surrender, and relations with Stalin had deteriorated when he, Churchill, and the Soviet leader met at Potsdam in July. However, Stalin was alarmed by the prospect of the United States controlling a defeated Japan and its conquered territories and so declared war on Tokyo to seize his share of the spoils.

The Red Army assembled 1.57 million troops, 3,700 tanks, 1,850 self-propelled guns and 3,720 aircraft for its offensive that Western historians subsequently codenamed August Storm. The attack would have three prongs: the Trans-Baikal Front (Marshal Rodion Malinovsky), 1st Far Eastern Front (Marshal Kirill Meretskov) and 2nd Far Eastern Front (General Maksim Purkayev). The three axes of attack would overpower Japanese defences with rapid armoured thrusts supported by airpower to invade and conquer Manchuria and drive south into Korea, halting at the 38th parallel in accordance with a prior agreement that permitted the Americans to conquer the southern half of the country.

POORLY EQUIPPED

Facing the Red onslaught was the Japanese Kwantung Army, commanded by General Otozo Yamada, which numbered 713,000 men in 24 divisions. On paper it had 1,215 armoured vehicles, 6,700 artillery pieces and 1,800 aircraft, but much of its equipment was obsolete and its units were suffering acute ammunition shortages. During the offensive the chief obstacle to the Red Army would not be the Japanese but the terrain: mountains, desert, swamp, marsh and forests, plus often-torrential rains. Thus, when the offensive opened on 8 August, Japanese units were swiftly outflanked and isolated. Ordinary Japanese soldiers became demoralised by massed Katyusha rocket barrages that preceded tank assaults. Red Army armoured columns advanced 149km (93 miles) on the first day and one unit, the Sixth Guards Tank Army, advanced 347km (217 miles) in four days. In the air Soviet aircraft soon established superiority over the Japanese. This allowed transports (Lend-Lease DC-3s) to supply armoured columns. In total 2,032 tonnes (2,000 tons) of fuel and 79 tonnes (78 tons) of ammunition were delivered to spearheads during the offensive. Aircraft were also used to transport troops, landing at Mukden and Changchun on 19 August to seize those cities' airfields (two days later Red Army tanks reached both places).

ROUTED

Japanese troops saw their anti-tank shells bounce off Soviet tanks and mounted Kamikaze attacks in a desperate attempt to halt the Russians. On 15 August, for example, 1,700 men, with officers wielding swords, mounted one such attack outside the city of Hualin. All were killed and the city fell to the Red Army three days later. On the same day, 18 August, the Soviets conducted amphibious landings in northern Korea and on the Sakhalin and Kurile Islands. Organised resistance in northern Korea, overrun by the 1st Far Eastern Front, had ended on 16 August. By 20 August the Soviets had reached the city of Harbin and the Japanese, ordered by their emperor to stop fighting, began surrendering.

So swift and total had been the Soviet victory that U.S. troops landed at the port city of Inchon in southern Korea to stop Red Army troops from occupying all of Korea. The Cold War map of the Far East was beginning to take shape. The price of victory was 12,000 Red Amy dead and 24,500 wounded. The Japanese fared much worse: up to 60,000 dead and 600,000 of their troops surrendering in Manchuria, Sakhalin, and the Kurile Islands. Most were transported to labour camps in Siberia where the majority died.

ABOVE Motorised Soviet infantry in Manchuria in August 1945.

INDEX

CREDITS